CAPTAIN AMERICA

TWO AMERICAS

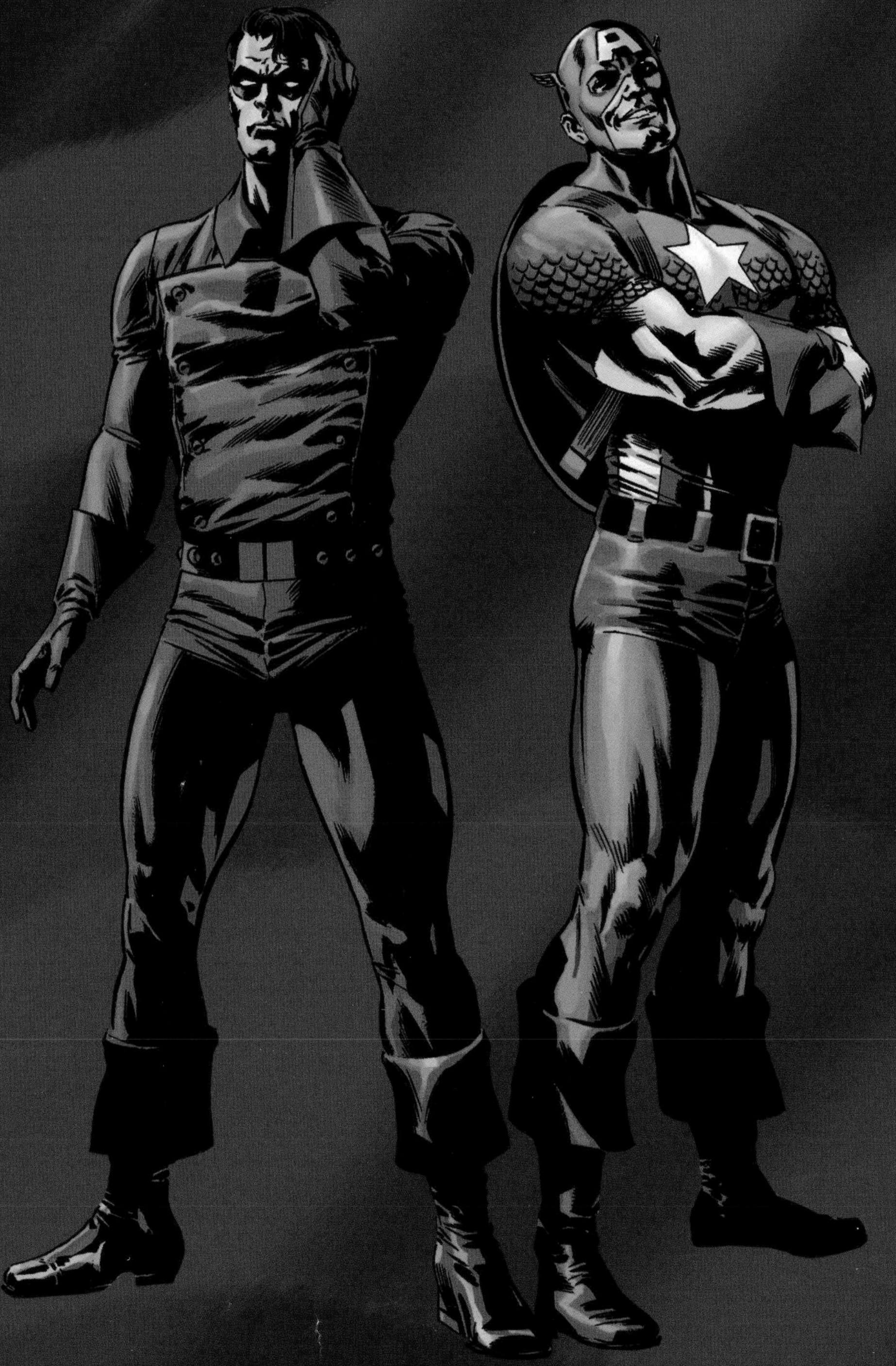

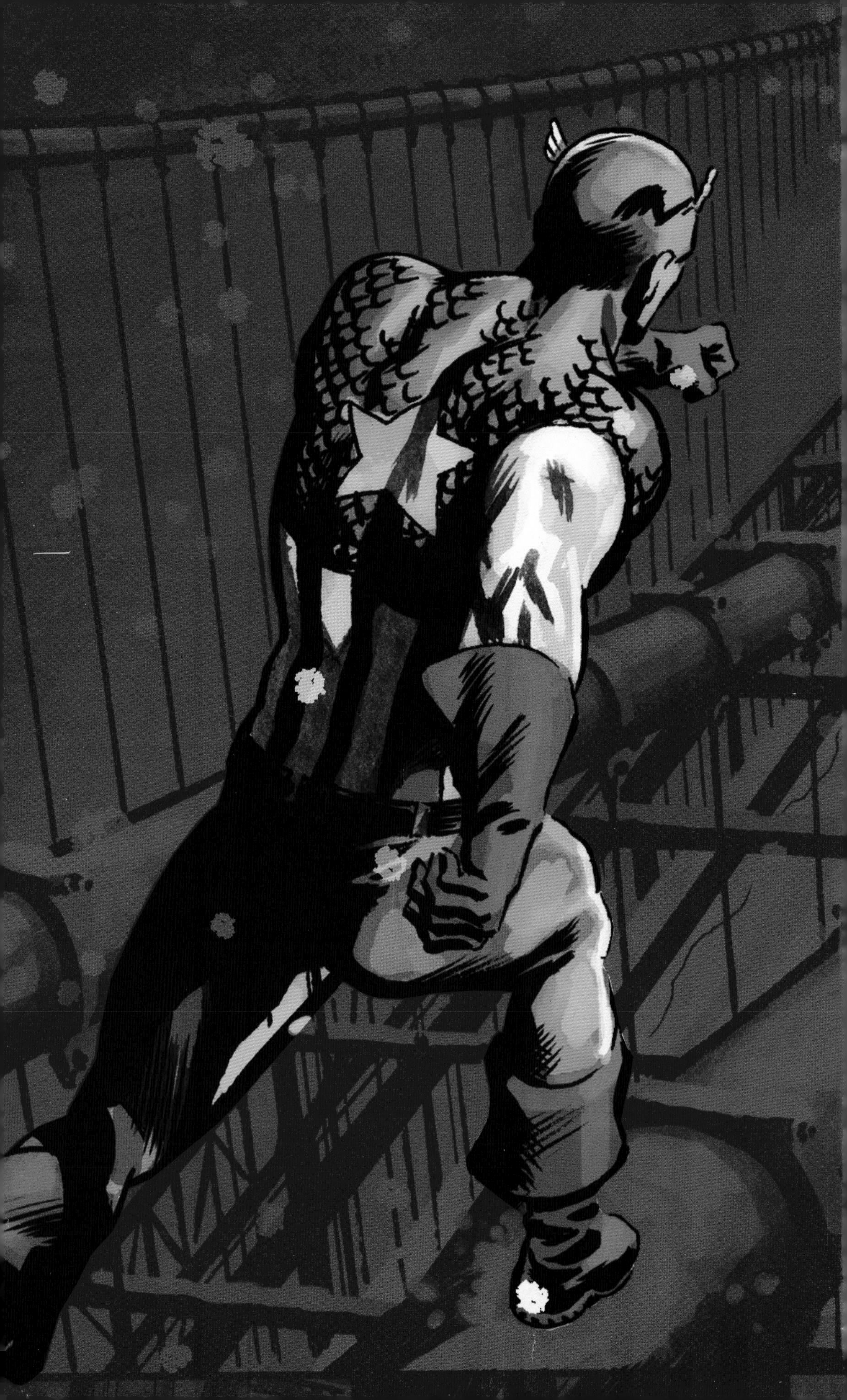

CAPTAIN AMERICA

TWO AMERICAS

WRITER: Ed Brubaker
PENCILS: Luke Ross
with Butch Guice (*Who Will Wield the Shield?*)

INKS: Butch Guice
with Luke Ross (*Who Will Wield the Shield?* & Issue #602)
& Rick Magyar (Issue #605)
COLOR ART: Dean White
LETTERERS: VC's Joe Caramagna
COVER ART: Gerald Parel
ASSOCIATE EDITOR: Lauren Sankovitch
EDITOR: Tom Brevoort

Captain America created by Joe Simon & Jack Kirby

Collection Editor: Jennifer Grünwald • Assistant Editor: Alex Starbuck
Associate Editor: John Denning • Editor, Special Projects: Mark D. Beazley
Senior Editor, Special Projects: Jeff Youngquist
Senior Vice President of Sales: David Gabriel

Editor in Chief: Joe Quesada • Publisher: Dan Buckley • Executive Producer: Alan Fine

CAPTAIN AMERICA: TWO AMERICAS. Contains material originally published in magazine form as CAPTAIN AMERICA #602-605 and CAPTAIN AMERICA: WHO WILL WIELD THE SHIELD? First printing 2010. Hardcover ISBN# 978-0-7851-4510-3. Softcover ISBN# 978-0-7851-4511-0. Published by MARVEL WORLDWIDE, INC., a subsidiary of MARVEL ENTERTAINMENT, LLC. OFFICE OF PUBLICATION: 417 5th Avenue, New York, NY 10016. Copyright © 2009 and 2010 Marvel Characters, Inc. All rights reserved. Hardcover: $19.99 per copy in the U.S. and $22.50 in Canada (GST #R127032852). Softcover: $14.99 per copy in the U.S. and $16.99 in Canada (GST #R127032852). Canadian Agreement #40668537. All characters featured in this issue and the distinctive names and likenesses thereof, and all related indicia are trademarks of Marvel Characters, Inc. No similarity between any of the names, characters, persons, and/or institutions in this magazine with those of any living or dead person or institution is intended, and any such similarity which may exist is purely coincidental. **Printed in the U.S.A.** ALAN FINE, EVP - Office of the President, Marvel Worldwide, Inc. and EVP & CMO Marvel Characters B.V.; DAN BUCKLEY, Chief Executive Officer and Publisher - Print, Animation & Digital Media; JIM SOKOLOWSKI, Chief Operating Officer; DAVID GABRIEL, SVP of Publishing Sales & Circulation; DAVID BOGART, SVP of Business Affairs & Talent Management; MICHAEL PASCIULLO, VP Merchandising & Communications; JIM O'KEEFE, VP of Operations & Logistics; DAN CARR, Executive Director of Publishing Technology; JUSTIN F. GABRIE, Director of Publishing & Editorial Operations; SUSAN CRESPI, Editorial Operations Manager; ALEX MORALES, Publishing Operations Manager; STAN LEE, Chairman Emeritus. For information regarding advertising in Marvel Comics or on Marvel.com, please contact Ron Stern, VP of Business Development, at rstern@marvel.com. For Marvel subscription inquiries, please call 800-217-9158. **Manufactured between 6/7/10 and 7/7/10 (hardcover), and 6/7/10 and 11/3/10 (softcover), by R.R. DONNELLEY, INC., SALEM, VA, USA.**

0987654321

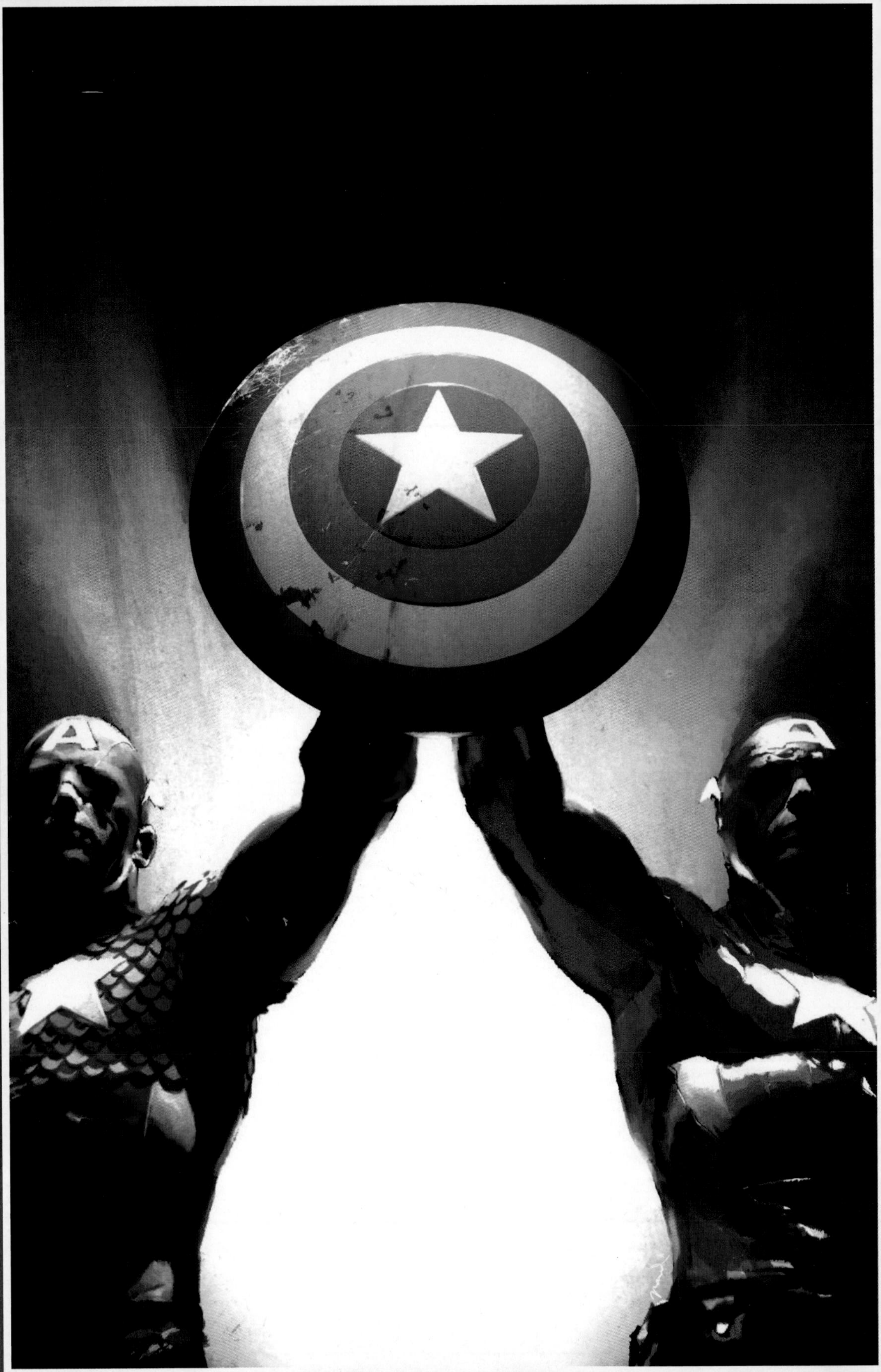

WHO WILL WIELD THE SHIELD?

CAPTAIN AMERICA

WHO WILL WIELD THE SHIELD?

In the wake of the superhuman Civil War, Captain America was to be arraigned for his violation of the Superhuman Registration Act...but Steve Rogers never made it to trial. On the steps of the federal courthouse Sharon Carter, Steve's lover, an agent of S.H.I.E.L.D. and unwilling puppet of the Red Skull, assassinated Captain America.

The Red Skull, trapped in a robot body and out for revenge against his greatest nemesis, had set a plan in motion. The gun Carter used, specially designed by renegade Nazi scientist Arnim Zola, severed Rogers' consciousness from his body, seemingly rendering him dead. Carter managed to break free from her conditioning in time to stop the Skull and Zola from carrying out their mysterious plot. As a result of her interference, Steve's consciousness became unhinged in time and he was forced to endure his entire history in an endless loop, unable to truly die.

With the help of Dr. Doom and Norman Osborn, the Red Skull reanimated Rogers' body, but kept Steve locked in his own subconscious. The Skull took over Captain America's body, planning to pose as the resurrected patriot to execute his master plan.

Carter, hoping to right her wrong, sought help from the Mighty Avengers, including James "Bucky" Barnes – Steve's old partner, the former Winter Soldier, and the new Captain America. Together, they discovered the Skull's endgame, and prepared to stop it.

On the steps of the Lincoln Memorial, Barnes and Rogers fought the Red Skull, both inside and out of Steve's body. Ultimately, Rogers won out, forcing the Red Skull from his mind. Before Steve recovered control of his body, though, he saw not only his past...but a glimpse of the future.

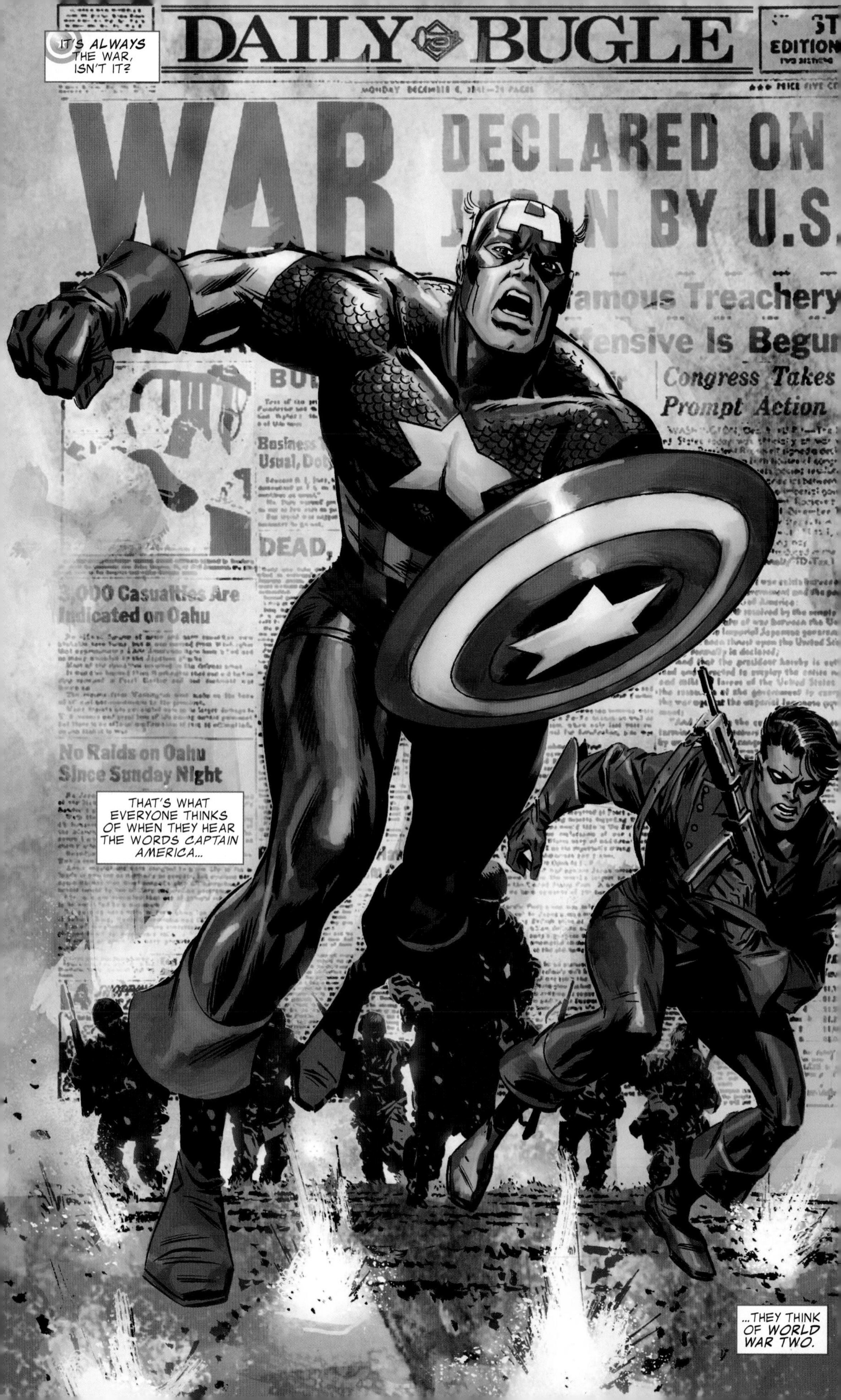
IT'S ALWAYS THE WAR, ISN'T IT?
DAILY BUGLE
WAR
DECLARED ON
BY U.S.
Congress Takes Prompt Action
DEAD,
3,000 Casualties Are Indicated on Oahu
No Raids on Oahu Since Sunday Night
THAT'S WHAT EVERYONE THINKS OF WHEN THEY HEAR THE WORDS CAPTAIN AMERICA...
...THEY THINK OF WORLD WAR TWO.

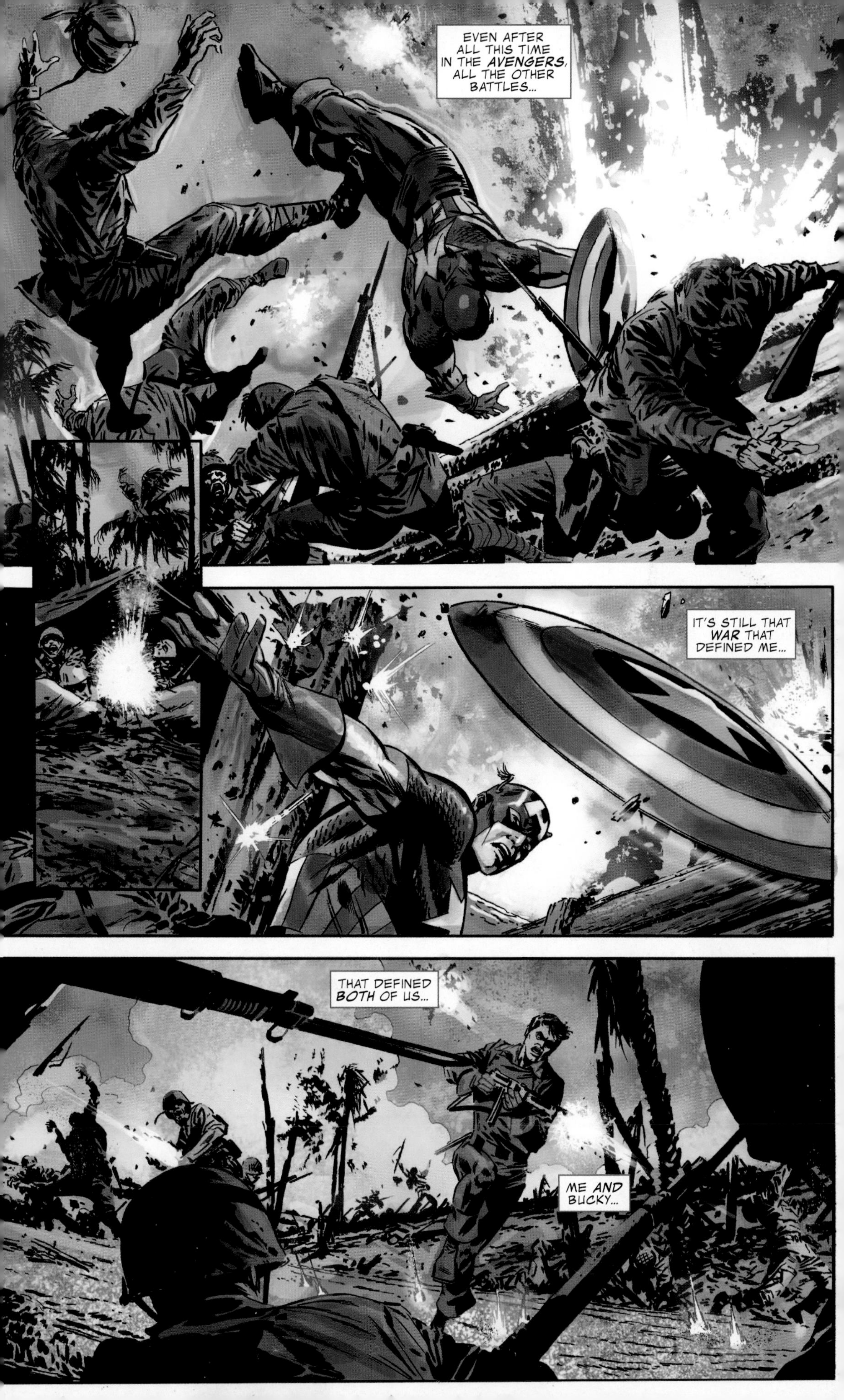
EVEN AFTER ALL THIS TIME IN THE AVENGERS, ALL THE OTHER BATTLES...
IT'S STILL THAT WAR THAT DEFINED ME...
THAT DEFINED BOTH OF US...
ME AND BUCKY...

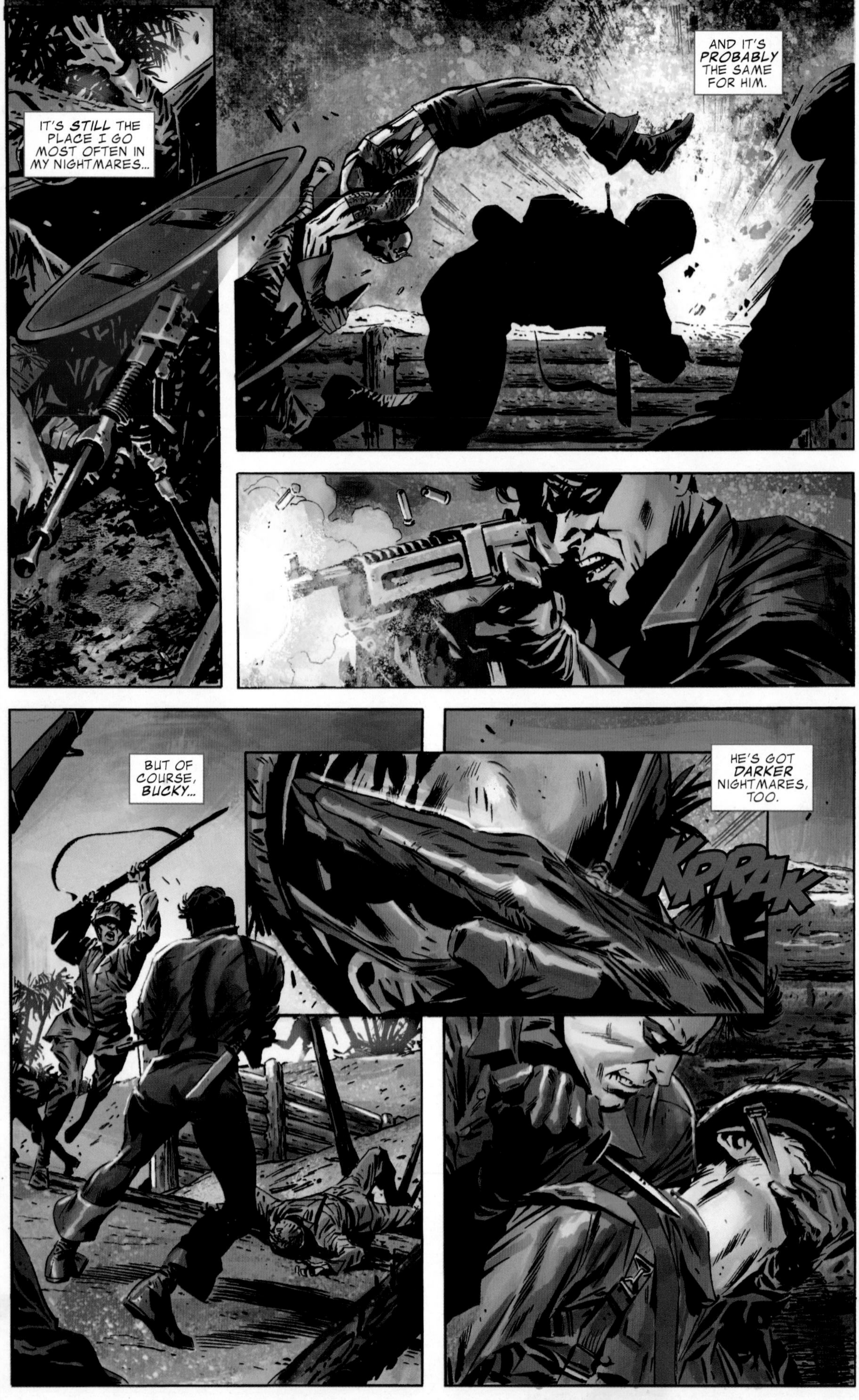
IT'S STILL THE PLACE I GO MOST OFTEN IN MY NIGHTMARES...
AND IT'S PROBABLY THE SAME FOR HIM.
BUT OF COURSE, BUCKY...
HE'S GOT DARKER NIGHTMARES, TOO.
KRRAK

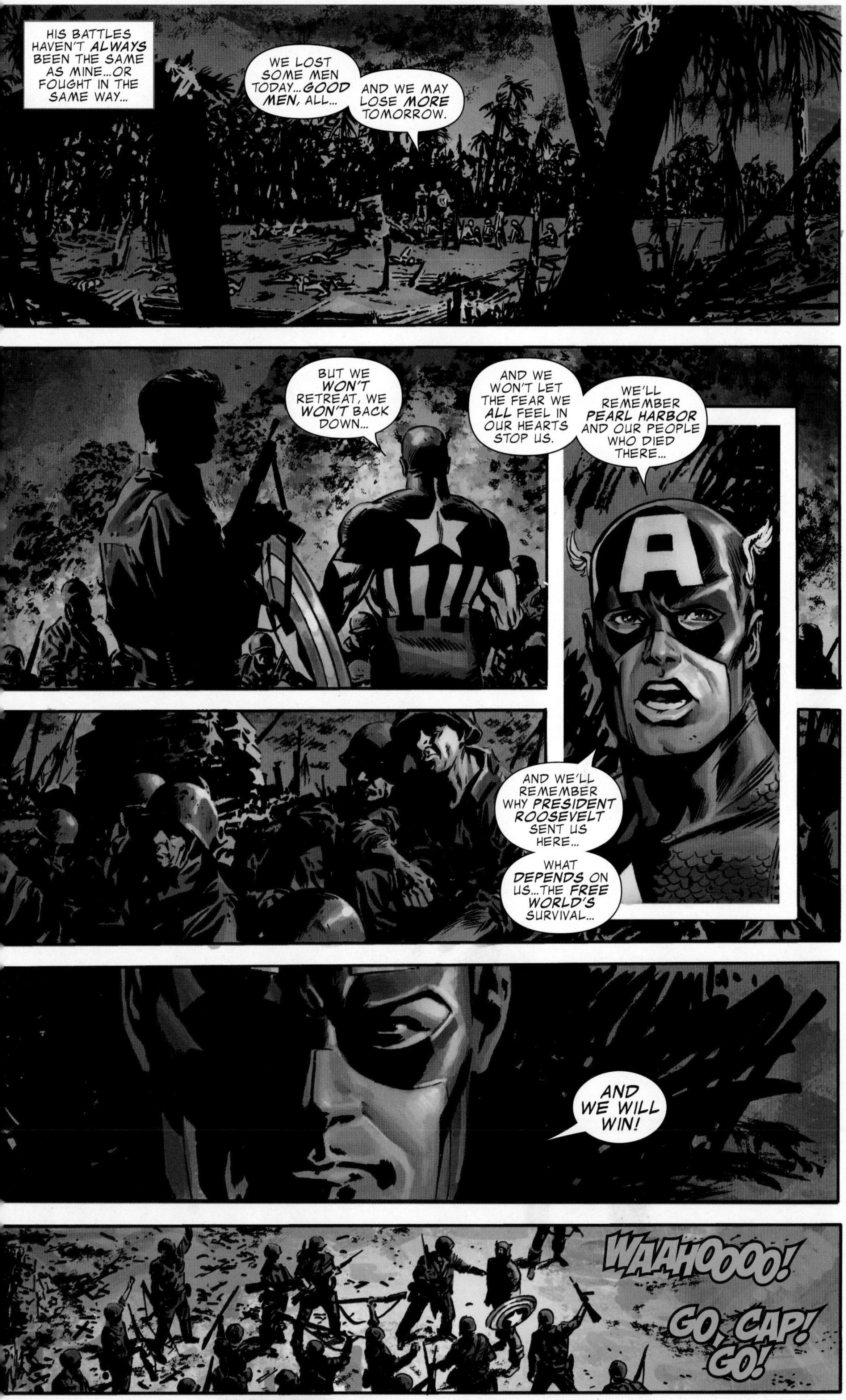
HIS BATTLES HAVEN'T ALWAYS BEEN THE SAME AS MINE...OR FOUGHT IN THE SAME WAY...
WE LOST SOME MEN TODAY...GOOD MEN, ALL...
AND WE MAY LOSE MORE TOMORROW.
BUT WE WON'T RETREAT, WE WON'T BACK DOWN...
AND WE WON'T LET THE FEAR WE ALL FEEL IN OUR HEARTS STOP US.
WE'LL REMEMBER PEARL HARBOR AND OUR PEOPLE WHO DIED THERE...
AND WE'LL REMEMBER WHY PRESIDENT ROOSEVELT SENT US HERE...
WHAT DEPENDS ON US...THE FREE WORLD'S SURVIVAL...
AND WE WILL WIN!
WAAHOOOO!
GO, CAP! GO!

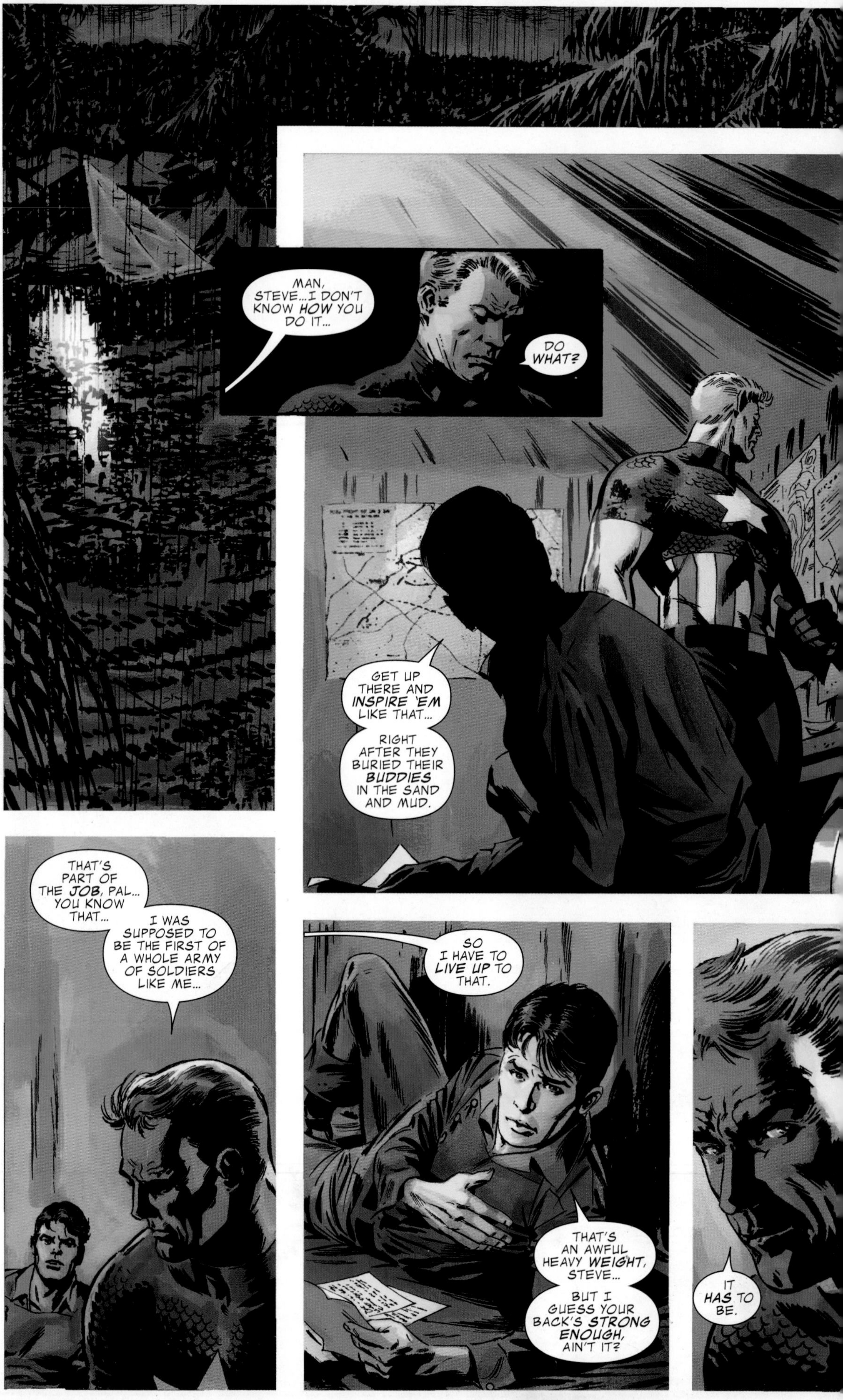
MAN, STEVE...I DON'T KNOW HOW YOU DO IT...
DO WHAT?
GET UP THERE AND INSPIRE 'EM LIKE THAT...
RIGHT AFTER THEY BURIED THEIR BUDDIES IN THE SAND AND MUD.
THAT'S PART OF THE JOB, PAL... YOU KNOW THAT...
I WAS SUPPOSED TO BE THE FIRST OF A WHOLE ARMY OF SOLDIERS LIKE ME...
SO I HAVE TO LIVE UP TO THAT.
THAT'S AN AWFUL HEAVY WEIGHT, STEVE...
BUT I GUESS YOUR BACK'S STRONG ENOUGH, AIN'T IT?
IT HAS TO BE.

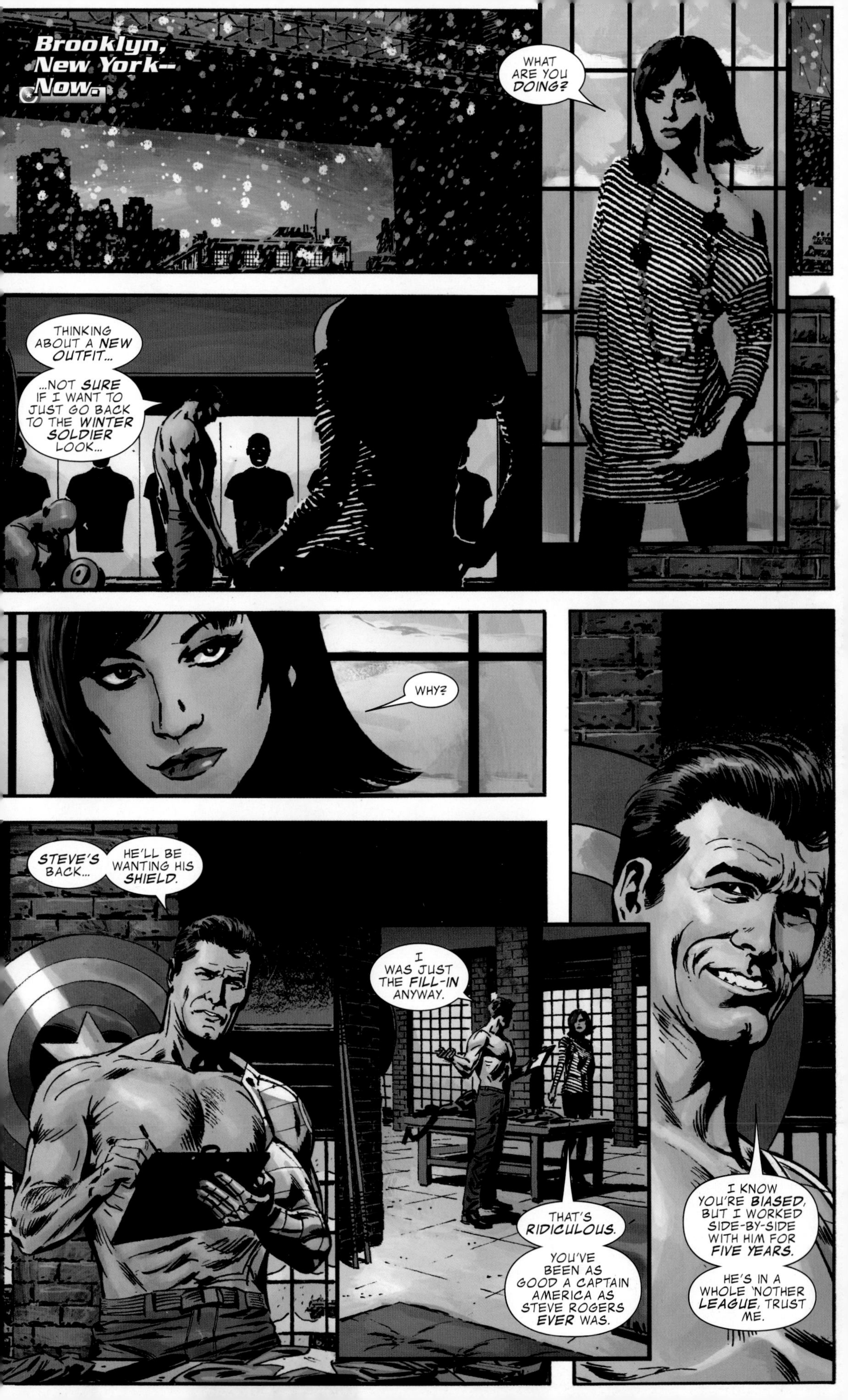

Brooklyn, New York-- Now.
WHAT ARE YOU DOING?
THINKING ABOUT A NEW OUTFIT...
...NOT SURE IF I WANT TO JUST GO BACK TO THE WINTER SOLDIER LOOK...
WHY?
STEVE'S BACK...
HE'LL BE WANTING HIS SHIELD.
I WAS JUST THE FILL-IN ANYWAY.
THAT'S RIDICULOUS.
YOU'VE BEEN AS GOOD A CAPTAIN AMERICA AS STEVE ROGERS EVER WAS.
I KNOW YOU'RE BIASED, BUT I WORKED SIDE-BY-SIDE WITH HIM FOR FIVE YEARS.
HE'S IN A WHOLE 'NOTHER LEAGUE, TRUST ME.

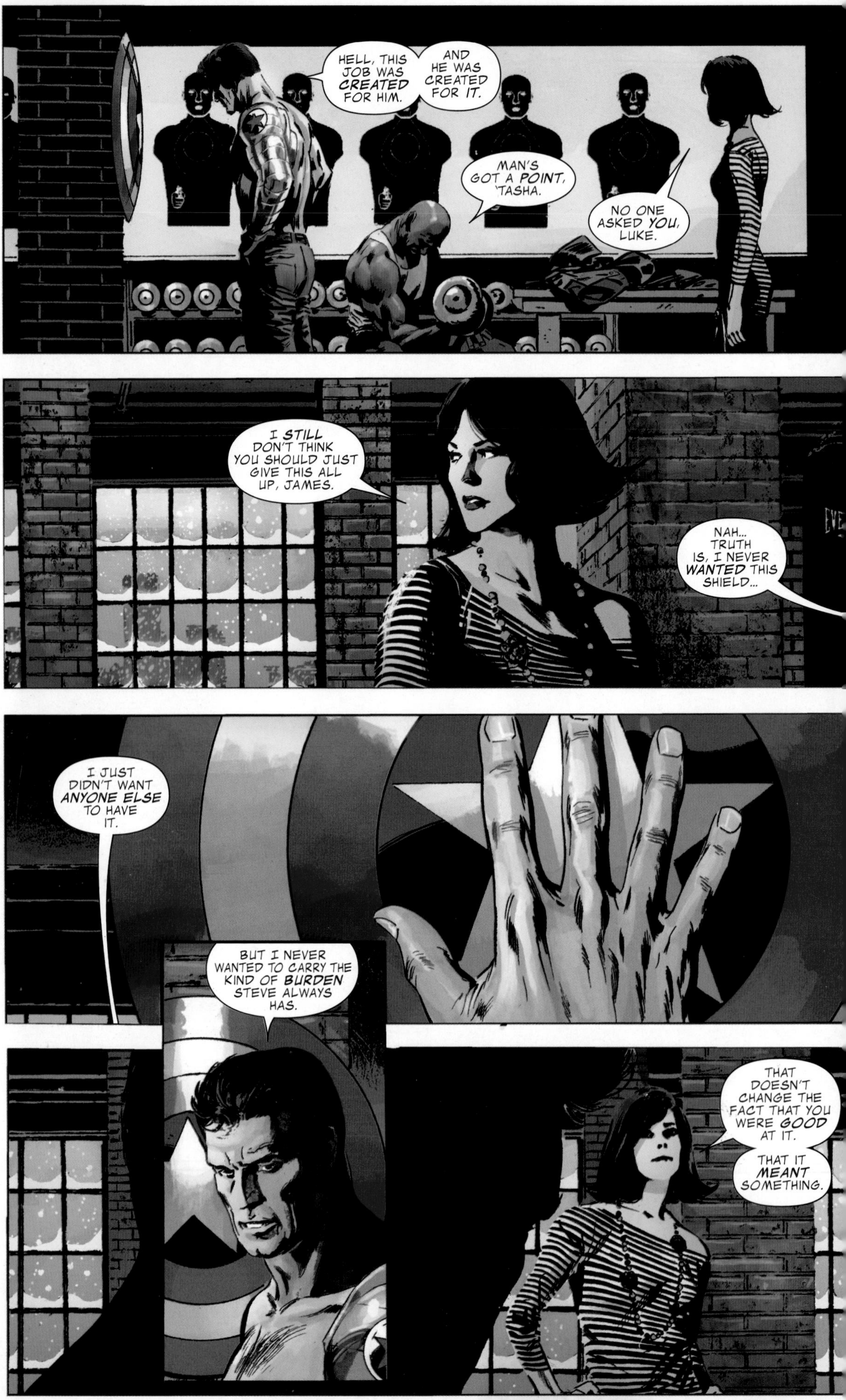
HELL, THIS JOB WAS CREATED FOR HIM.
AND HE WAS CREATED FOR IT.
MAN'S GOT A POINT, 'TASHA.
NO ONE ASKED YOU, LUKE.
I STILL DON'T THINK YOU SHOULD JUST GIVE THIS ALL UP, JAMES.
NAH... TRUTH IS, I NEVER WANTED THIS SHIELD...
I JUST DIDN'T WANT ANYONE ELSE TO HAVE IT.
BUT I NEVER WANTED TO CARRY THE KIND OF BURDEN STEVE ALWAYS HAS.
THAT DOESN'T CHANGE THE FACT THAT YOU WERE GOOD AT IT.
THAT IT MEANT SOMETHING.

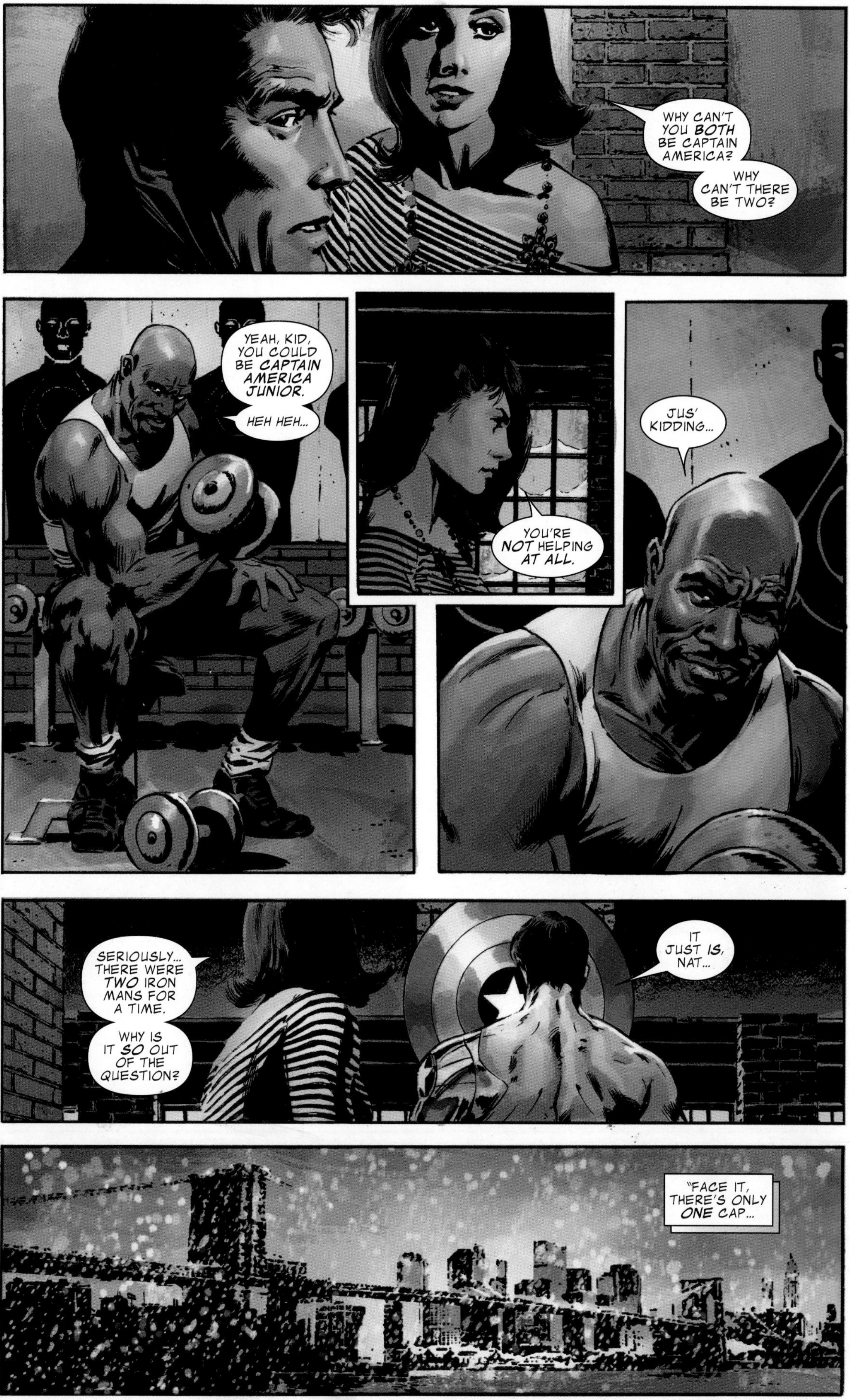
WHY CAN'T YOU BOTH BE CAPTAIN AMERICA?
WHY CAN'T THERE BE TWO?
YEAH, KID, YOU COULD BE CAPTAIN AMERICA JUNIOR.
HEH HEH...
YOU'RE NOT HELPING AT ALL.
JUS' KIDDING...
SERIOUSLY... THERE WERE TWO IRON MANS FOR A TIME.
WHY IS IT SO OUT OF THE QUESTION?
IT JUST IS, NAT...
"FACE IT, THERE'S ONLY ONE CAP...

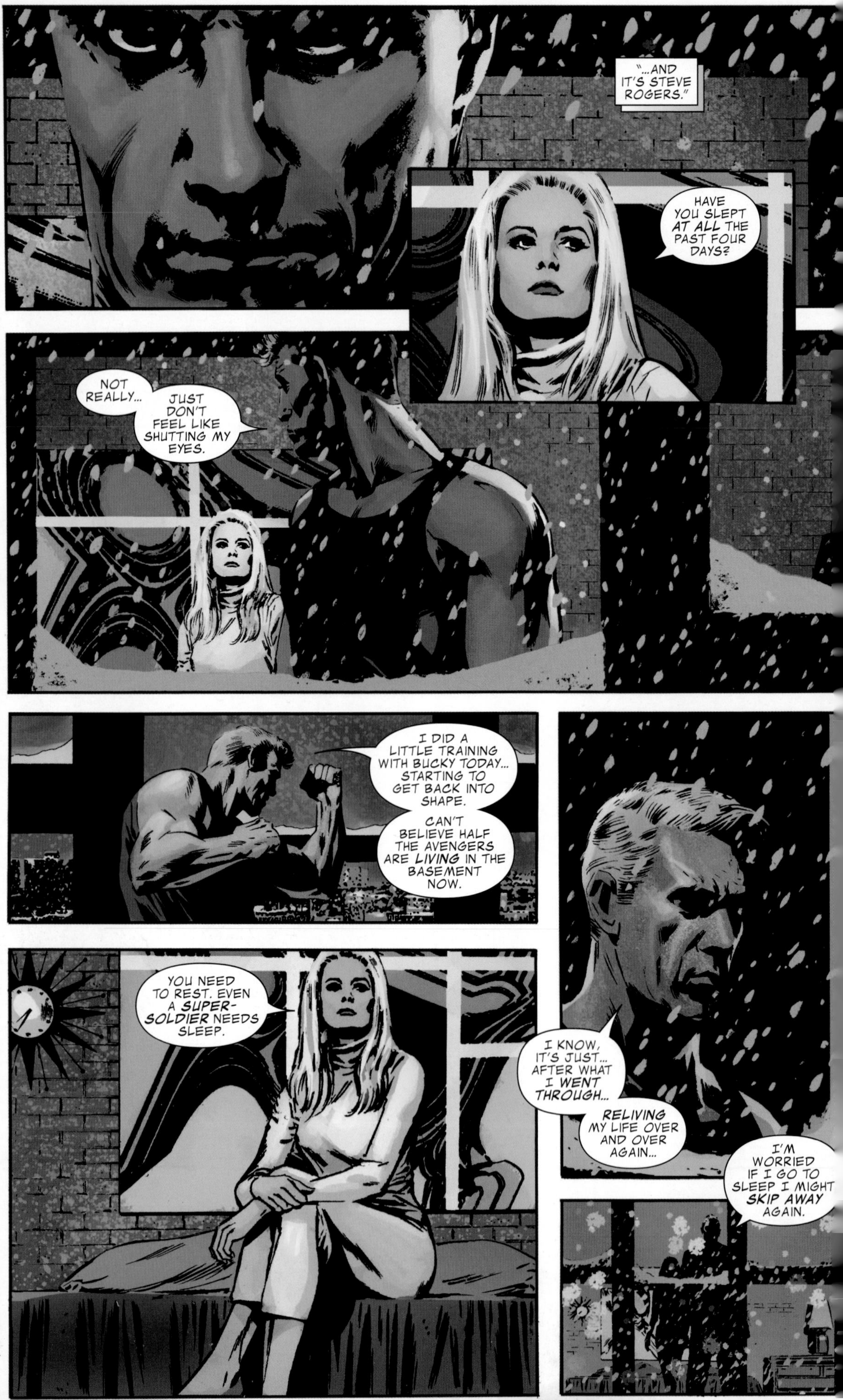

"...AND IT'S STEVE ROGERS."
HAVE YOU SLEPT AT ALL THE PAST FOUR DAYS?
NOT REALLY...
JUST DON'T FEEL LIKE SHUTTING MY EYES.
I DID A LITTLE TRAINING WITH BUCKY TODAY... STARTING TO GET BACK INTO SHAPE.
CAN'T BELIEVE HALF THE AVENGERS ARE LIVING IN THE BASEMENT NOW.
YOU NEED TO REST. EVEN A SUPER-SOLDIER NEEDS SLEEP.
I KNOW, IT'S JUST... AFTER WHAT I WENT THROUGH...
RELIVING MY LIFE OVER AND OVER AGAIN...
I'M WORRIED IF I GO TO SLEEP I MIGHT SKIP AWAY AGAIN.

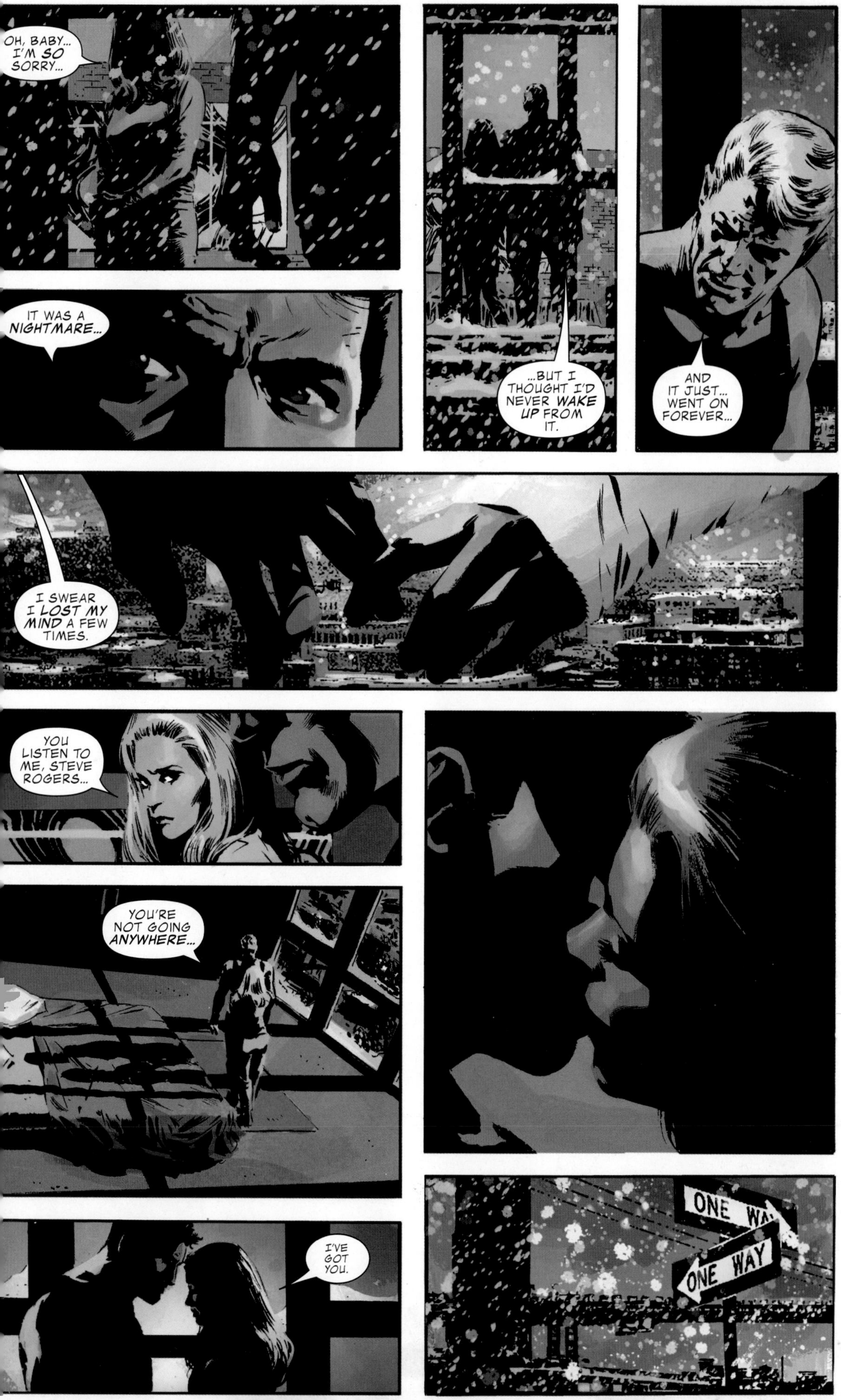

OH, BABY... I'M SO SORRY...
IT WAS A NIGHTMARE...
...BUT I THOUGHT I'D NEVER WAKE UP FROM IT.
AND IT JUST... WENT ON FOREVER...
I SWEAR I LOST MY MIND A FEW TIMES.
YOU LISTEN TO ME, STEVE ROGERS...
YOU'RE NOT GOING ANYWHERE...
I'VE GOT YOU.
ONE WAY
ONE WAY

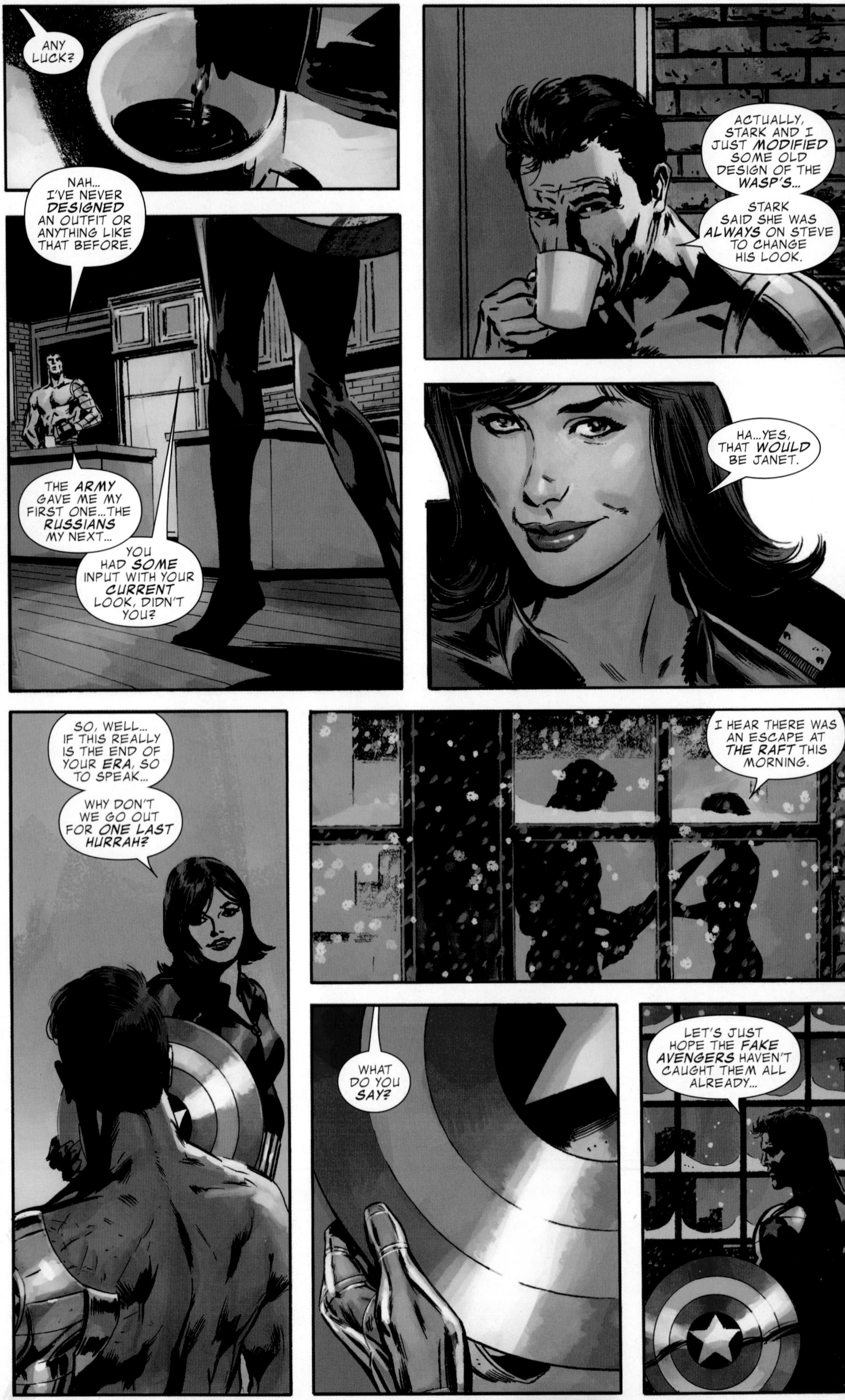
ANY LUCK?
ACTUALLY, STARK AND I JUST MODIFIED SOME OLD DESIGN OF THE WASP'S...
STARK SAID SHE WAS ALWAYS ON STEVE TO CHANGE HIS LOOK.
NAH... I'VE NEVER DESIGNED AN OUTFIT OR ANYTHING LIKE THAT BEFORE.
THE ARMY GAVE ME MY FIRST ONE...THE RUSSIANS MY NEXT...
YOU HAD SOME INPUT WITH YOUR CURRENT LOOK, DIDN'T YOU?
HA...YES, THAT WOULD BE JANET.
SO, WELL... IF THIS REALLY IS THE END OF YOUR ERA, SO TO SPEAK...
WHY DON'T WE GO OUT FOR ONE LAST HURRAH?
I HEAR THERE WAS AN ESCAPE AT THE RAFT THIS MORNING.
WHAT DO YOU SAY?
LET'S JUST HOPE THE FAKE AVENGERS HAVEN'T CAUGHT THEM ALL ALREADY...

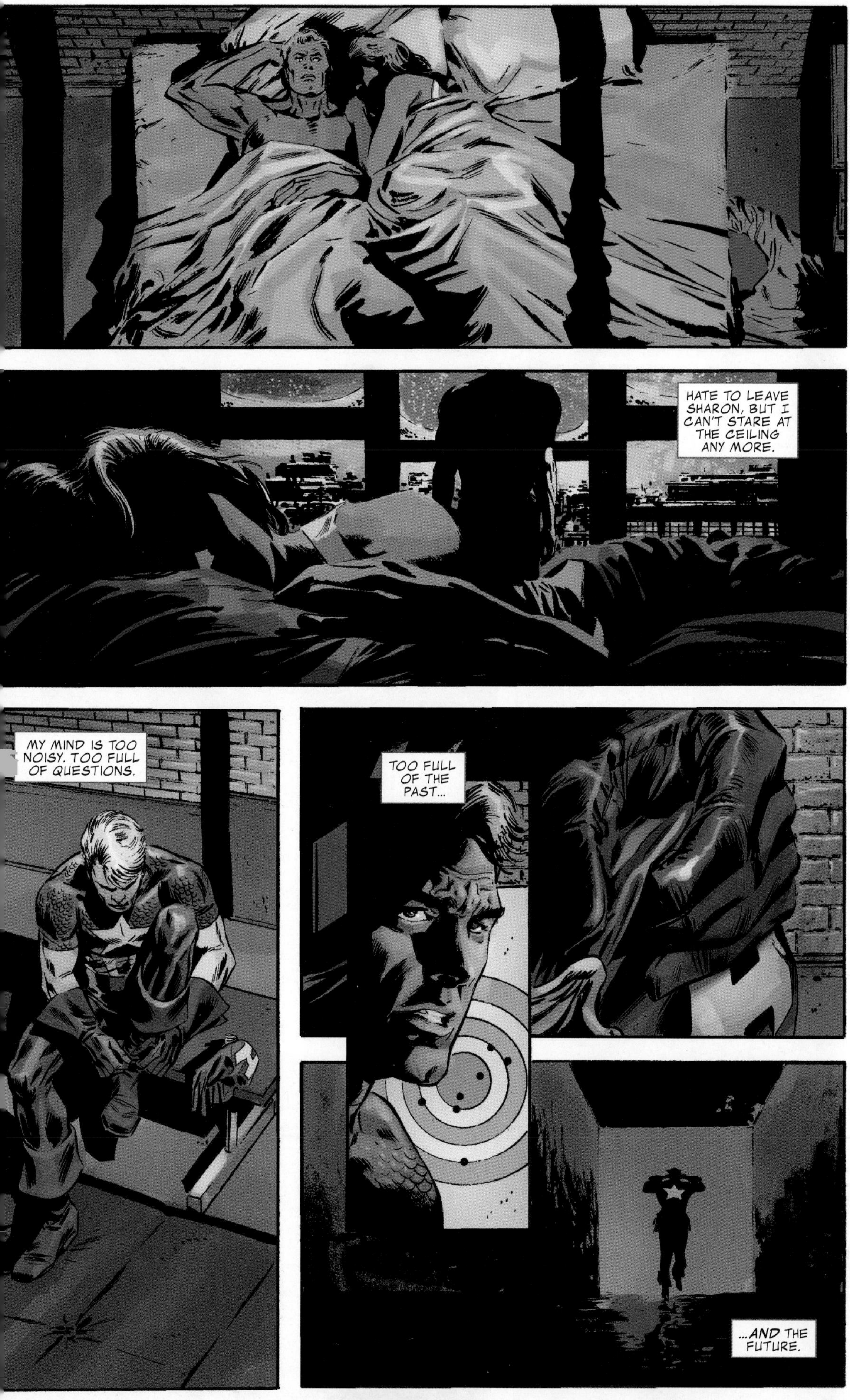
HATE TO LEAVE SHARON, BUT I CAN'T STARE AT THE CEILING ANY MORE.
MY MIND IS TOO NOISY. TOO FULL OF QUESTIONS.
TOO FULL OF THE PAST...
...AND THE FUTURE.

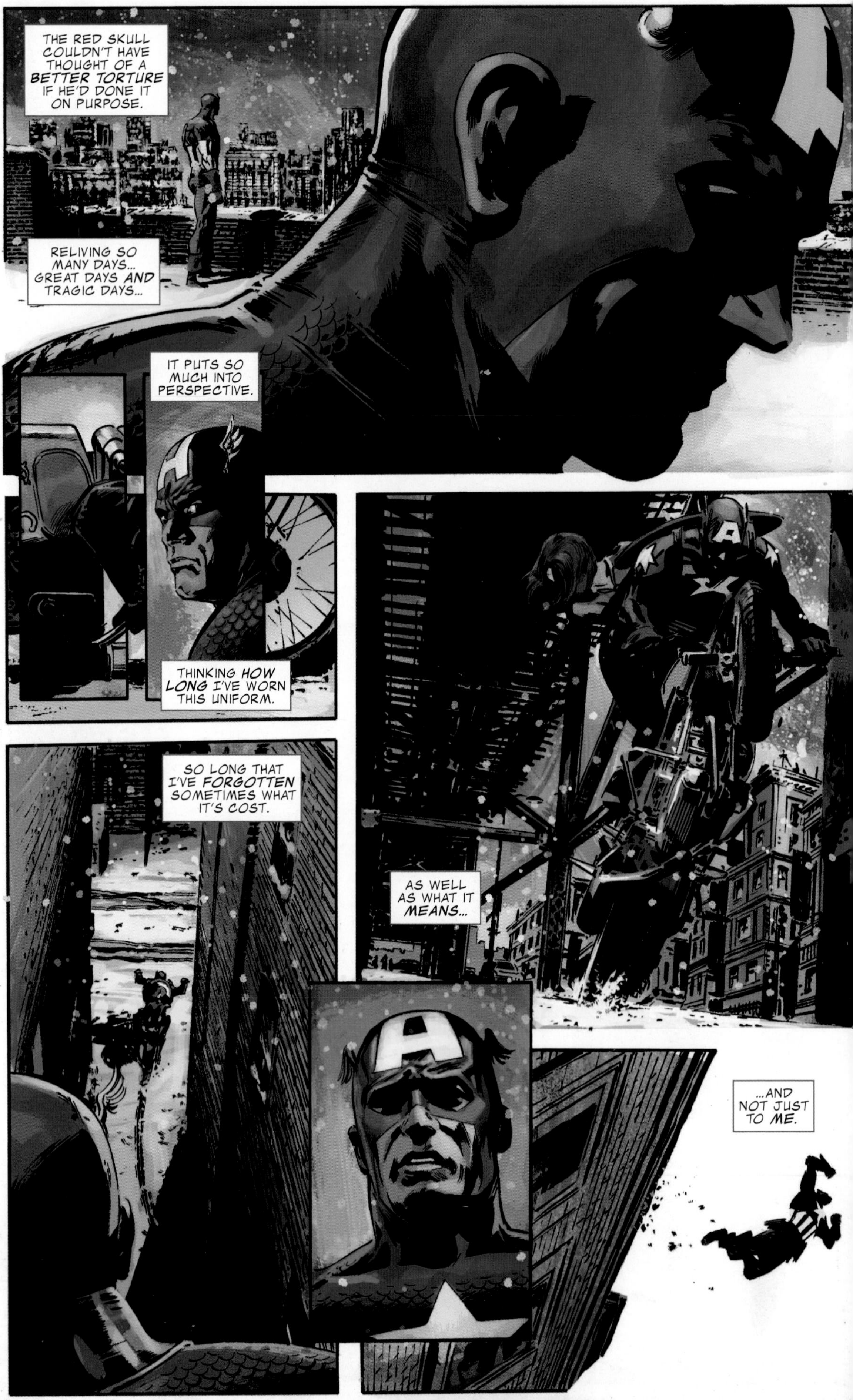
THE RED SKULL COULDN'T HAVE THOUGHT OF A BETTER TORTURE IF HE'D DONE IT ON PURPOSE.
RELIVING SO MANY DAYS... GREAT DAYS AND TRAGIC DAYS...
IT PUTS SO MUCH INTO PERSPECTIVE.
THINKING HOW LONG I'VE WORN THIS UNIFORM.
SO LONG THAT I'VE FORGOTTEN SOMETIMES WHAT IT'S COST.
AS WELL AS WHAT IT MEANS...
...AND NOT JUST TO ME.

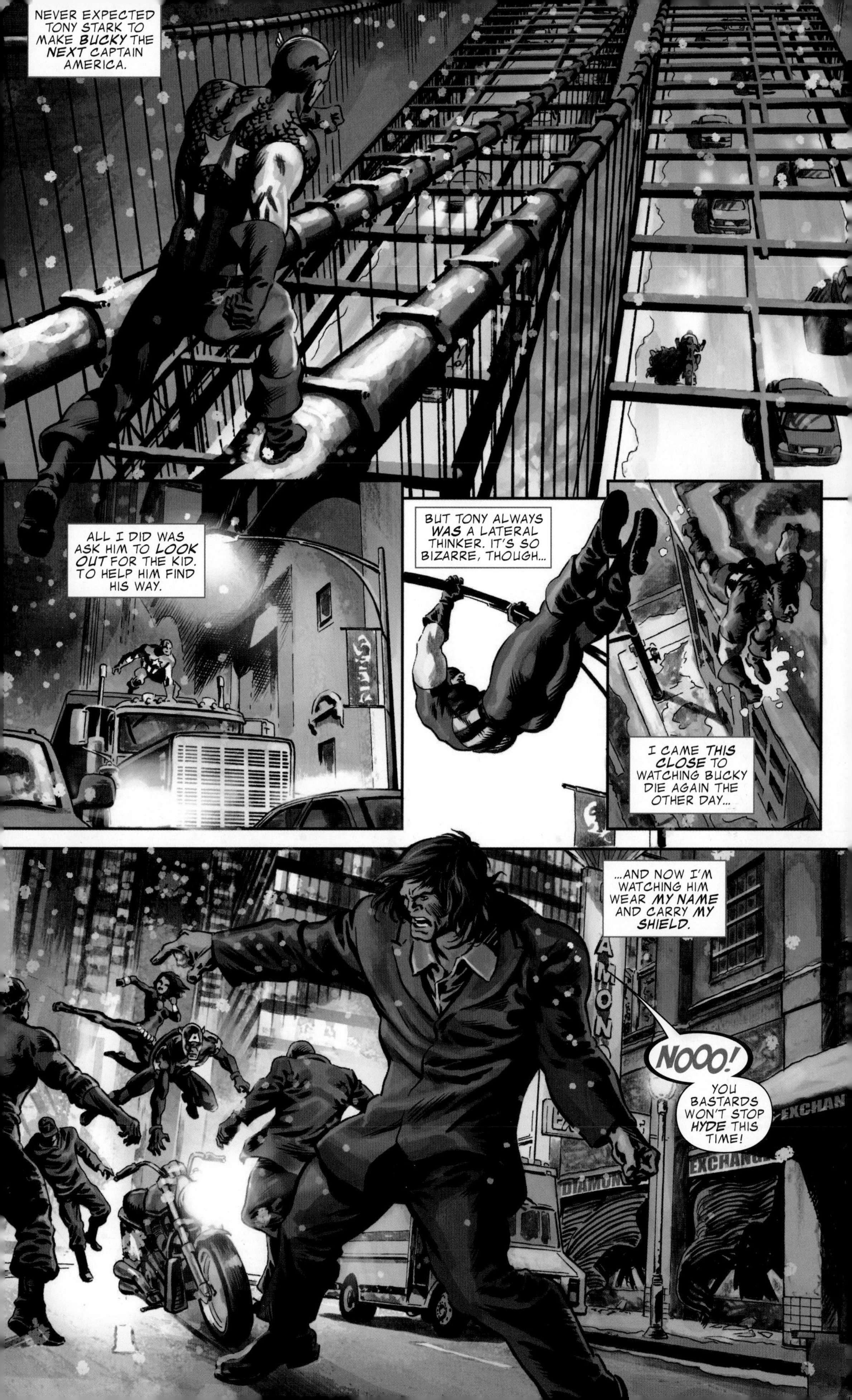
NEVER EXPECTED TONY STARK TO MAKE BUCKY THE NEXT CAPTAIN AMERICA.
ALL I DID WAS ASK HIM TO LOOK OUT FOR THE KID. TO HELP HIM FIND HIS WAY.
BUT TONY ALWAYS WAS A LATERAL THINKER. IT'S SO BIZARRE, THOUGH...
I CAME THIS CLOSE TO WATCHING BUCKY DIE AGAIN THE OTHER DAY...
...AND NOW I'M WATCHING HIM WEAR MY NAME AND CARRY MY SHIELD.
NOOO!
YOU BASTARDS WON'T STOP HYDE THIS TIME!
EXCHAN
EXCHANGE
DIAMON

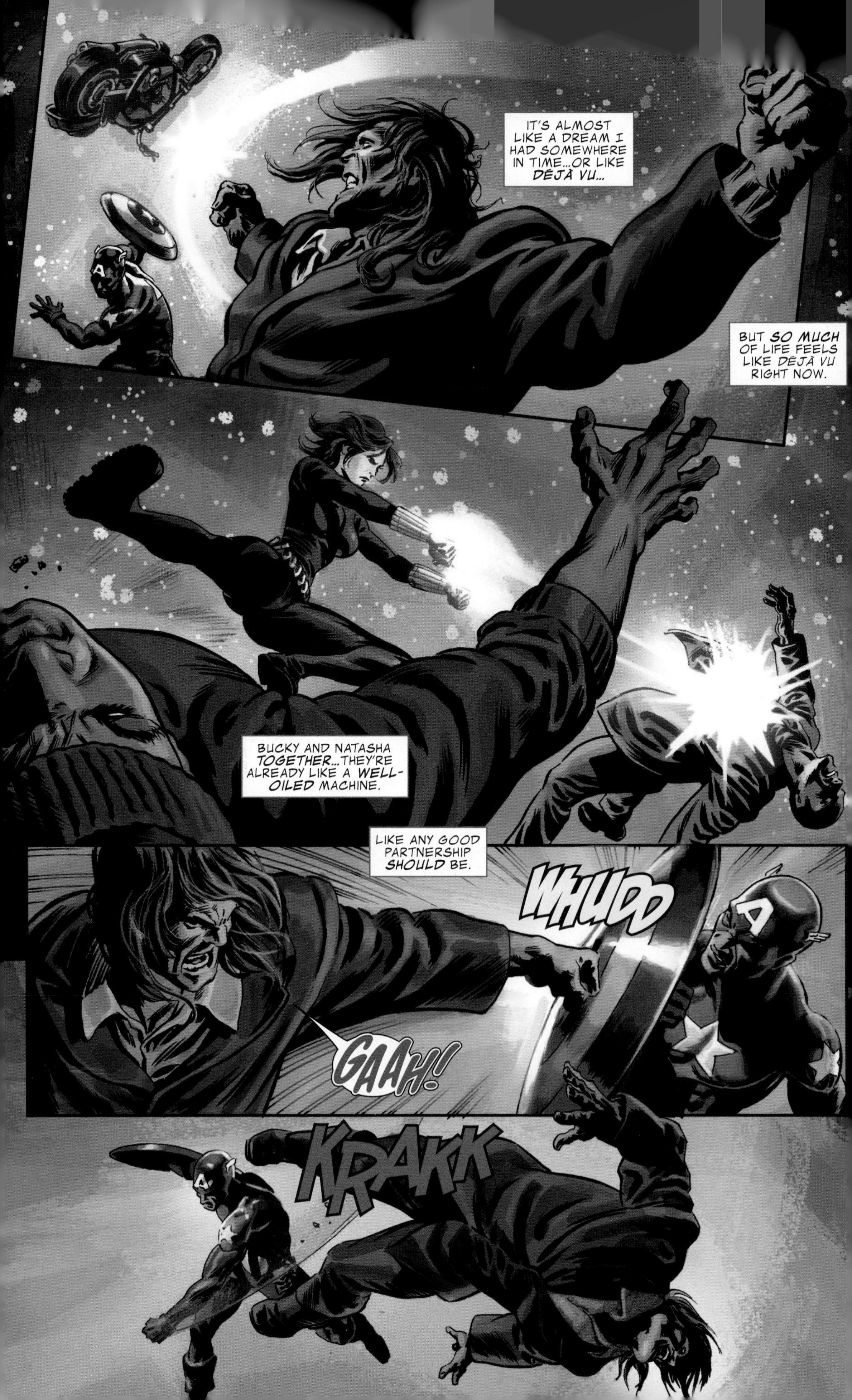
IT'S ALMOST LIKE A DREAM I HAD SOMEWHERE IN TIME...OR LIKE DÉJÀ VU...
BUT SO MUCH OF LIFE FEELS LIKE DÉJÀ VU RIGHT NOW.
BUCKY AND NATASHA TOGETHER...THEY'RE ALREADY LIKE A WELL-OILED MACHINE.
LIKE ANY GOOD PARTNERSHIP SHOULD BE.
WHUDD
GAAH!
KRAKK

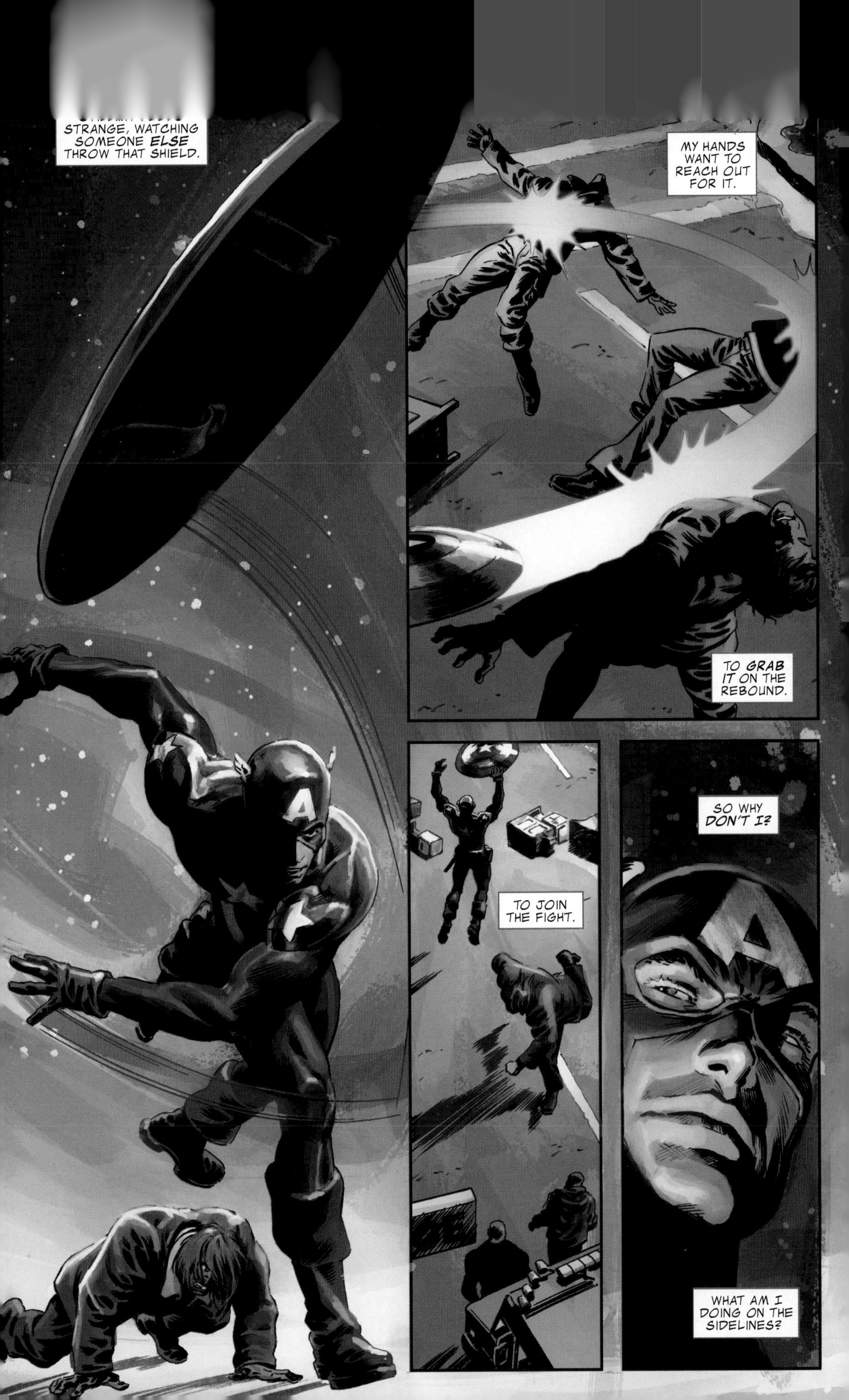

STRANGE, WATCHING SOMEONE *ELSE* THROW THAT SHIELD.
MY HANDS WANT TO REACH OUT FOR IT.
TO *GRAB IT* ON THE REBOUND.
TO JOIN THE FIGHT.
SO WHY *DON'T I?*
WHAT AM I DOING ON THE SIDELINES?

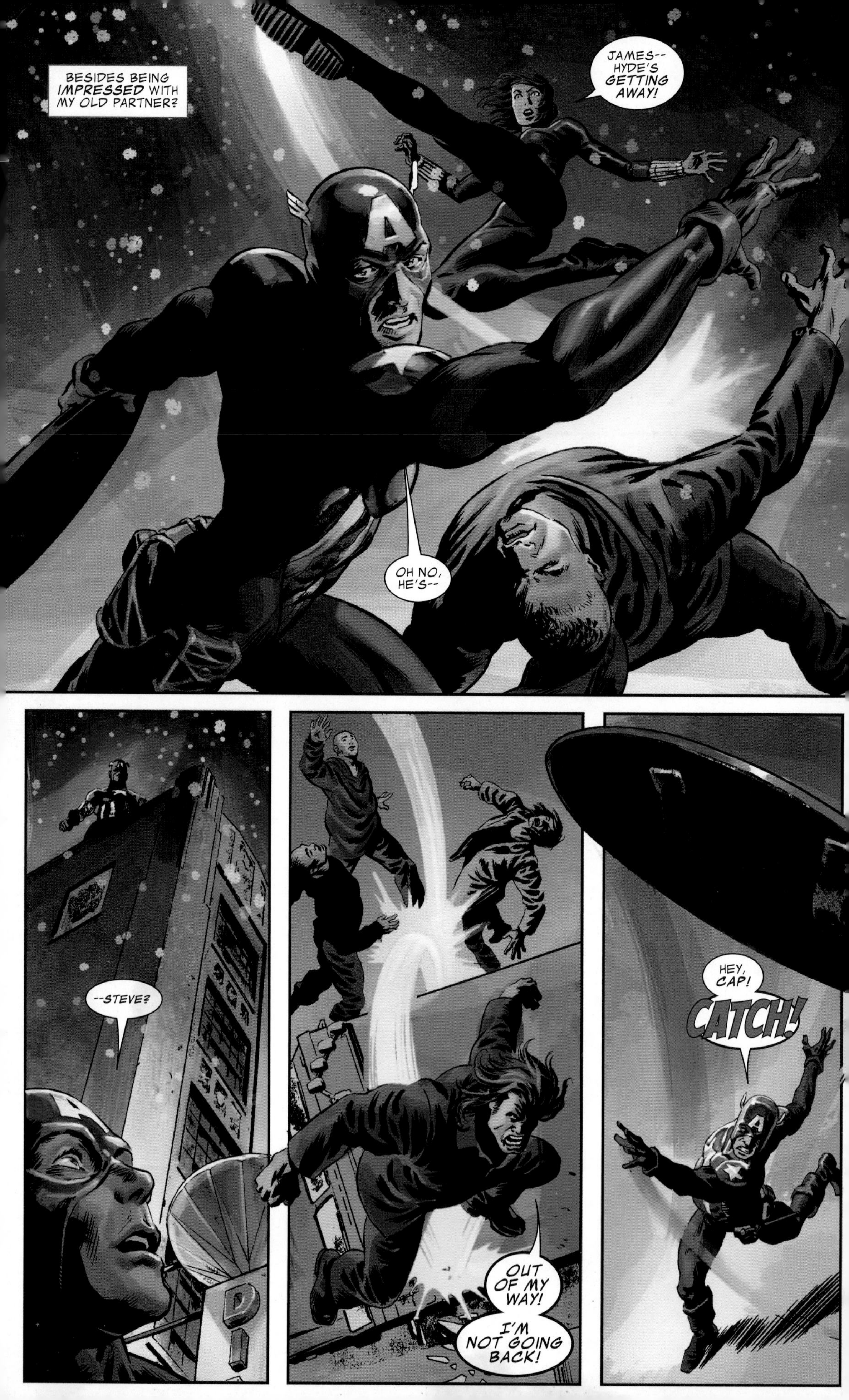
BESIDES BEING IMPRESSED WITH MY OLD PARTNER?
JAMES-- HYDE'S GETTING AWAY!
OH NO, HE'S--
--STEVE?
OUT OF MY WAY!
I'M NOT GOING BACK!
HEY, CAP!
CATCH!

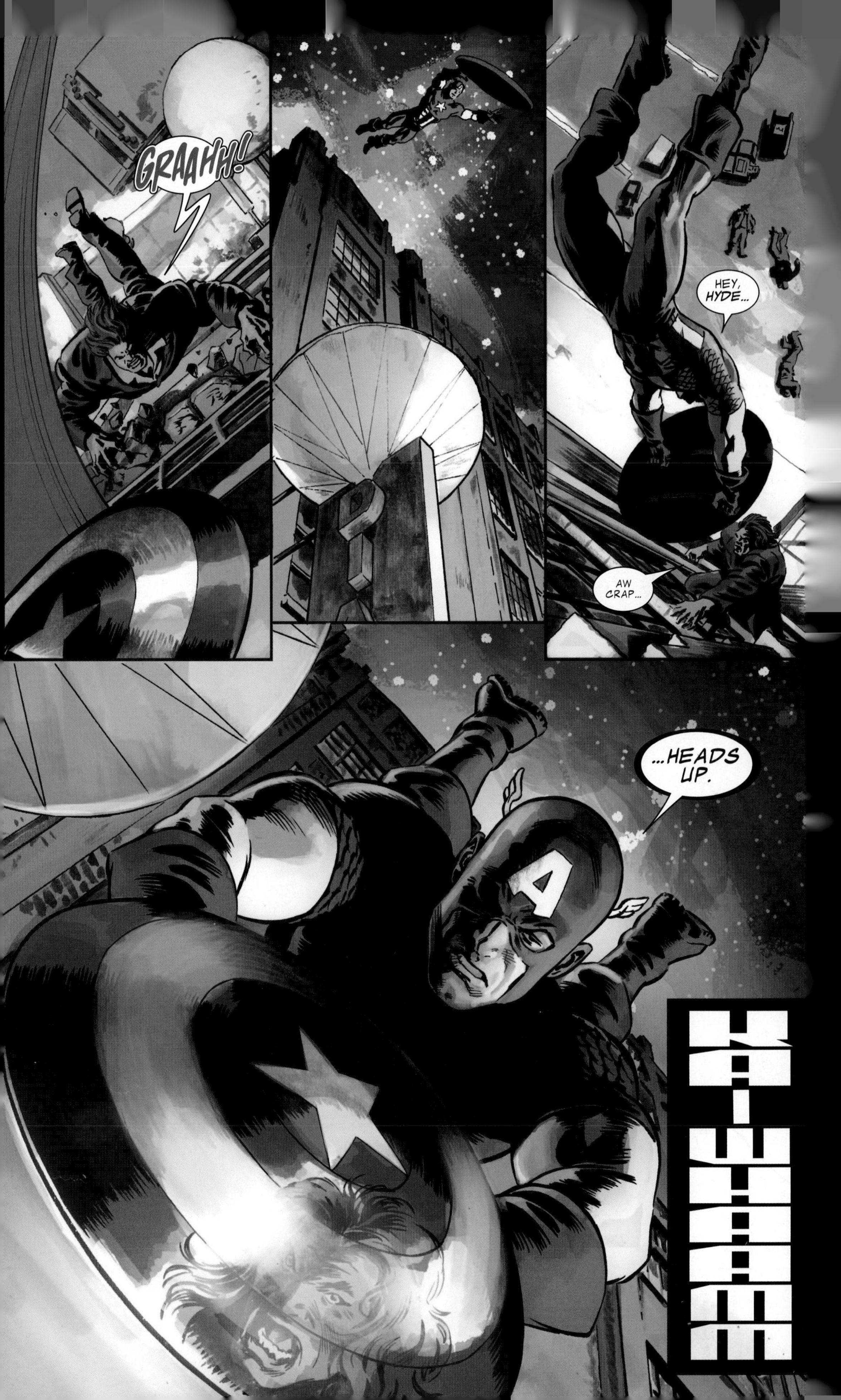
GRAAHH!
HEY, HYDE...
AW CRAP...
...HEADS UP.
KA-WHAAMM

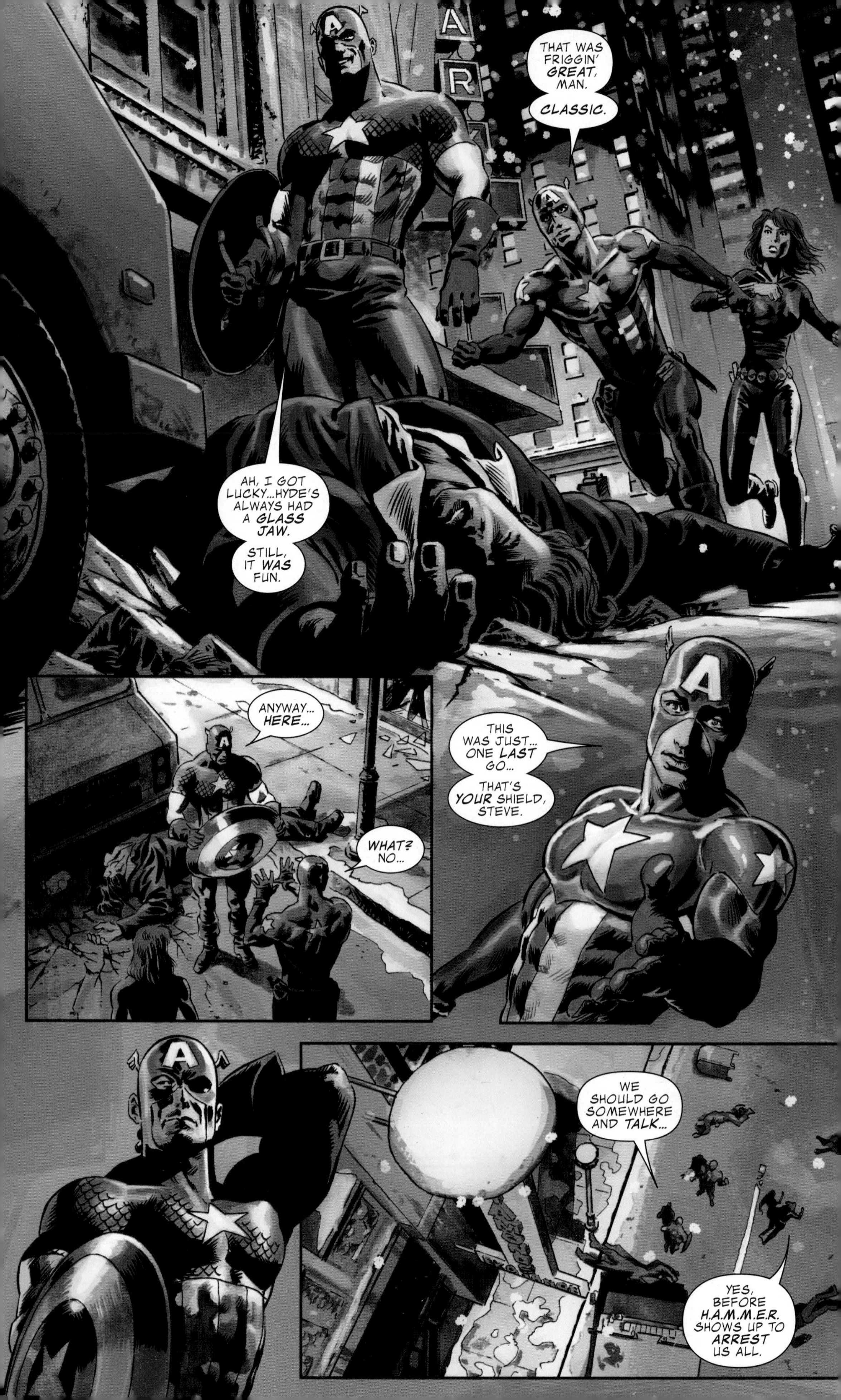
THAT WAS FRIGGIN' GREAT, MAN.
CLASSIC.
AH, I GOT LUCKY...HYDE'S ALWAYS HAD A GLASS JAW.
STILL, IT WAS FUN.
ANYWAY... HERE...
WHAT? NO...
THIS WAS JUST... ONE LAST GO...
THAT'S YOUR SHIELD, STEVE.
WE SHOULD GO SOMEWHERE AND TALK...
YES, BEFORE H.A.M.M.E.R. SHOWS UP TO ARREST US ALL.

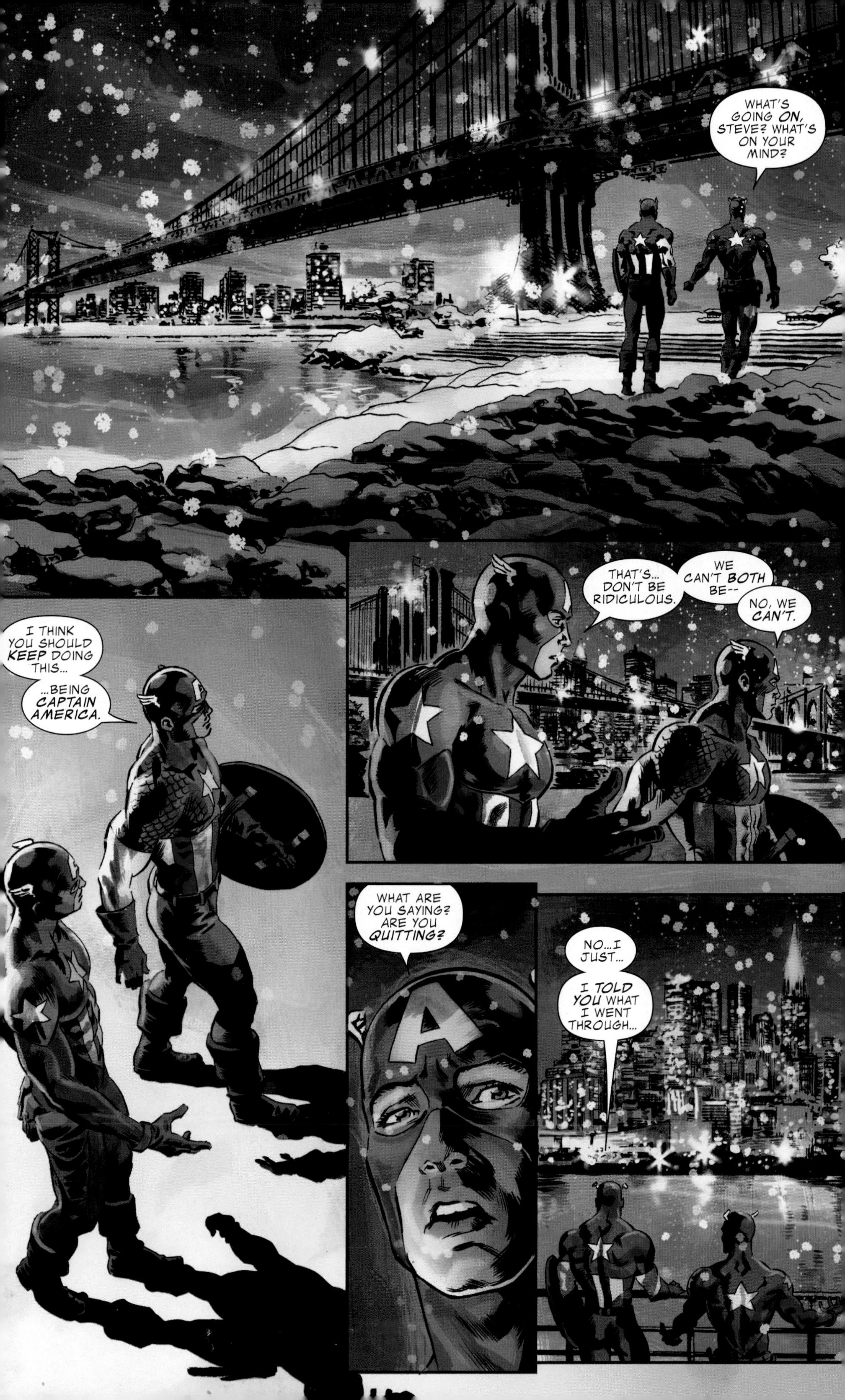
WHAT'S GOING ON, STEVE? WHAT'S ON YOUR MIND?
I THINK YOU SHOULD KEEP DOING THIS...
...BEING CAPTAIN AMERICA.
THAT'S... DON'T BE RIDICULOUS.
WE CAN'T BOTH BE--
NO, WE CAN'T.
WHAT ARE YOU SAYING? ARE YOU QUITTING?
NO...I JUST...
I TOLD YOU WHAT I WENT THROUGH...

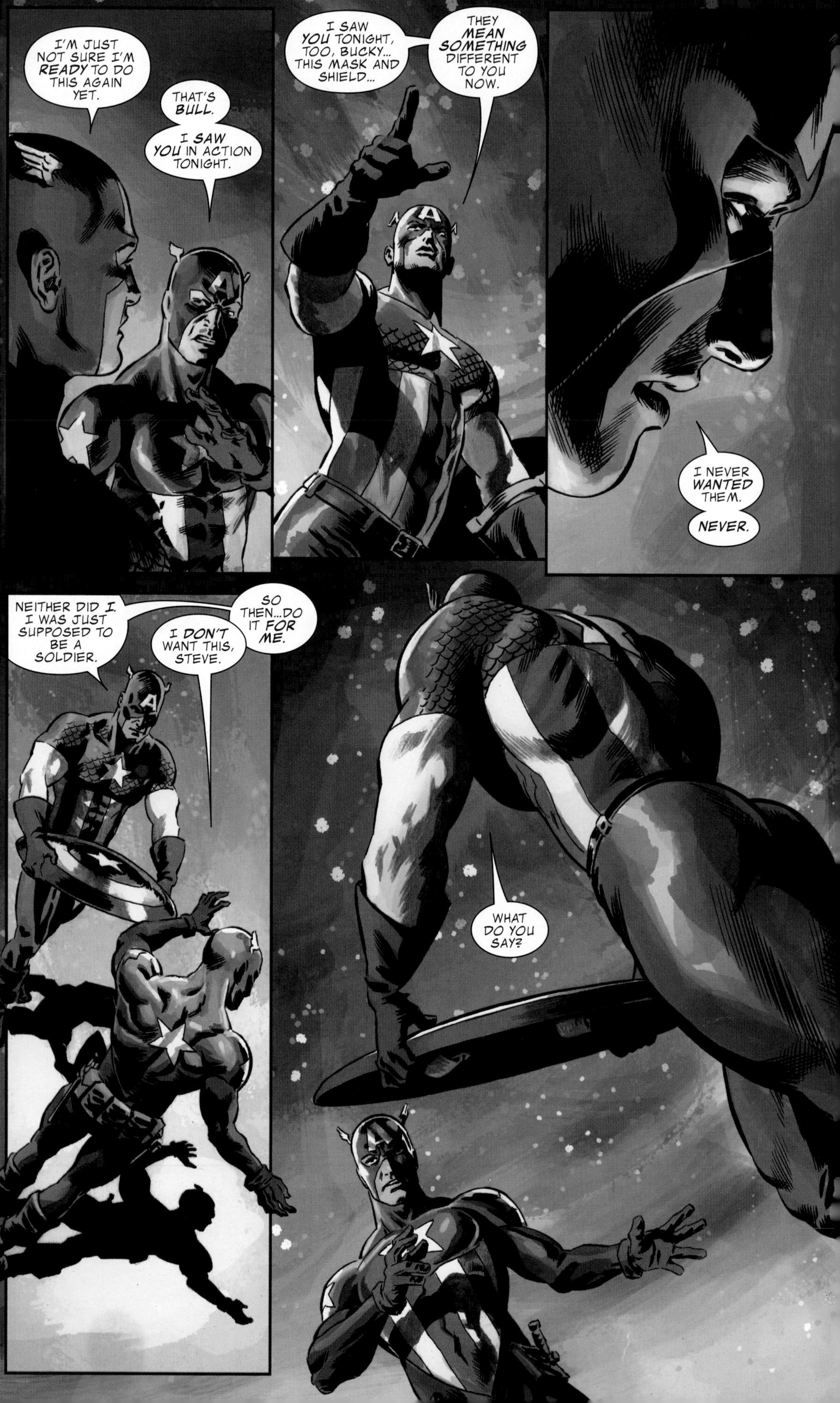
I'M JUST NOT SURE I'M READY TO DO THIS AGAIN YET.
THAT'S BULL.
I SAW YOU IN ACTION TONIGHT.
I SAW YOU TONIGHT, TOO, BUCKY... THIS MASK AND SHIELD...
THEY MEAN SOMETHING DIFFERENT TO YOU NOW.
I NEVER WANTED THEM.
NEVER.
NEITHER DID I. I WAS JUST SUPPOSED TO BE A SOLDIER.
I DON'T WANT THIS, STEVE.
SO THEN...DO IT FOR ME.
WHAT DO YOU SAY?

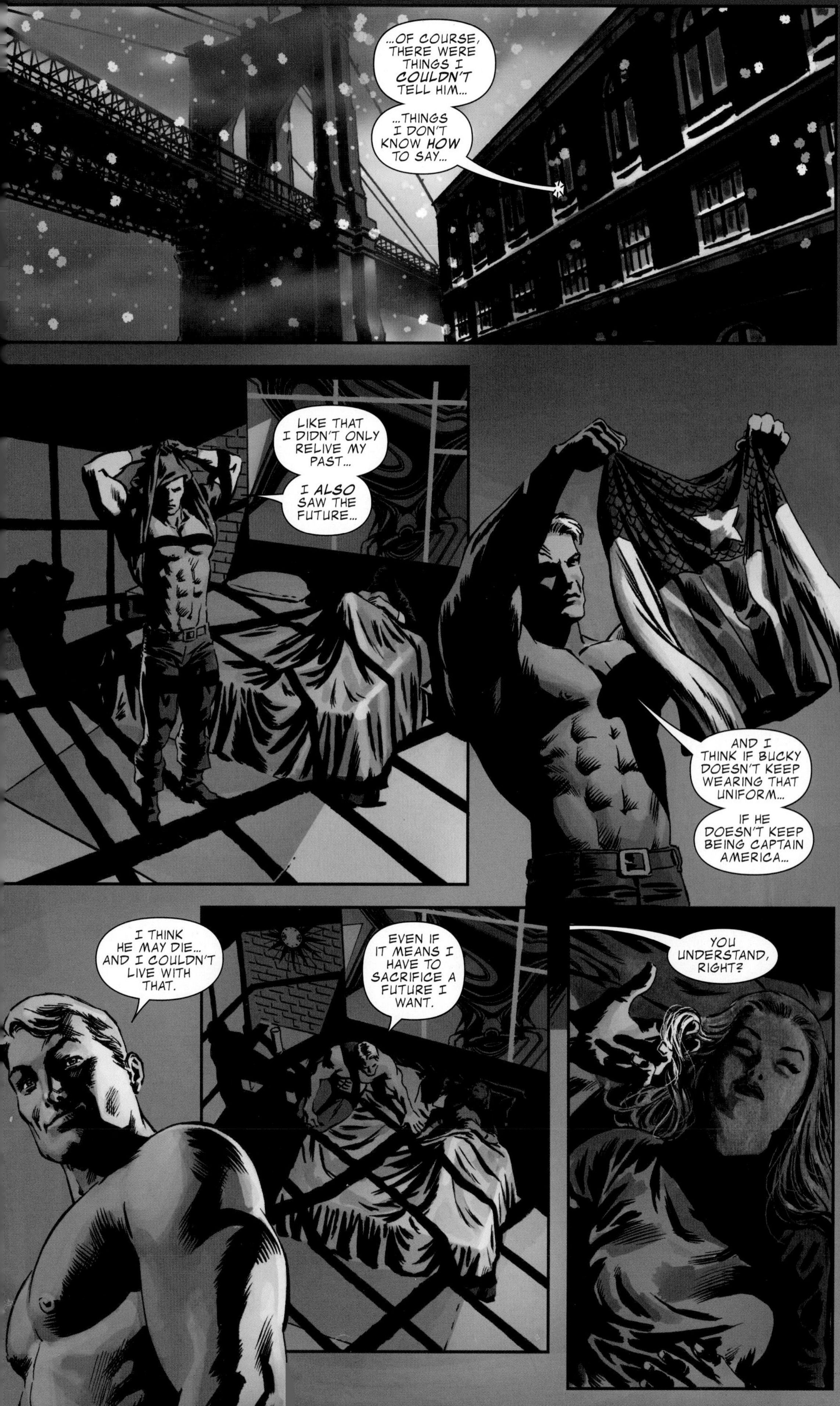

...OF COURSE, THERE WERE THINGS I COULDN'T TELL HIM...
...THINGS I DON'T KNOW HOW TO SAY...
LIKE THAT I DIDN'T ONLY RELIVE MY PAST...
I ALSO SAW THE FUTURE...
AND I THINK IF BUCKY DOESN'T KEEP WEARING THAT UNIFORM...
IF HE DOESN'T KEEP BEING CAPTAIN AMERICA...
I THINK HE MAY DIE... AND I COULDN'T LIVE WITH THAT.
EVEN IF IT MEANS I HAVE TO SACRIFICE A FUTURE I WANT.
YOU UNDERSTAND, RIGHT?

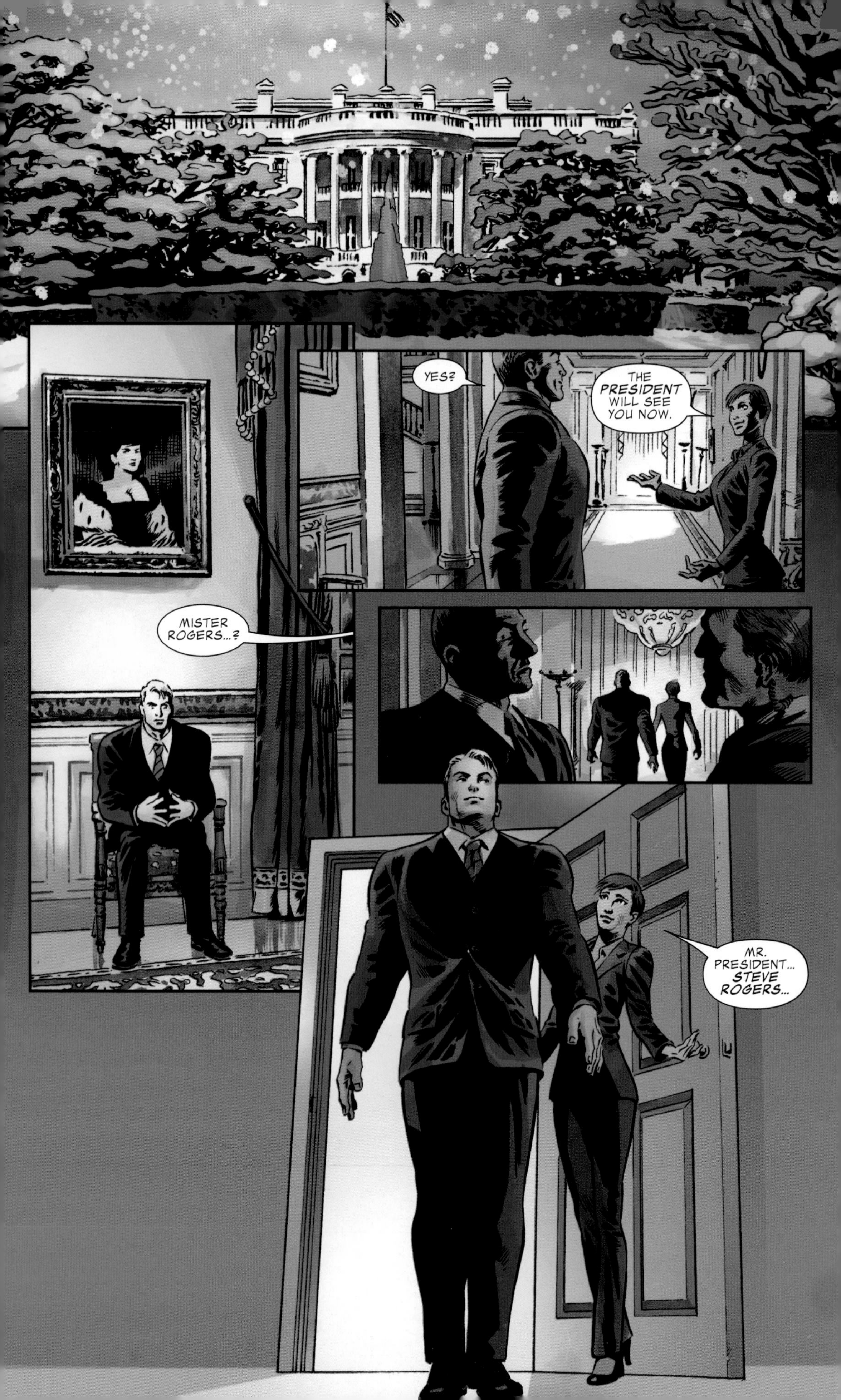

MISTER ROGERS...?
YES?
THE PRESIDENT WILL SEE YOU NOW.
MR. PRESIDENT... STEVE ROGERS...

MR. PRESIDENT. IT'S AN *HONOR*.

PLEASE, STOP THAT... THE HONOR'S ALL *MINE*, CAPTAIN.

I'M JUST GLAD TO SEE YOU'RE STILL *WITH US*.

I DIDN'T KNOW WHAT TO THINK WHEN THIS *OLD PHONE* OF FDR'S STARTED RINGING.

YES. HE CALLED IT THE *HOTLINE*.

HE HAD QUITE A SENSE OF HUMOR.

SO I SEE.

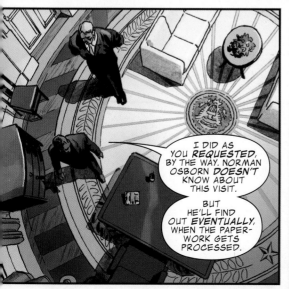

I DID AS YOU *REQUESTED*, BY THE WAY. NORMAN OSBORN *DOESN'T* KNOW ABOUT THIS VISIT.

BUT HE'LL FIND OUT *EVENTUALLY*, WHEN THE PAPER-WORK GETS PROCESSED.

THAT'S FINE.

I JUST WANTED TO BE SURE WE HAD ONE CHANCE TO TALK ALONE.

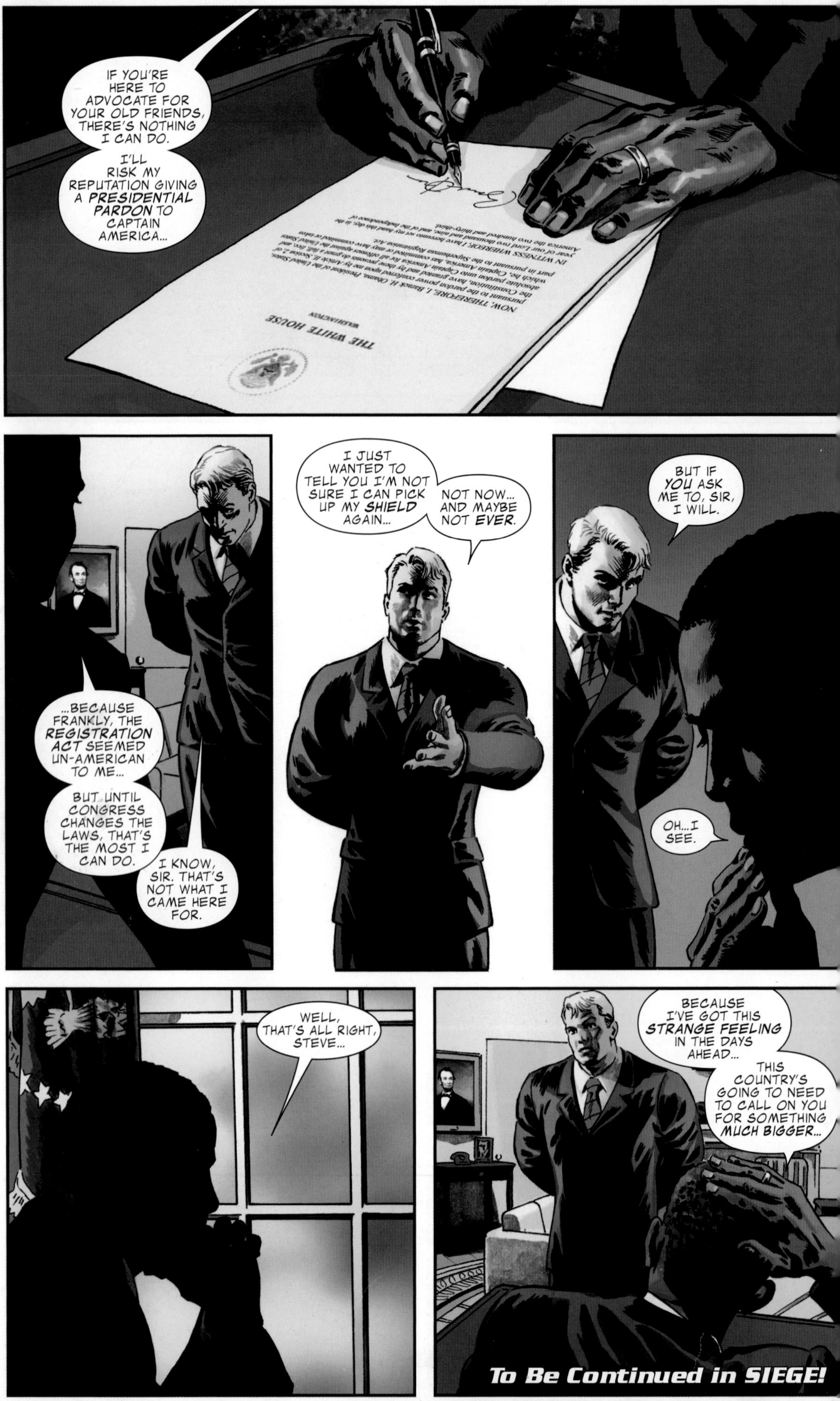

IF YOU'RE HERE TO ADVOCATE FOR YOUR OLD FRIENDS, THERE'S NOTHING I CAN DO.
I'LL RISK MY REPUTATION GIVING A PRESIDENTIAL PARDON TO CAPTAIN AMERICA...
...BECAUSE FRANKLY, THE REGISTRATION ACT SEEMED UN-AMERICAN TO ME...
BUT UNTIL CONGRESS CHANGES THE LAWS, THAT'S THE MOST I CAN DO.
I KNOW, SIR. THAT'S NOT WHAT I CAME HERE FOR.
I JUST WANTED TO TELL YOU I'M NOT SURE I CAN PICK UP MY SHIELD AGAIN...
NOT NOW... AND MAYBE NOT EVER.
BUT IF YOU ASK ME TO, SIR, I WILL.
OH...I SEE.
WELL, THAT'S ALL RIGHT, STEVE...
BECAUSE I'VE GOT THIS STRANGE FEELING IN THE DAYS AHEAD...
THIS COUNTRY'S GOING TO NEED TO CALL ON YOU FOR SOMETHING MUCH BIGGER...
To Be Continued in SIEGE!

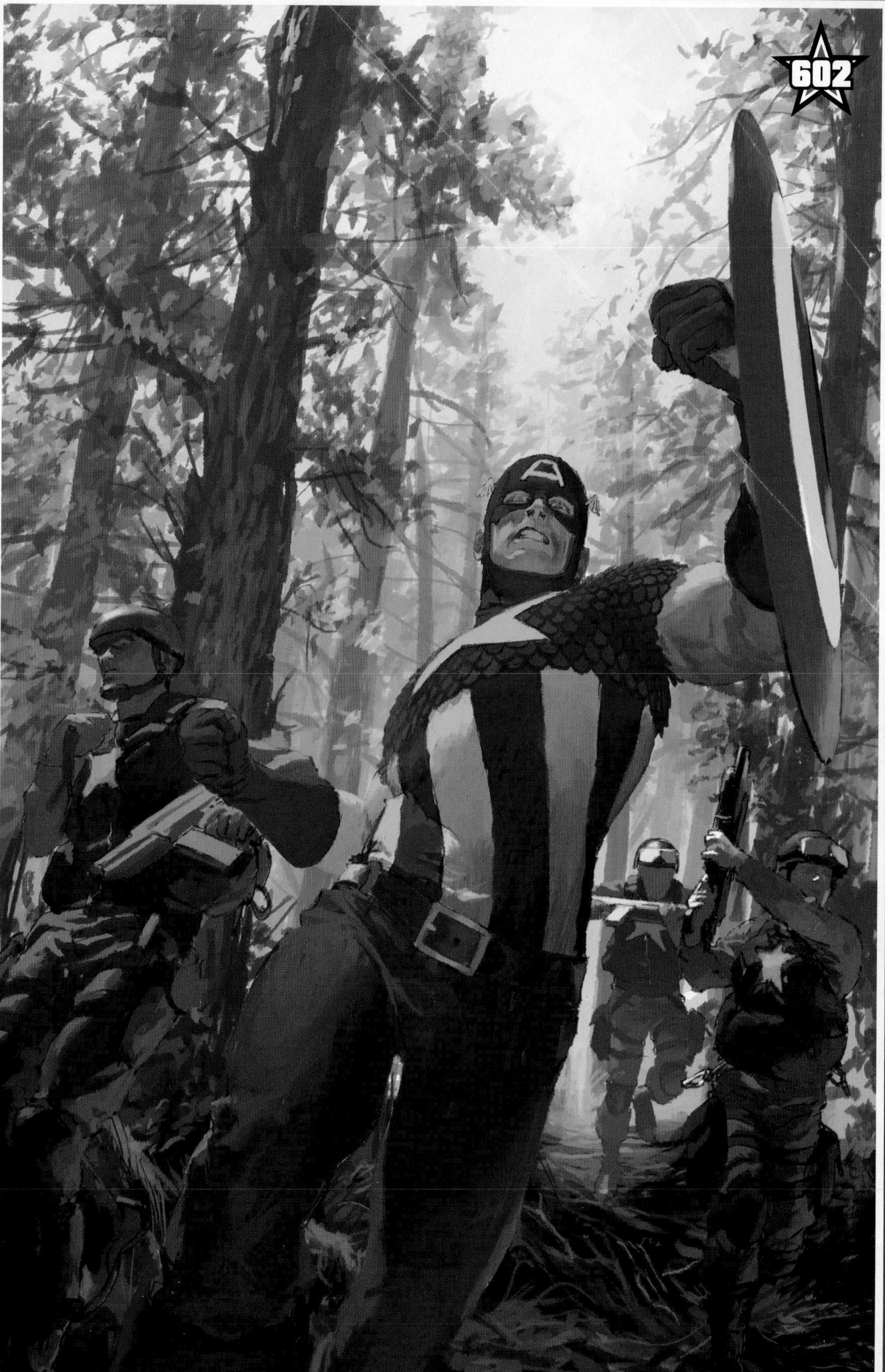
602

TWO AMERICAS PART 1

Congress Takes
Prompt Action

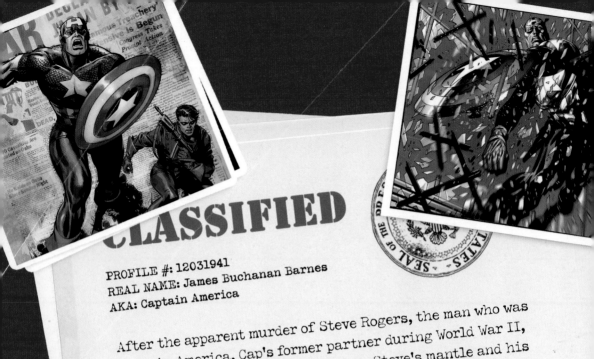

CLASSIFIED

PROFILE #: 12031941
REAL NAME: James Buchanan Barnes
AKA: Captain America

After the apparent murder of Steve Rogers, the man who was Captain America, Cap's former partner during World War II, James "Bucky" Barnes, has taken on Steve's mantle and his mission. Even now that Steve Rogers has returned from the grave, Bucky continues to wield the shield as Captain America.

During the 1950s, while the original Cap was in suspended animation, another Captain America was created. While a nearly perfect physical match for Steve Rogers, this new Cap became severely mentally unstable and eventually had to be taken down.

Recently, Bucky clashed with a newly revived, but still deranged, 1950s Captain America who then escaped. No one has seen him since.

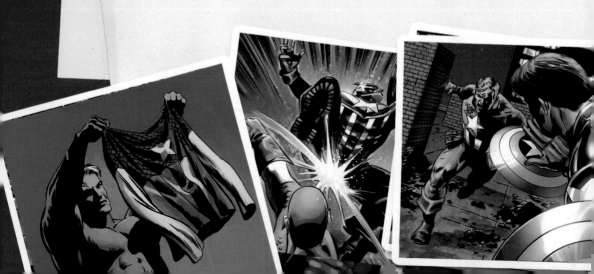

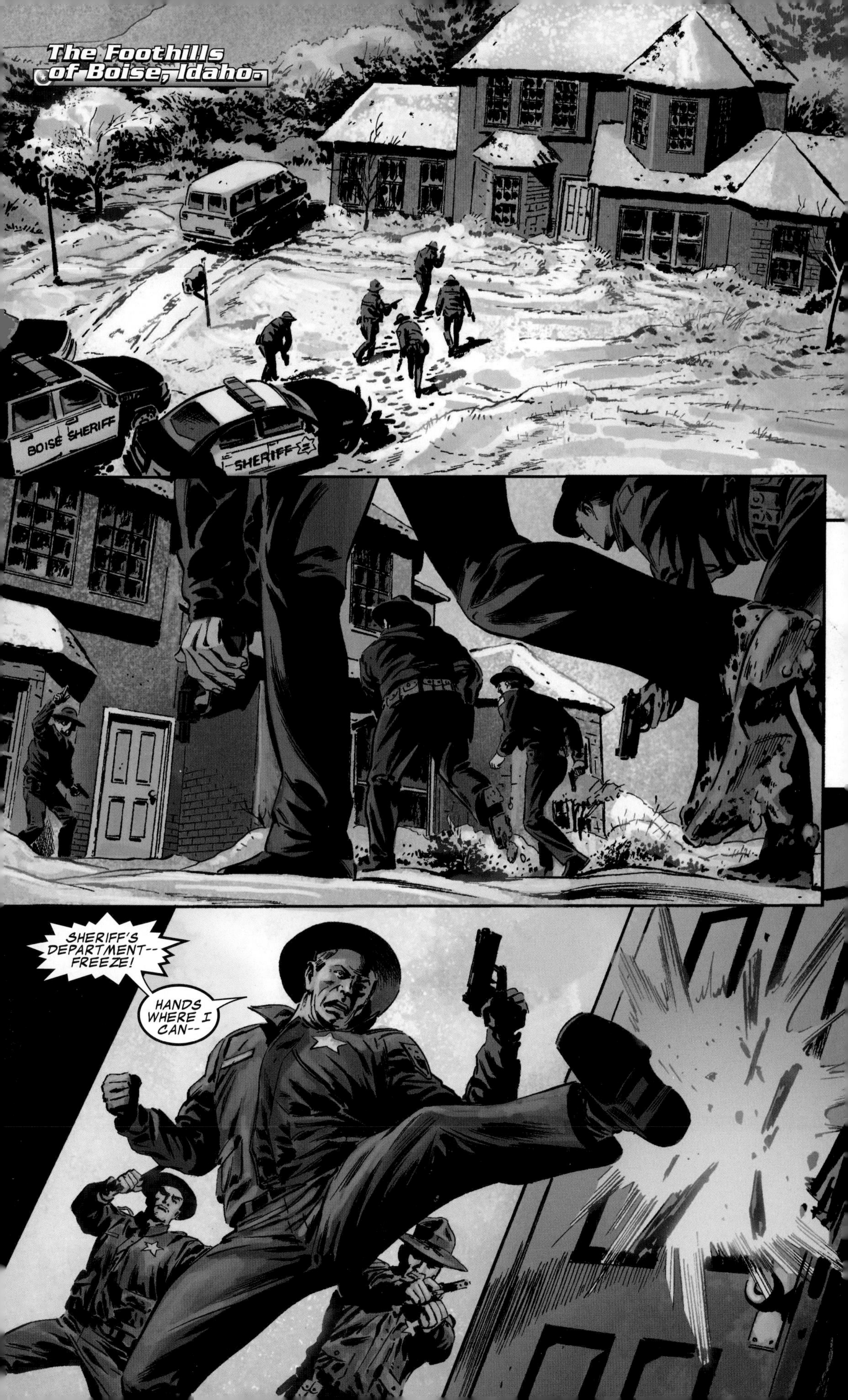

The Foothills of Boise, Idaho.
BOISE SHERIFF
SHERIFF
SHERIFF'S DEPARTMENT-- FREEZE!
HANDS WHERE I CAN--

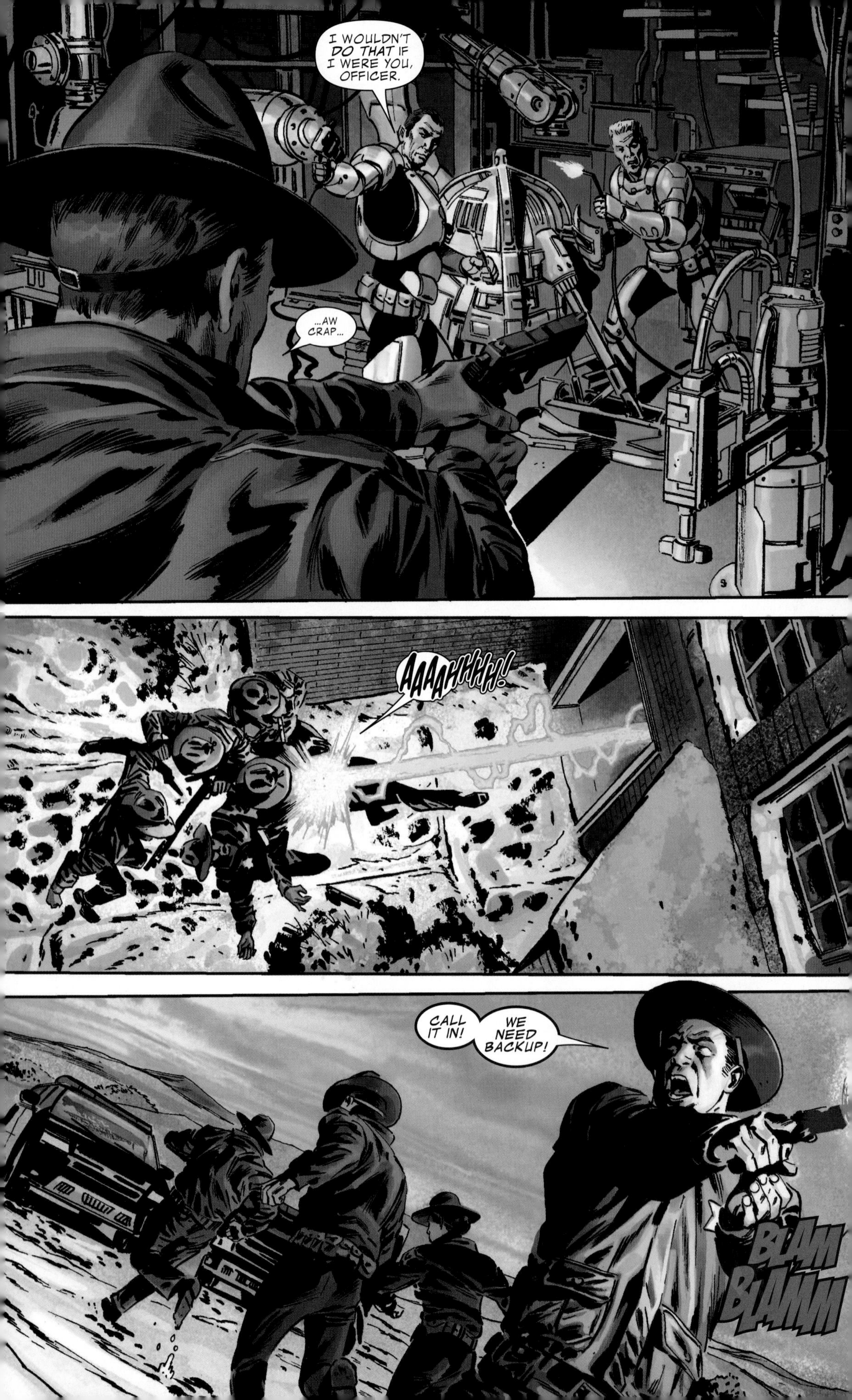
I WOULDN'T DO THAT IF I WERE YOU, OFFICER.
...AW CRAP...
AAAAHHHHH!
CALL IT IN!
WE NEED BACKUP!
BLAM
BLAMM

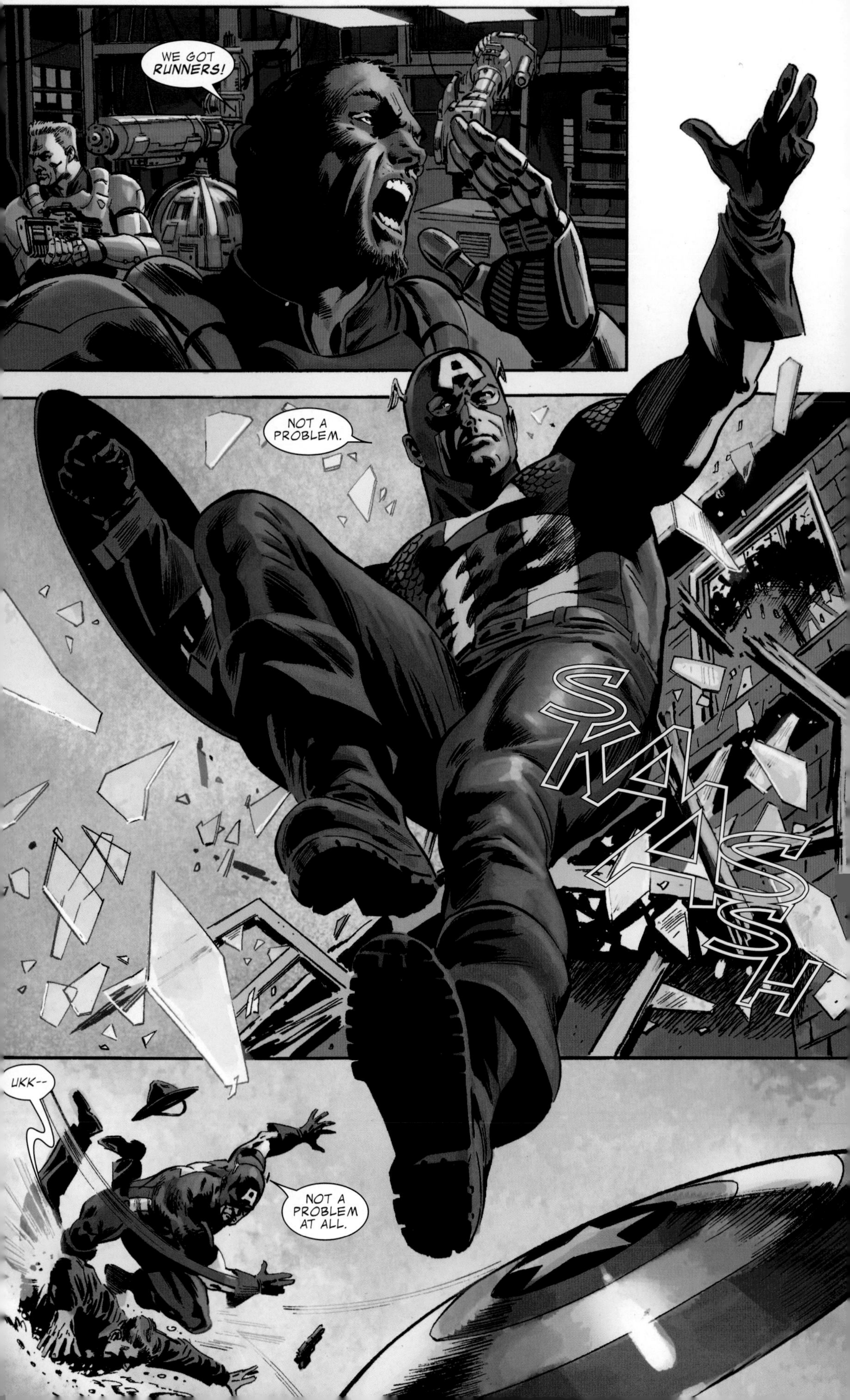
WE GOT RUNNERS!
NOT A PROBLEM.
SKRASH
UKK--
NOT A PROBLEM AT ALL.

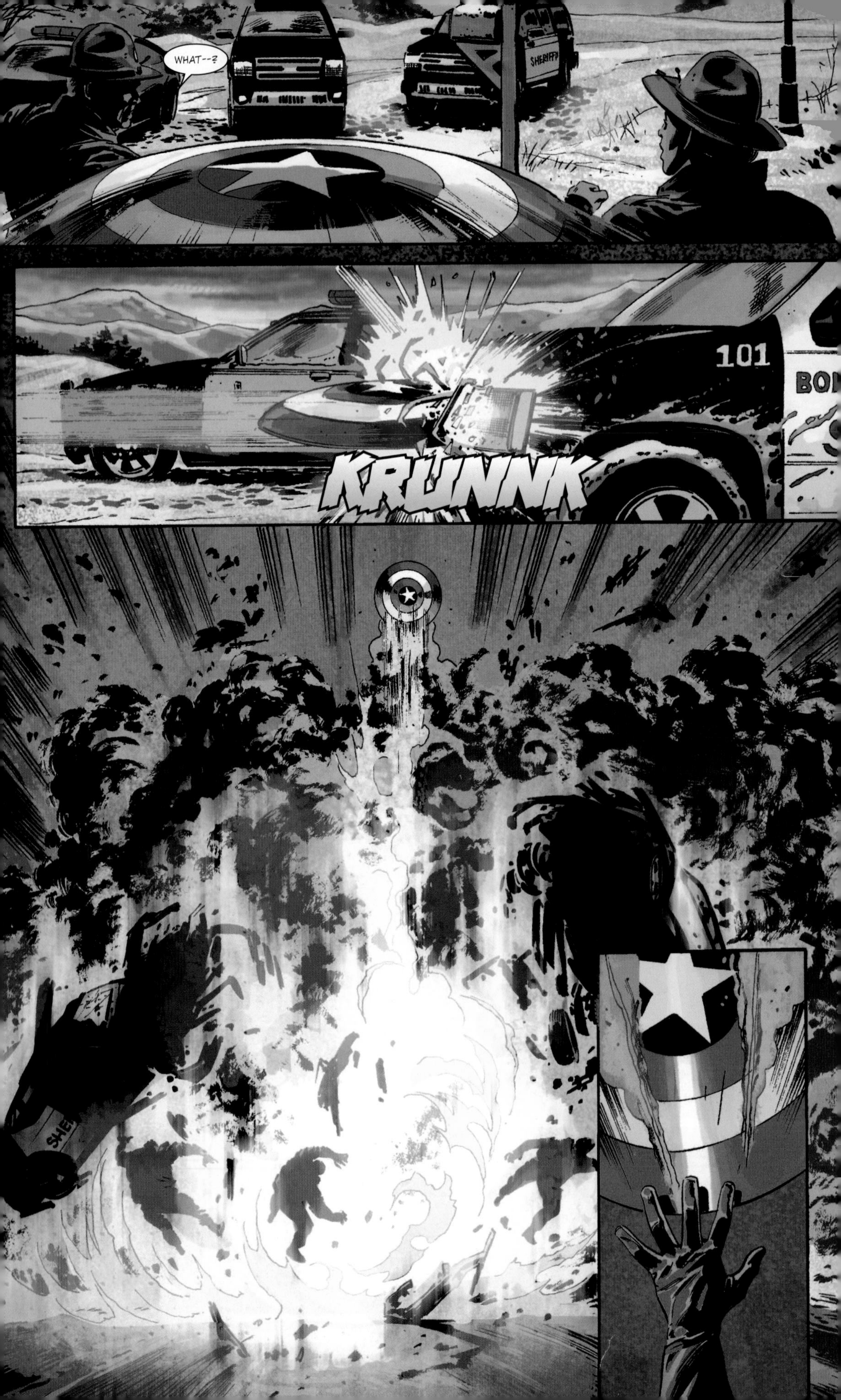
WHAT--?
SHERIFF
101
KRUNNK

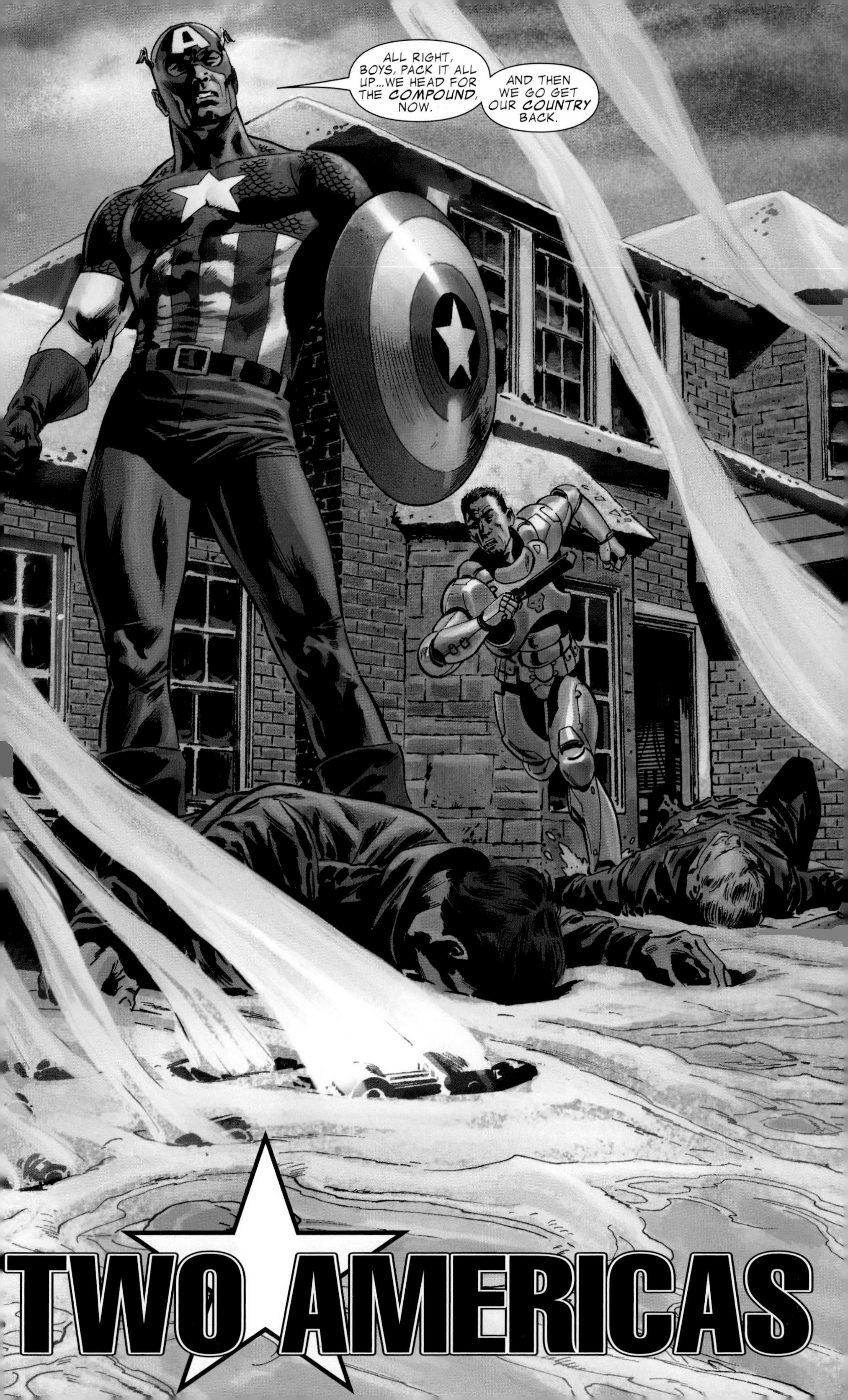
ALL RIGHT, BOYS, PACK IT ALL UP...WE HEAD FOR THE COMPOUND, NOW.
AND THEN WE GO GET OUR COUNTRY BACK.
TWO AMERICAS

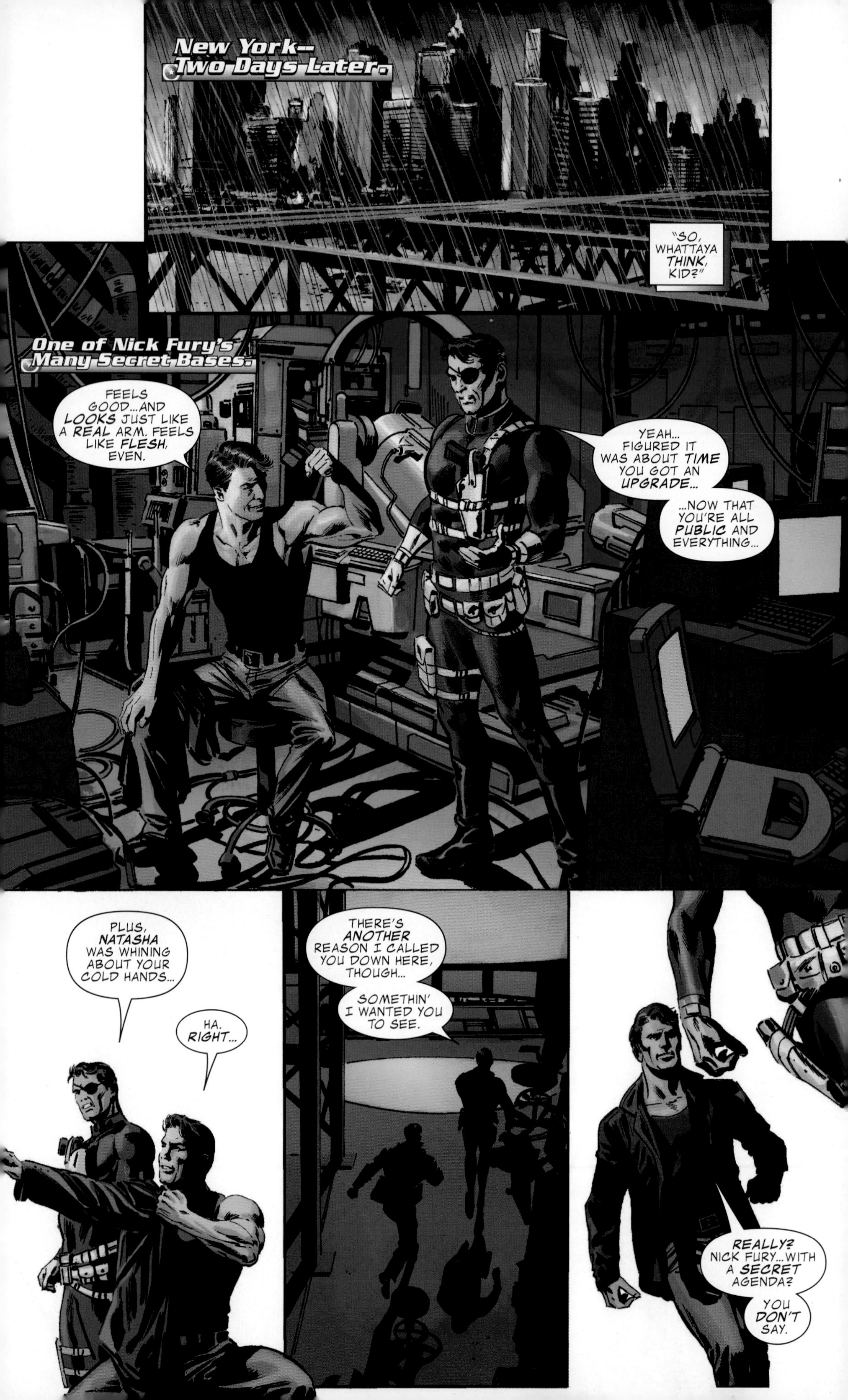
New York-- Two Days Later.
"SO, WHATTAYA THINK, KID?"
One of Nick Fury's Many Secret Bases.
FEELS GOOD...AND LOOKS JUST LIKE A REAL ARM. FEELS LIKE FLESH, EVEN.
YEAH... FIGURED IT WAS ABOUT TIME YOU GOT AN UPGRADE...
...NOW THAT YOU'RE ALL PUBLIC AND EVERYTHING...
PLUS, NATASHA WAS WHINING ABOUT YOUR COLD HANDS...
HA. RIGHT...
THERE'S ANOTHER REASON I CALLED YOU DOWN HERE, THOUGH...
SOMETHIN' I WANTED YOU TO SEE.
REALLY? NICK FURY...WITH A SECRET AGENDA?
YOU DON'T SAY.

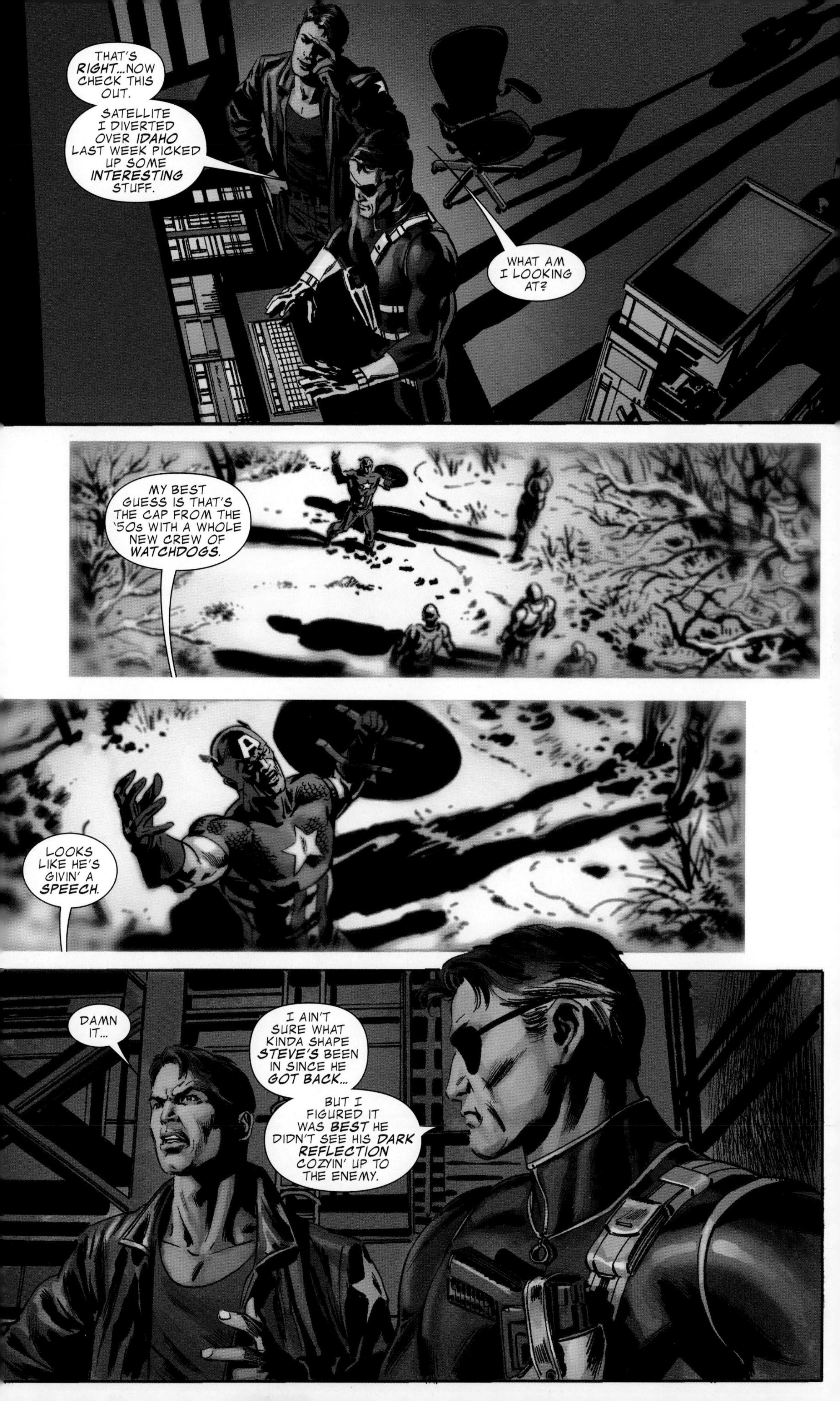
THAT'S RIGHT...NOW CHECK THIS OUT.
SATELLITE I DIVERTED OVER IDAHO LAST WEEK PICKED UP SOME INTERESTING STUFF.
WHAT AM I LOOKING AT?
MY BEST GUESS IS THAT'S THE CAP FROM THE '50s WITH A WHOLE NEW CREW OF WATCHDOGS.
LOOKS LIKE HE'S GIVIN' A SPEECH.
DAMN IT...
I AIN'T SURE WHAT KINDA SHAPE STEVE'S BEEN IN SINCE HE GOT BACK...
BUT I FIGURED IT WAS BEST HE DIDN'T SEE HIS DARK REFLECTION COZYIN' UP TO THE ENEMY.

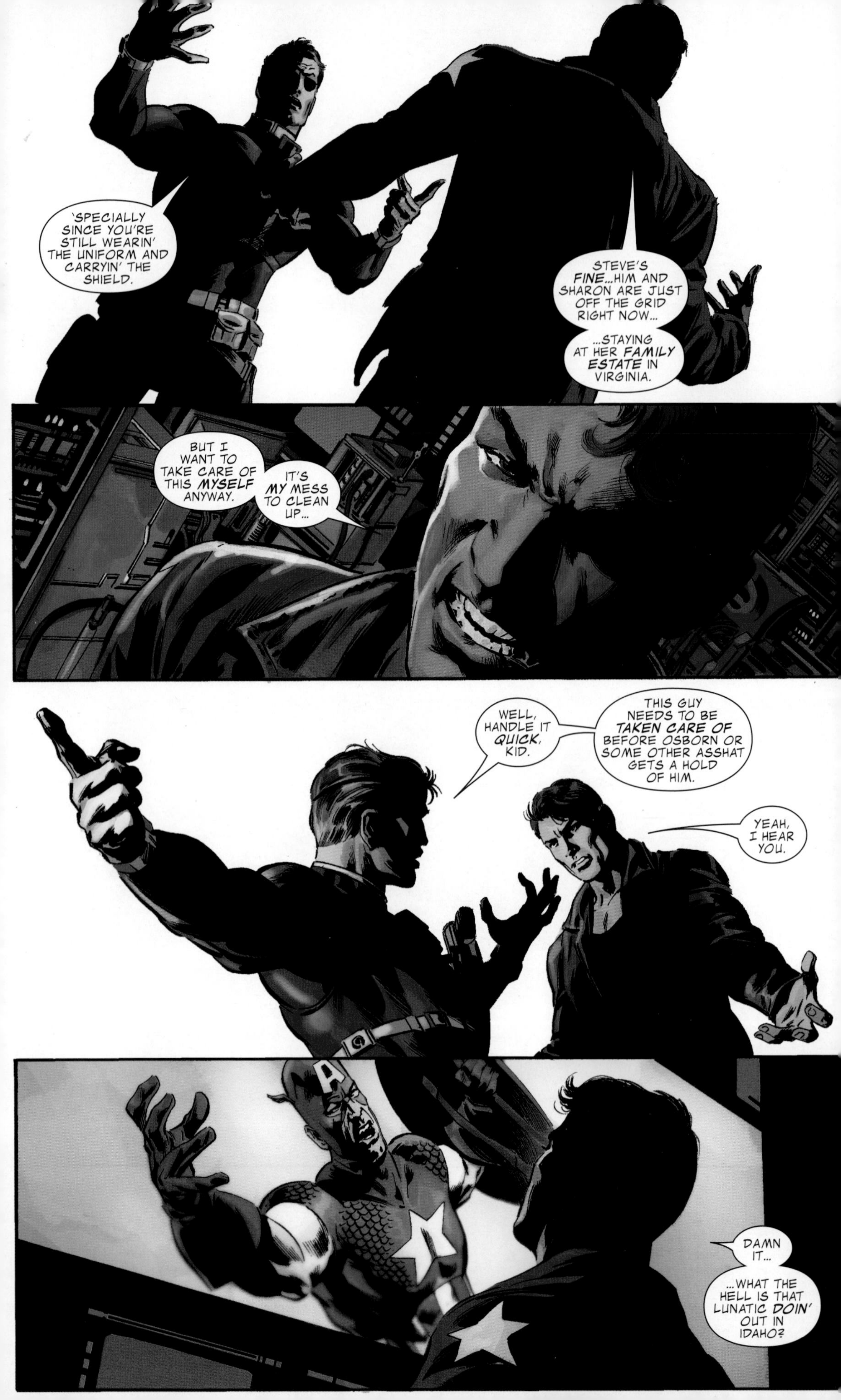
'SPECIALLY SINCE YOU'RE STILL WEARIN' THE UNIFORM AND CARRYIN' THE SHIELD.
STEVE'S FINE...HIM AND SHARON ARE JUST OFF THE GRID RIGHT NOW...
...STAYING AT HER FAMILY ESTATE IN VIRGINIA.
BUT I WANT TO TAKE CARE OF THIS MYSELF ANYWAY.
IT'S MY MESS TO CLEAN UP...
WELL, HANDLE IT QUICK, KID.
THIS GUY NEEDS TO BE TAKEN CARE OF BEFORE OSBORN OR SOME OTHER ASSHAT GETS A HOLD OF HIM.
YEAH, I HEAR YOU.
DAMN IT...
...WHAT THE HELL IS THAT LUNATIC DOIN' OUT IN IDAHO?

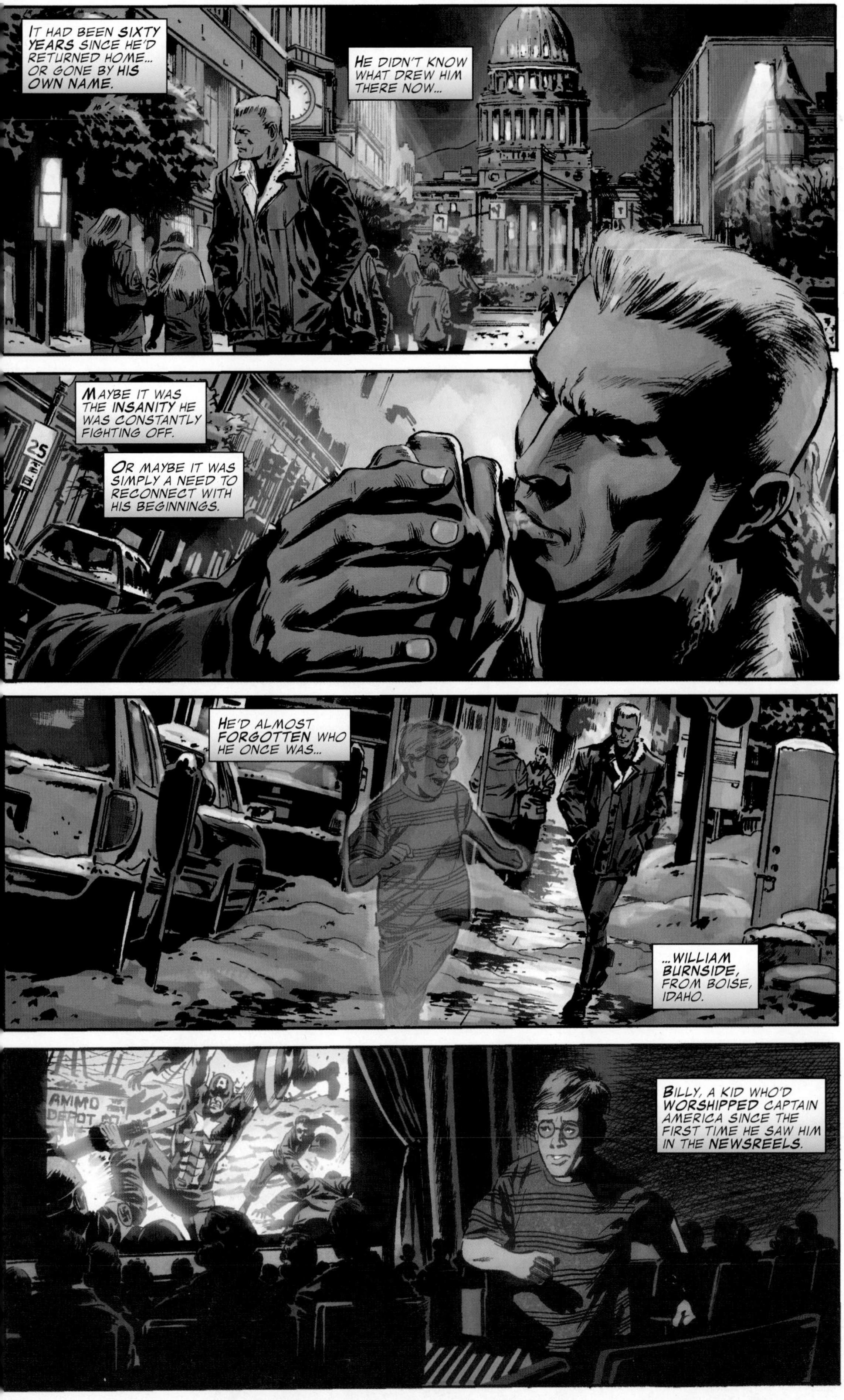
IT HAD BEEN SIXTY YEARS SINCE HE'D RETURNED HOME... OR GONE BY HIS OWN NAME.
HE DIDN'T KNOW WHAT DREW HIM THERE NOW...
MAYBE IT WAS THE INSANITY HE WAS CONSTANTLY FIGHTING OFF.
OR MAYBE IT WAS SIMPLY A NEED TO RECONNECT WITH HIS BEGINNINGS.
HE'D ALMOST FORGOTTEN WHO HE ONCE WAS...
...WILLIAM BURNSIDE, FROM BOISE, IDAHO.
BILLY, A KID WHO'D WORSHIPPED CAPTAIN AMERICA SINCE THE FIRST TIME HE SAW HIM IN THE NEWSREELS.

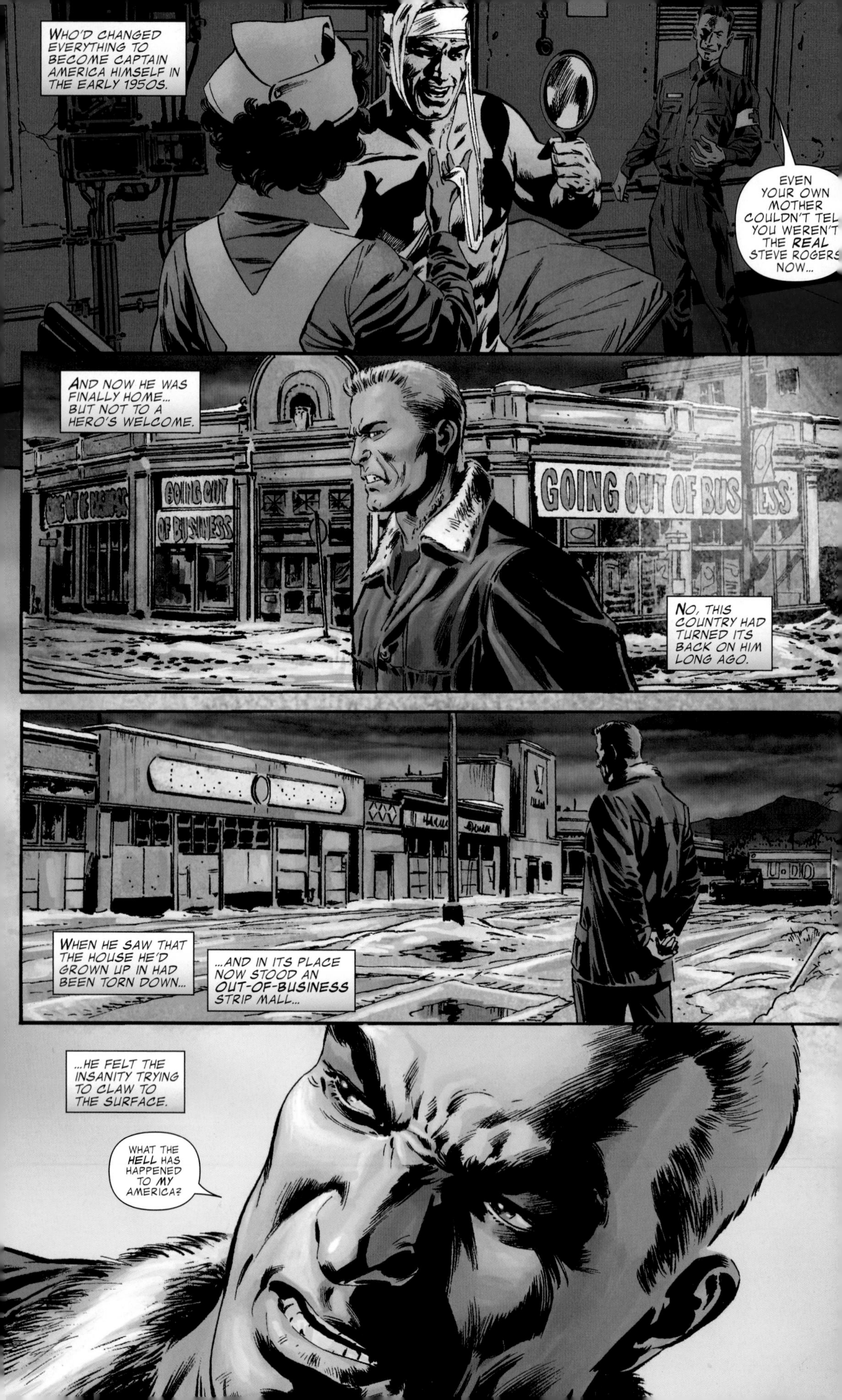

WHO'D CHANGED EVERYTHING TO BECOME CAPTAIN AMERICA HIMSELF IN THE EARLY 1950S.
EVEN YOUR OWN MOTHER COULDN'T TEL YOU WEREN'T THE REAL STEVE ROGERS NOW...
AND NOW HE WAS FINALLY HOME... BUT NOT TO A HERO'S WELCOME.
GOING OUT OF BUSINESS
GOING OUT OF BUS ESS
NO, THIS COUNTRY HAD TURNED ITS BACK ON HIM LONG AGO.
WHEN HE SAW THAT THE HOUSE HE'D GROWN UP IN HAD BEEN TORN DOWN...
...AND IN ITS PLACE NOW STOOD AN OUT-OF-BUSINESS STRIP MALL...
...HE FELT THE INSANITY TRYING TO CLAW TO THE SURFACE.
WHAT THE HELL HAS HAPPENED TO MY AMERICA?

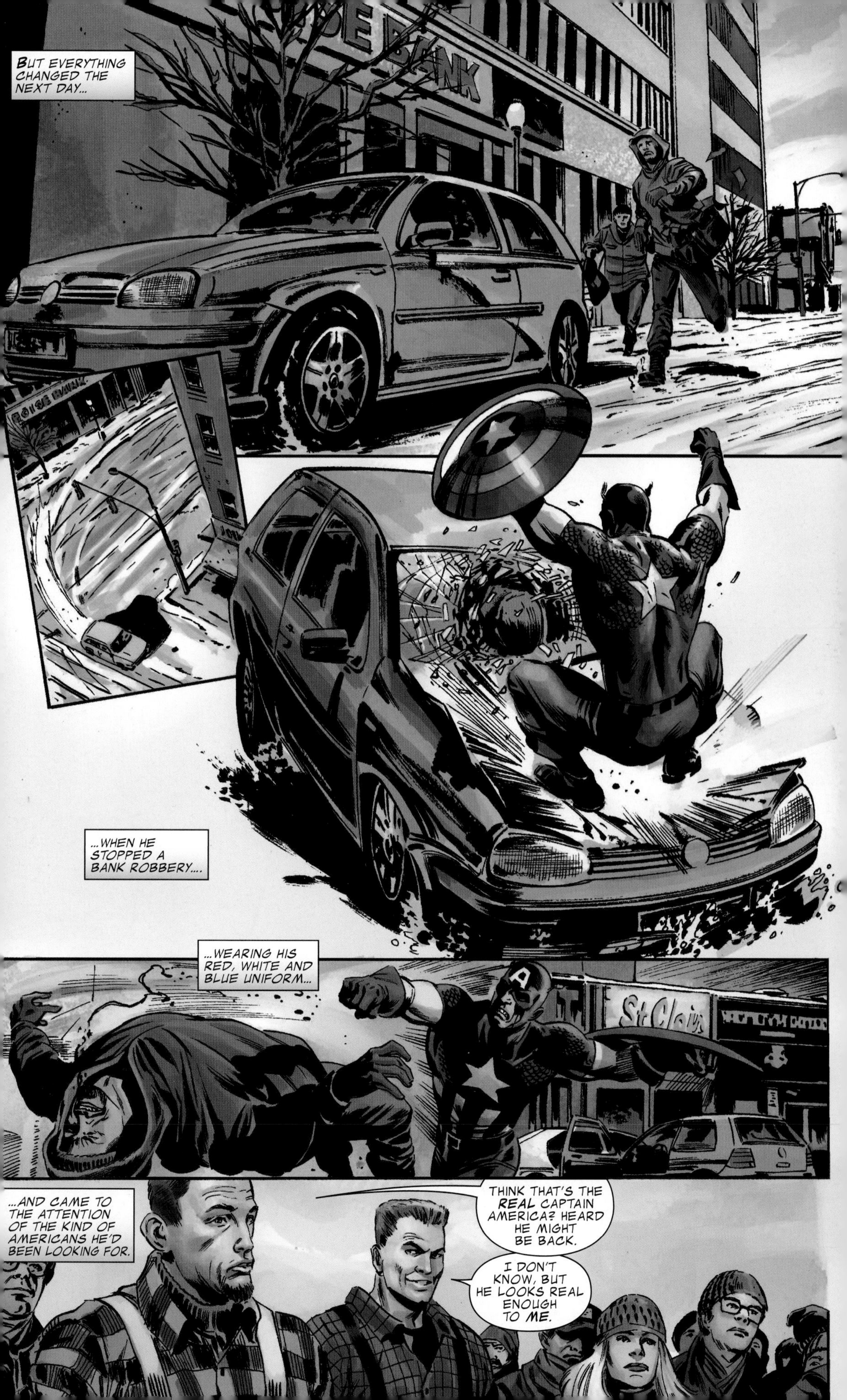
BUT EVERYTHING CHANGED THE NEXT DAY...
...WHEN HE STOPPED A BANK ROBBERY....
...WEARING HIS RED, WHITE AND BLUE UNIFORM...
St Clair's
...AND CAME TO THE ATTENTION OF THE KIND OF AMERICANS HE'D BEEN LOOKING FOR.
THINK THAT'S THE REAL CAPTAIN AMERICA? HEARD HE MIGHT BE BACK.
I DON'T KNOW, BUT HE LOOKS REAL ENOUGH TO ME.

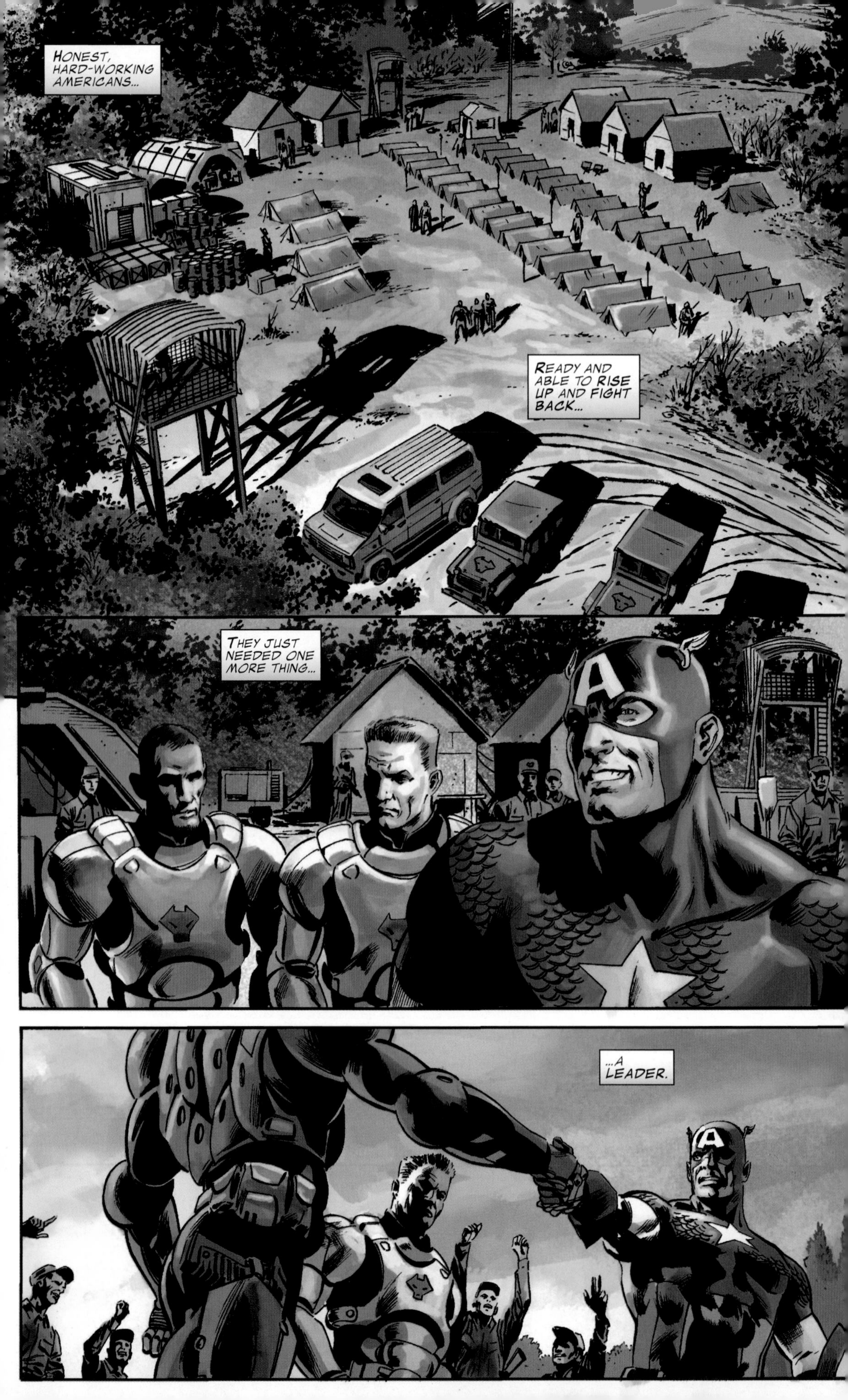
HONEST, HARD-WORKING AMERICANS...
READY AND ABLE TO RISE UP AND FIGHT BACK...
THEY JUST NEEDED ONE MORE THING...
...A LEADER.

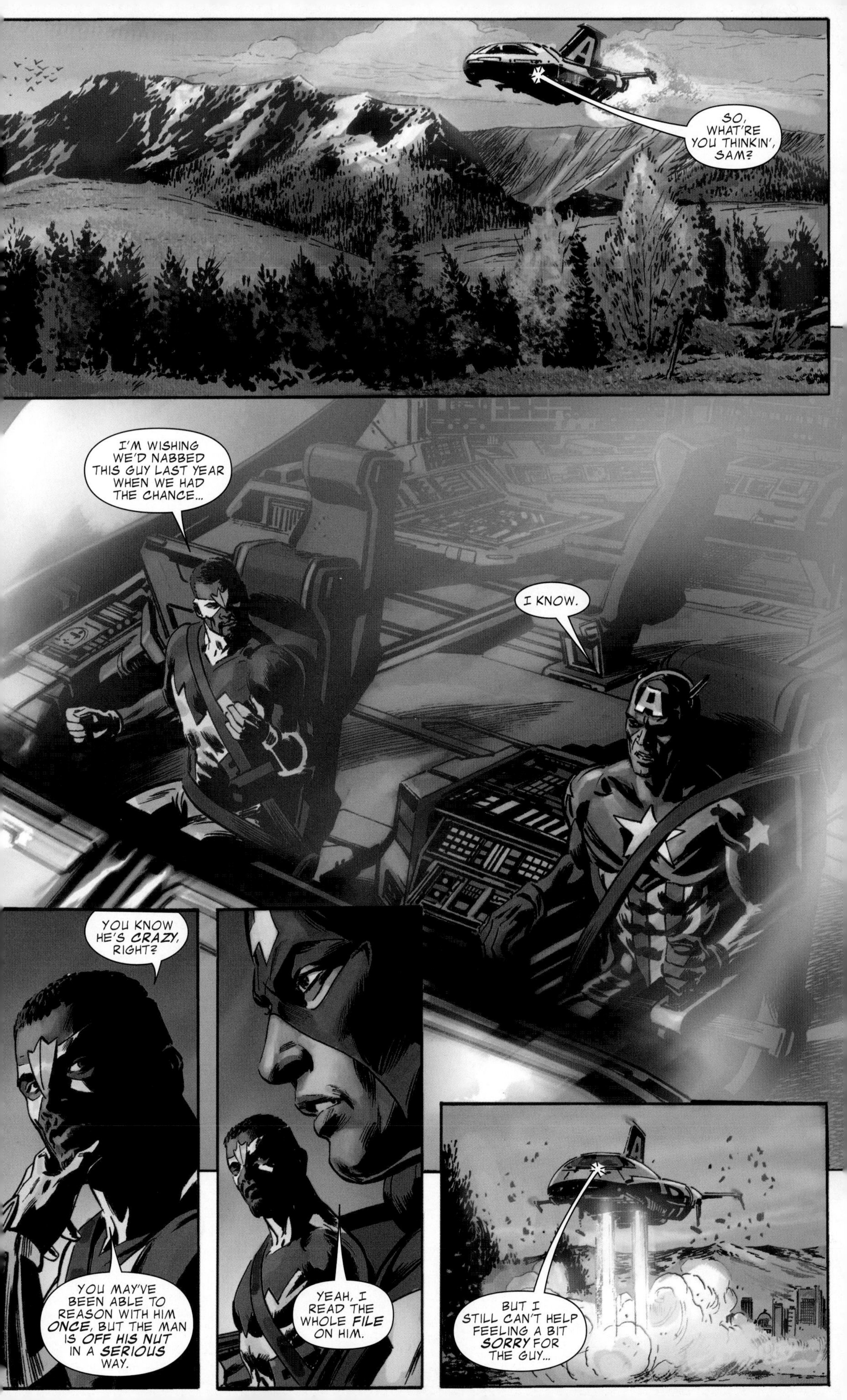
SO, WHAT'RE YOU THINKIN', SAM?
I'M WISHING WE'D NABBED THIS GUY LAST YEAR WHEN WE HAD THE CHANCE...
I KNOW.
YOU KNOW HE'S *CRAZY*, RIGHT?
YOU MAY'VE BEEN ABLE TO REASON WITH HIM *ONCE*, BUT THE MAN IS *OFF HIS NUT* IN A *SERIOUS* WAY.
YEAH, I READ THE WHOLE *FILE* ON HIM.
BUT I STILL CAN'T HELP FEELING A BIT *SORRY* FOR THE GUY...

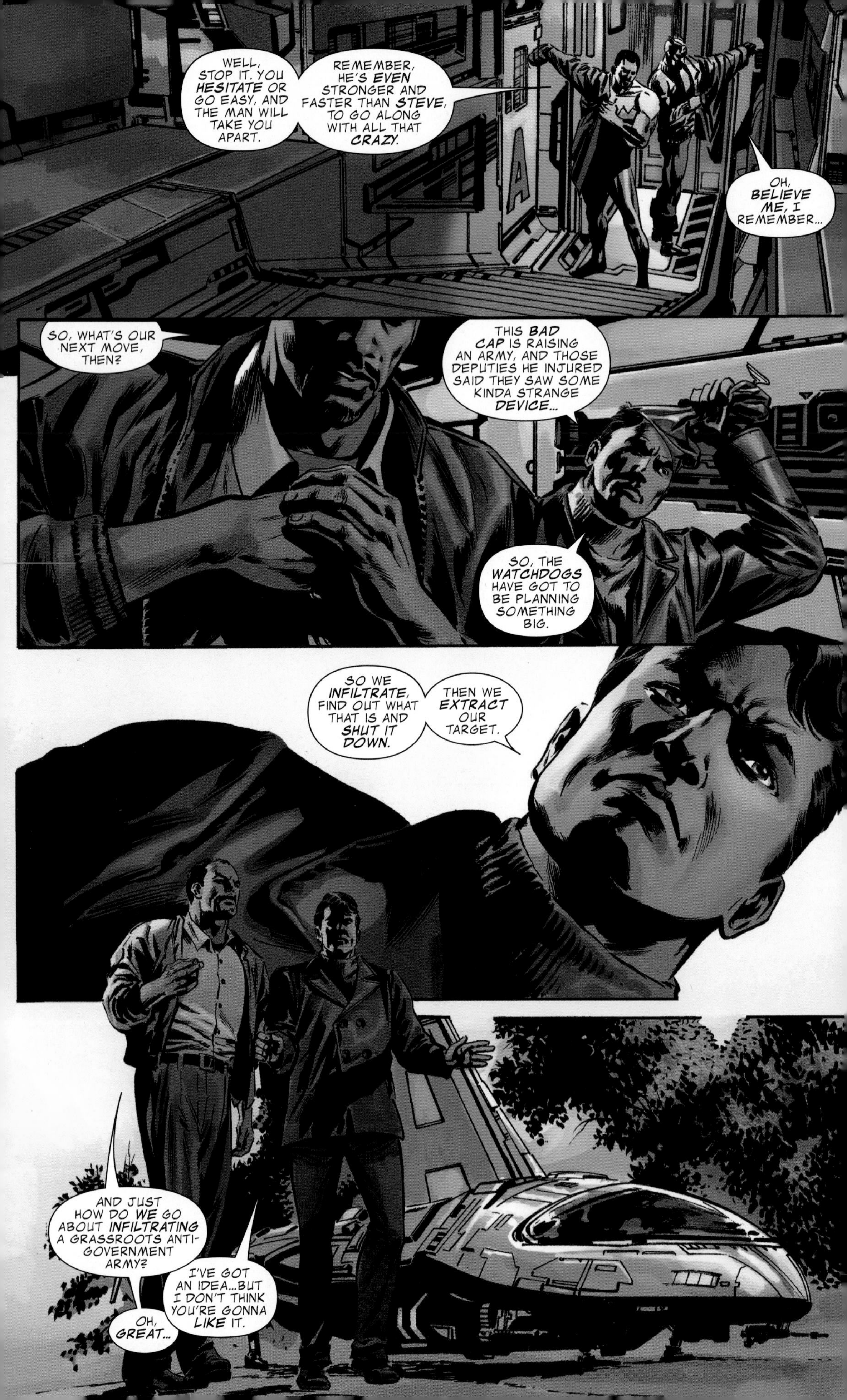
WELL, STOP IT. YOU HESITATE OR GO EASY, AND THE MAN WILL TAKE YOU APART.
REMEMBER, HE'S EVEN STRONGER AND FASTER THAN STEVE, TO GO ALONG WITH ALL THAT CRAZY.
OH, BELIEVE ME, I REMEMBER...
SO, WHAT'S OUR NEXT MOVE, THEN?
THIS BAD CAP IS RAISING AN ARMY, AND THOSE DEPUTIES HE INJURED SAID THEY SAW SOME KINDA STRANGE DEVICE...
SO, THE WATCHDOGS HAVE GOT TO BE PLANNING SOMETHING BIG.
SO WE INFILTRATE, FIND OUT WHAT THAT IS AND SHUT IT DOWN.
THEN WE EXTRACT OUR TARGET.
AND JUST HOW DO WE GO ABOUT INFILTRATING A GRASSROOTS ANTI-GOVERNMENT ARMY?
I'VE GOT AN IDEA...BUT I DON'T THINK YOU'RE GONNA LIKE IT.
OH, GREAT...

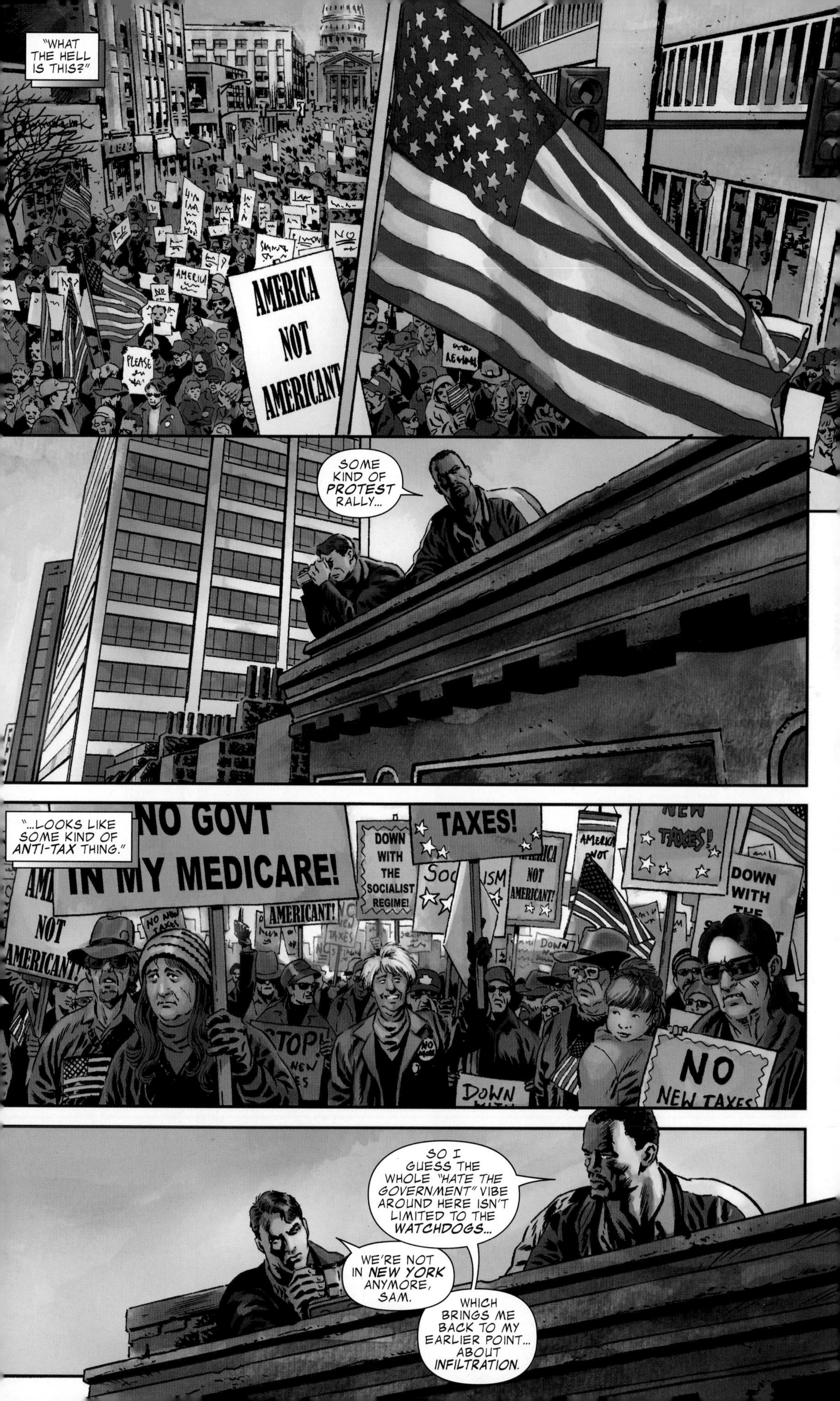
"WHAT THE HELL IS THIS?"
AMERICA NOT AMERICANT
PLEASE
SOME KIND OF PROTEST RALLY...
"...LOOKS LIKE SOME KIND OF ANTI-TAX THING."
NO GOVT IN MY MEDICARE!
DOWN WITH THE SOCIALIST REGIME!
TAXES!
AMERICA NOT AMERICANT!
AMERICANT!
NOT AMERICANT!
STOP!
NO NEW TAXES
SO I GUESS THE WHOLE "HATE THE GOVERNMENT" VIBE AROUND HERE ISN'T LIMITED TO THE WATCHDOGS...
WE'RE NOT IN NEW YORK ANYMORE, SAM.
WHICH BRINGS ME BACK TO MY EARLIER POINT... ABOUT INFILTRATION.

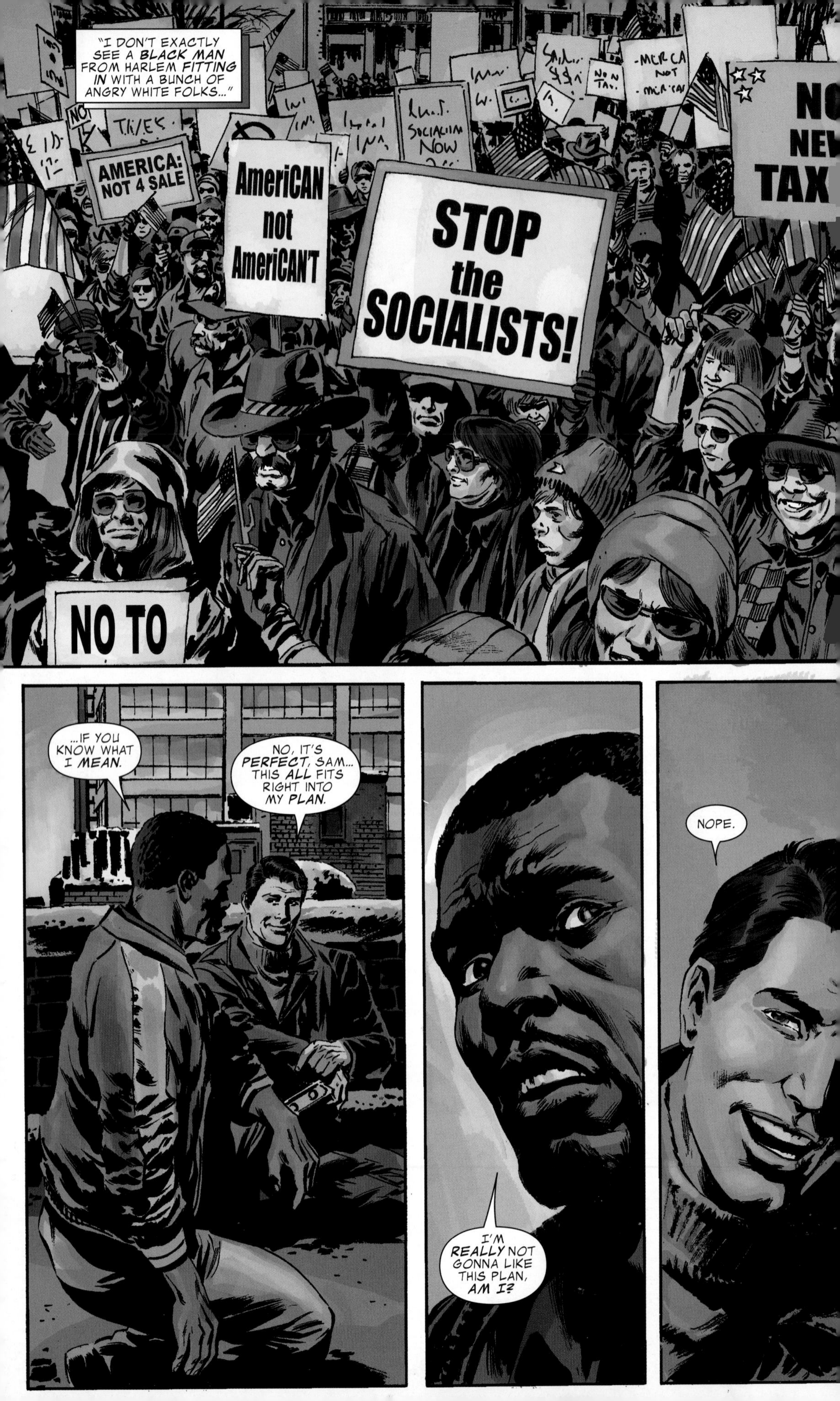
"I DON'T EXACTLY SEE A BLACK MAN FROM HARLEM FITTING IN WITH A BUNCH OF ANGRY WHITE FOLKS..."
AMERICA: NOT 4 SALE
AmeriCAN not AmeriCAN'T
STOP the SOCIALISTS!
NO NEW TAX
NO TO
...IF YOU KNOW WHAT I MEAN.
NO, IT'S PERFECT, SAM... THIS ALL FITS RIGHT INTO MY PLAN.
I'M REALLY NOT GONNA LIKE THIS PLAN, AM I?
NOPE.

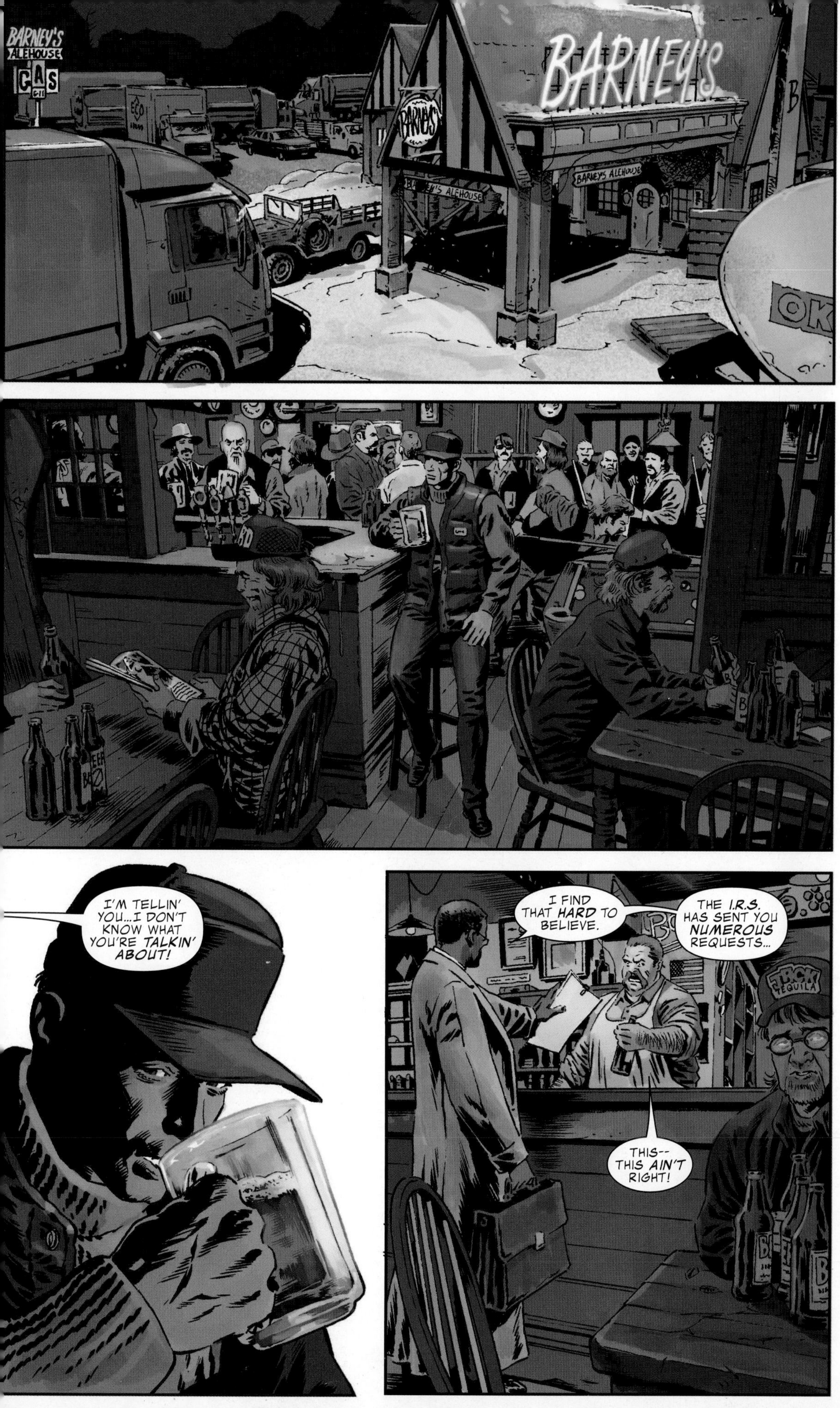
BARNEY'S ALEHOUSE
GAS
BARNEY'S
BARNEY'S ALEHOUSE
BARNEY'S ALEHOUSE
I'M TELLIN' YOU...I DON'T KNOW WHAT YOU'RE *TALKIN'* *ABOUT!*
I FIND THAT *HARD* TO BELIEVE.
THE *I.R.S.* HAS SENT YOU *NUMEROUS* REQUESTS...
THIS-- THIS *AIN'T* RIGHT!

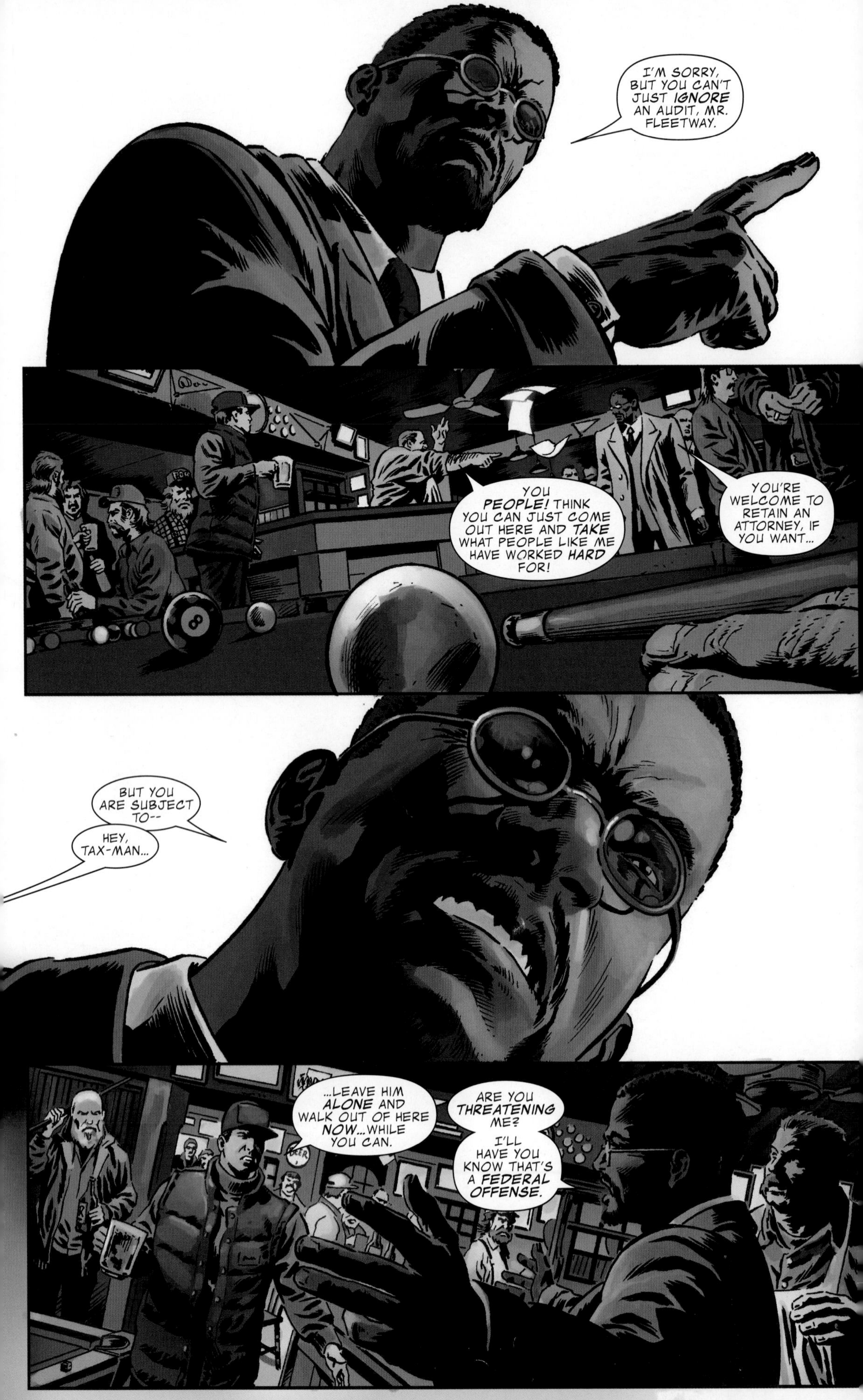
I'M SORRY, BUT YOU CAN'T JUST IGNORE AN AUDIT, MR. FLEETWAY.
YOU PEOPLE! THINK YOU CAN JUST COME OUT HERE AND TAKE WHAT PEOPLE LIKE ME HAVE WORKED HARD FOR!
YOU'RE WELCOME TO RETAIN AN ATTORNEY, IF YOU WANT...
BUT YOU ARE SUBJECT TO--
HEY, TAX-MAN...
...LEAVE HIM ALONE AND WALK OUT OF HERE NOW... WHILE YOU CAN.
ARE YOU THREATENING ME?
I'LL HAVE YOU KNOW THAT'S A FEDERAL OFFENSE.

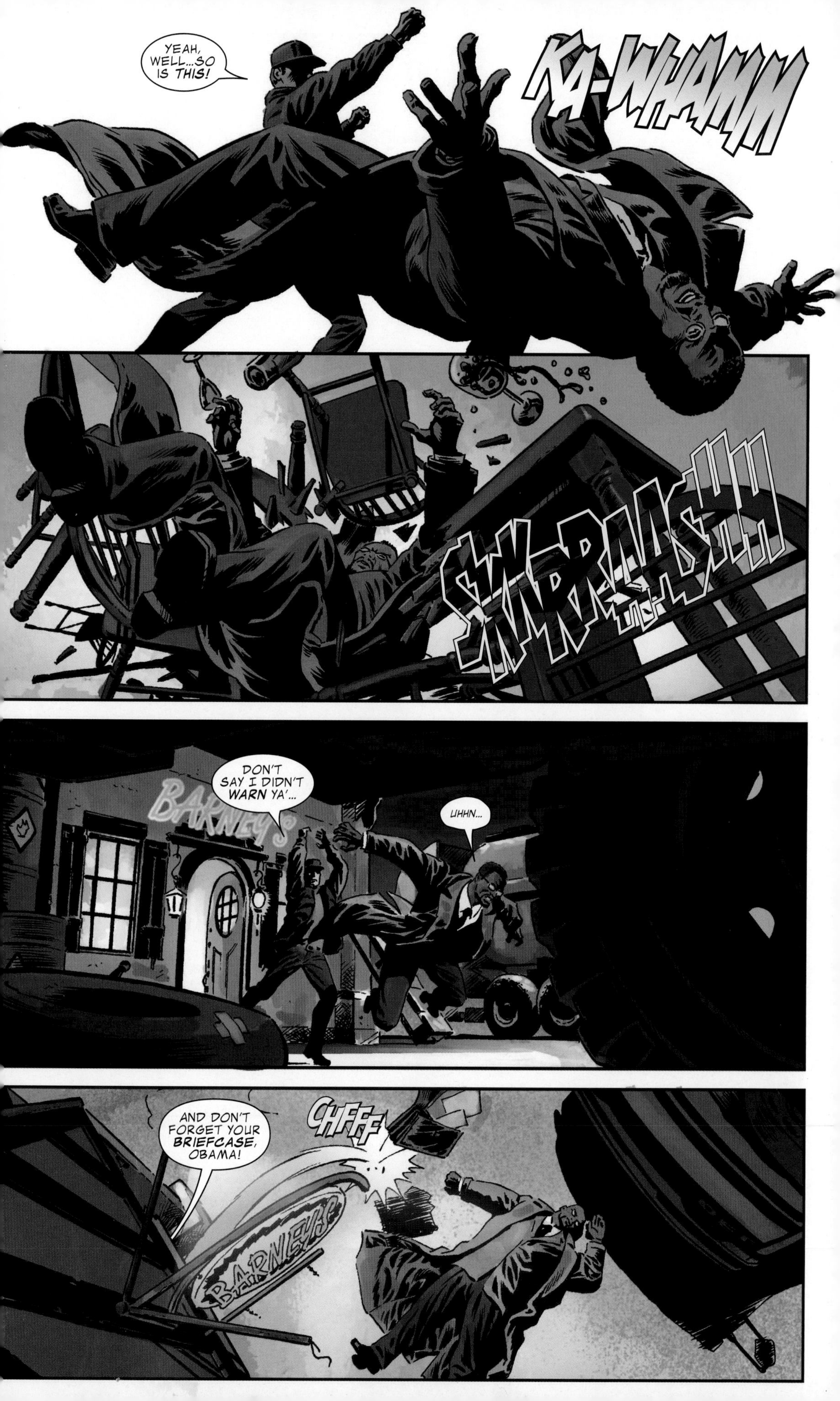

YEAH, WELL...SO IS THIS!
KA-WHAMM
SKKRAASHH
DON'T SAY I DIDN'T WARN YA'...
BARNEY'S
UHHN...
AND DON'T FORGET YOUR BRIEFCASE, OBAMA!
CHFFF
BARNEY'S

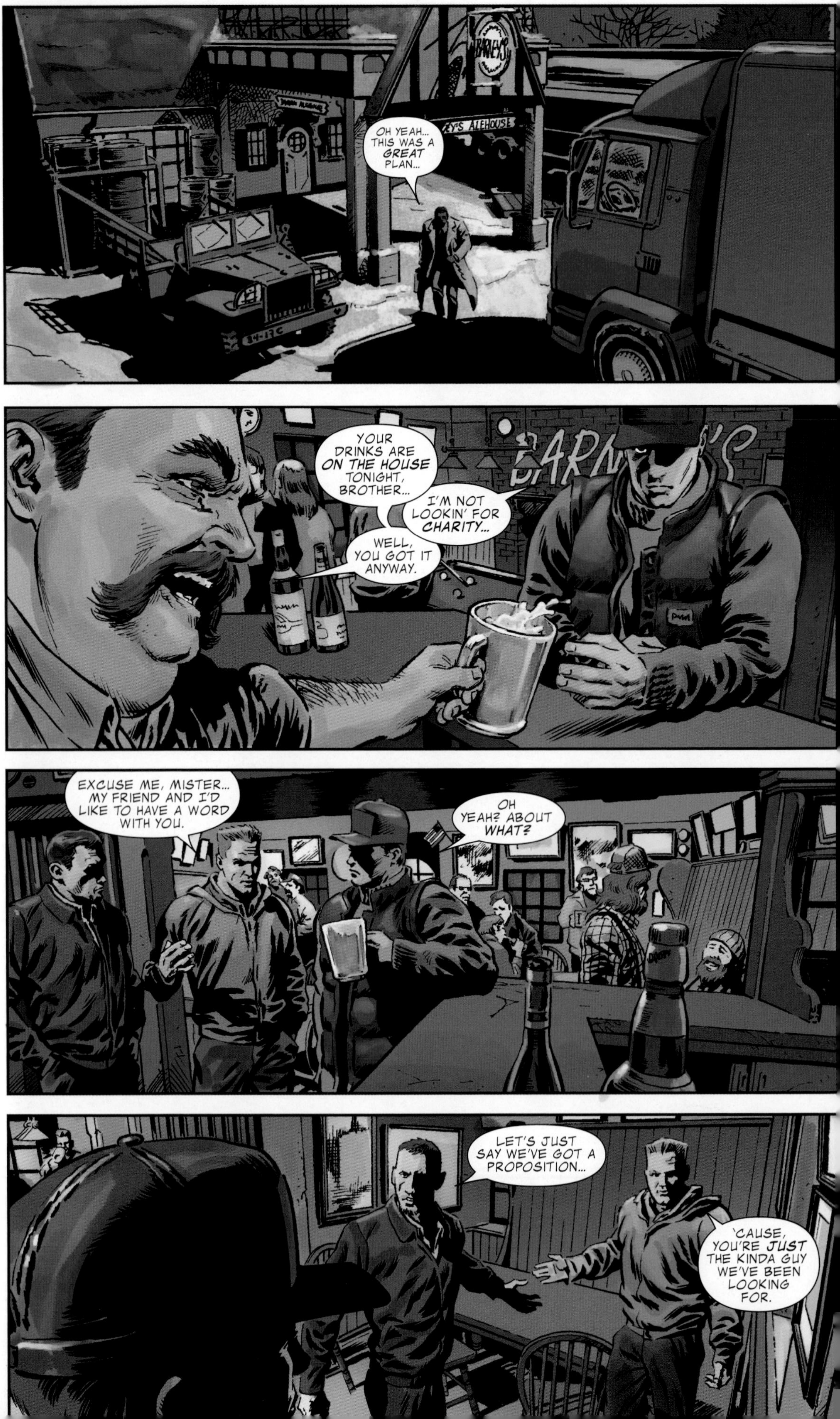
BARLEY'S
BARLEY'S ALEHOUSE
OH YEAH... THIS WAS A GREAT PLAN...
YOUR DRINKS ARE ON THE HOUSE TONIGHT, BROTHER...
I'M NOT LOOKIN' FOR CHARITY...
WELL, YOU GOT IT ANYWAY.
EXCUSE ME, MISTER... MY FRIEND AND I'D LIKE TO HAVE A WORD WITH YOU.
OH YEAH? ABOUT WHAT?
LET'S JUST SAY WE'VE GOT A PROPOSITION...
'CAUSE, YOU'RE JUST THE KINDA GUY WE'VE BEEN LOOKING FOR.

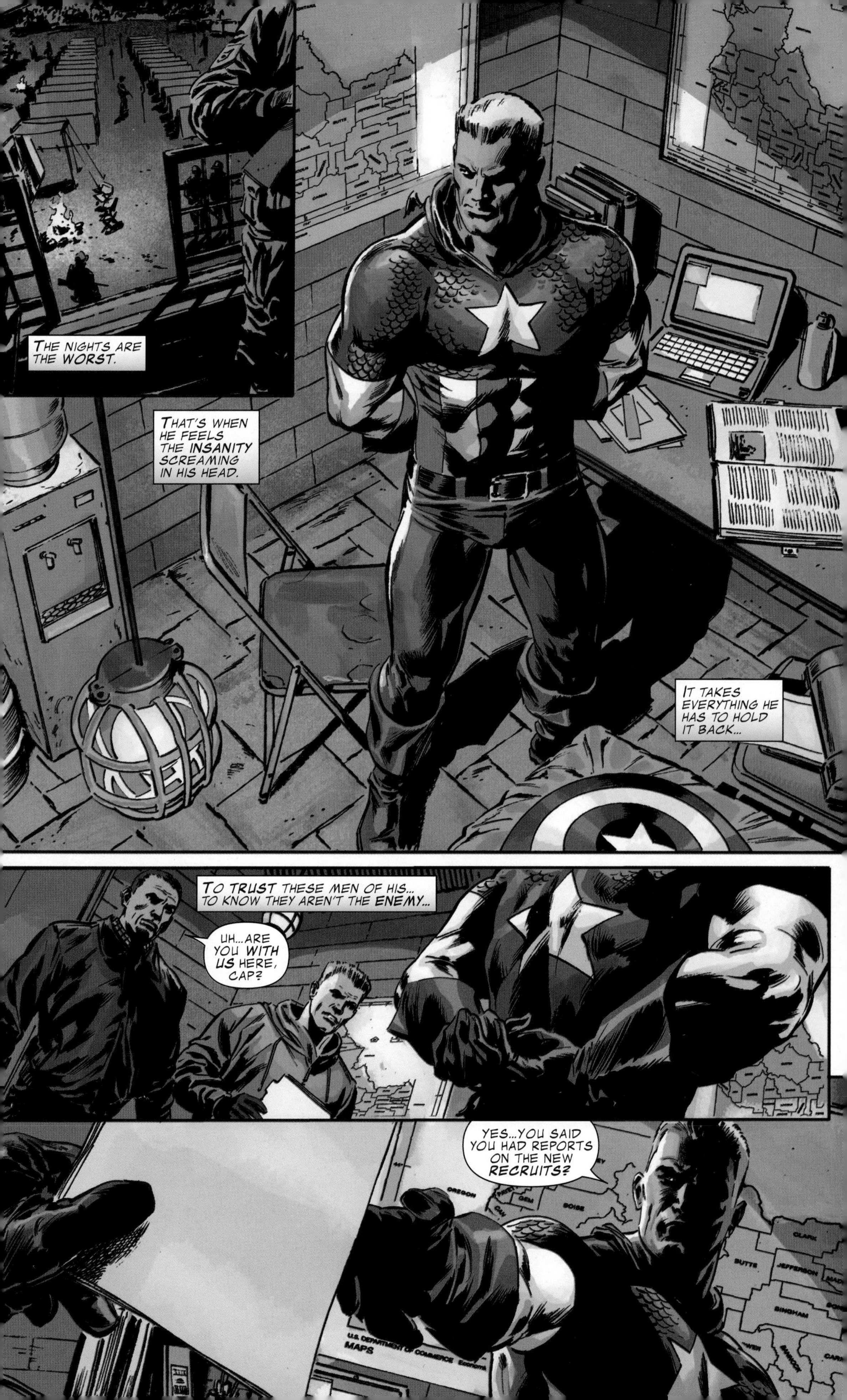
THE NIGHTS ARE THE WORST.
THAT'S WHEN HE FEELS THE INSANITY SCREAMING IN HIS HEAD.
IT TAKES EVERYTHING HE HAS TO HOLD IT BACK...
TO TRUST THESE MEN OF HIS... TO KNOW THEY AREN'T THE ENEMY...
UH...ARE YOU WITH US HERE, CAP?
YES...YOU SAID YOU HAD REPORTS ON THE NEW RECRUITS?

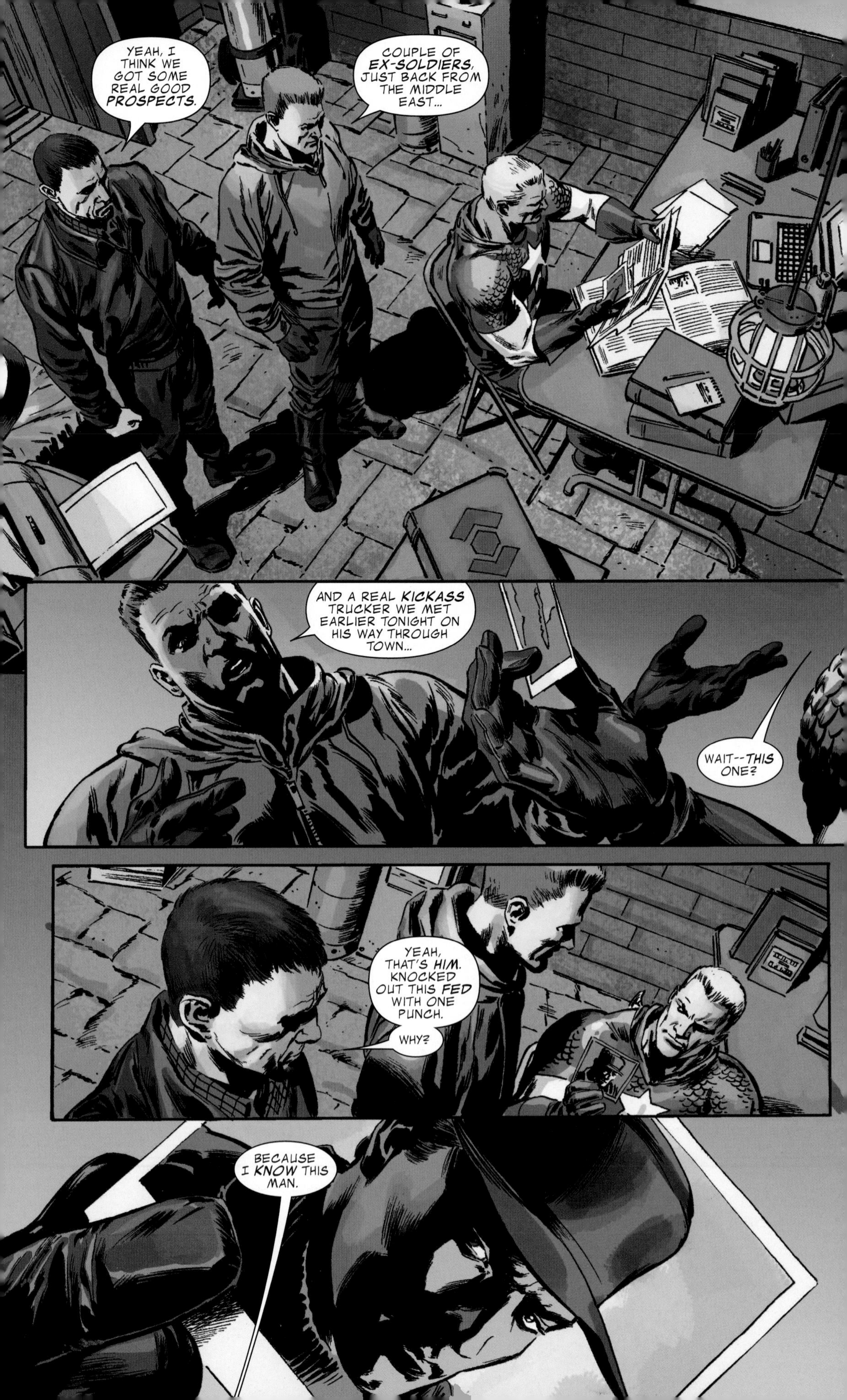
YEAH, I THINK WE GOT SOME REAL GOOD PROSPECTS.
COUPLE OF EX-SOLDIERS, JUST BACK FROM THE MIDDLE EAST...
AND A REAL KICKASS TRUCKER WE MET EARLIER TONIGHT ON HIS WAY THROUGH TOWN...
WAIT--THIS ONE?
YEAH, THAT'S HIM. KNOCKED OUT THIS FED WITH ONE PUNCH.
WHY?
BECAUSE I KNOW THIS MAN.

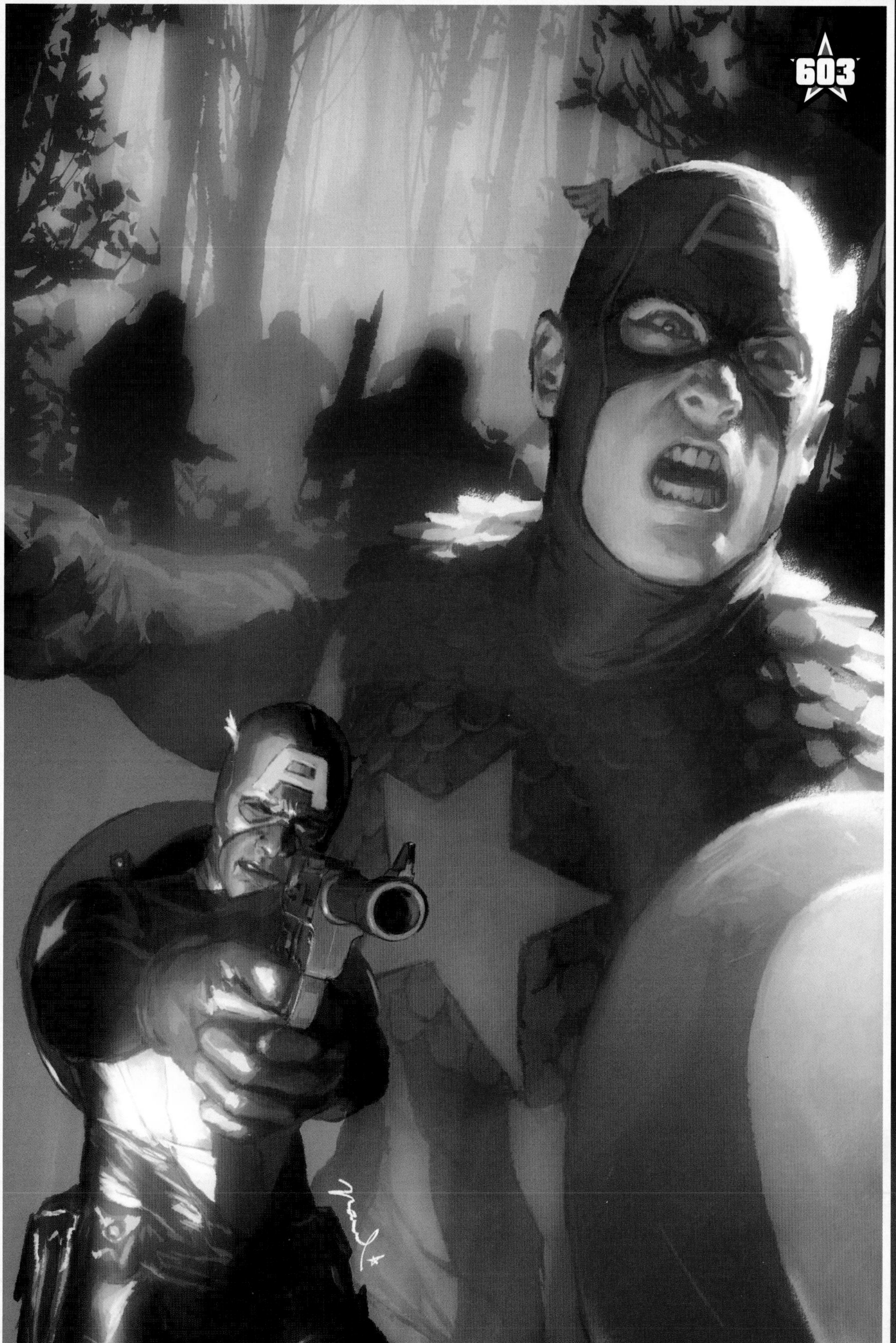
603

TWO AMERICAS PART 2

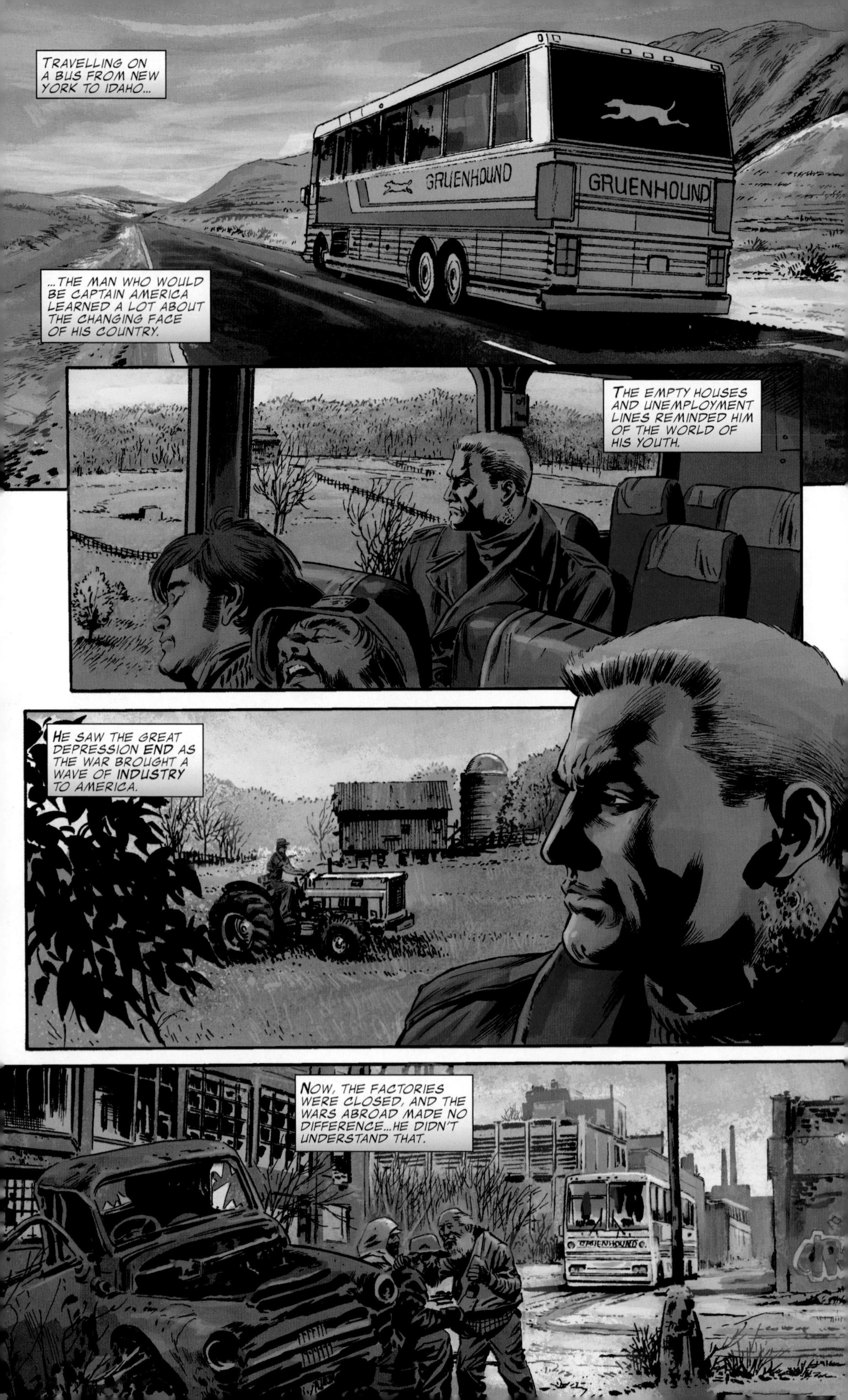
TRAVELLING ON A BUS FROM NEW YORK TO IDAHO...
GRUENHOUND
GRUENHOUND
...THE MAN WHO WOULD BE CAPTAIN AMERICA LEARNED A LOT ABOUT THE CHANGING FACE OF HIS COUNTRY.
THE EMPTY HOUSES AND UNEMPLOYMENT LINES REMINDED HIM OF THE WORLD OF HIS YOUTH.
HE SAW THE GREAT DEPRESSION END AS THE WAR BROUGHT A WAVE OF INDUSTRY TO AMERICA.
NOW, THE FACTORIES WERE CLOSED, AND THE WARS ABROAD MADE NO DIFFERENCE...HE DIDN'T UNDERSTAND THAT.
GRUENHOUND

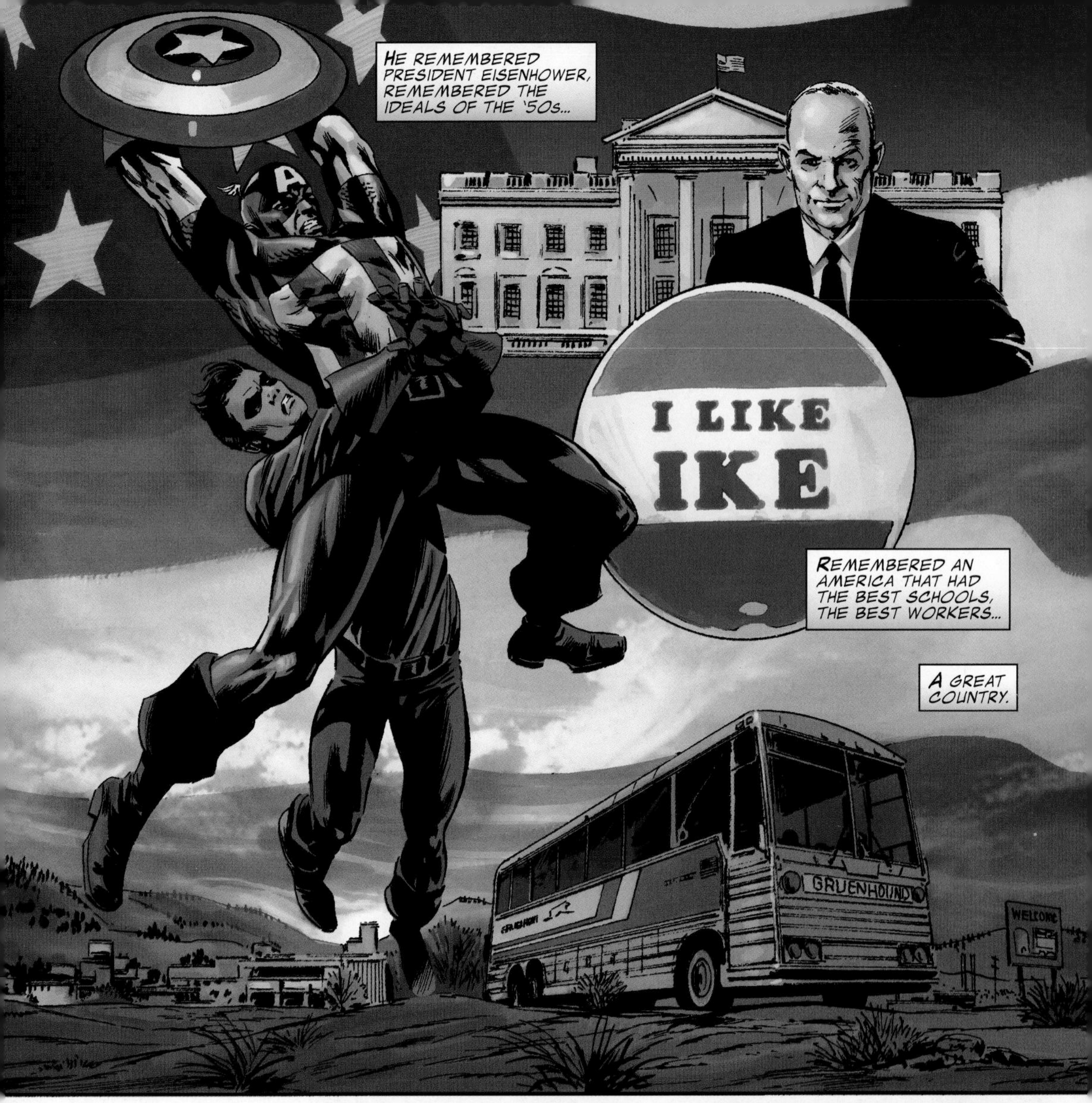
HE REMEMBERED PRESIDENT EISENHOWER, REMEMBERED THE IDEALS OF THE '50s...
I LIKE IKE
REMEMBERED AN AMERICA THAT HAD THE BEST SCHOOLS, THE BEST WORKERS...
A GREAT COUNTRY.
GRUENHOUND
WELCOME

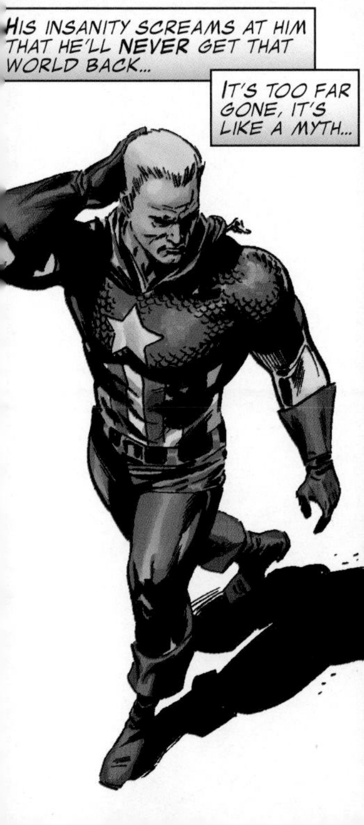
HIS INSANITY SCREAMS AT HIM THAT HE'LL NEVER GET THAT WORLD BACK...
IT'S TOO FAR GONE, IT'S LIKE A MYTH...

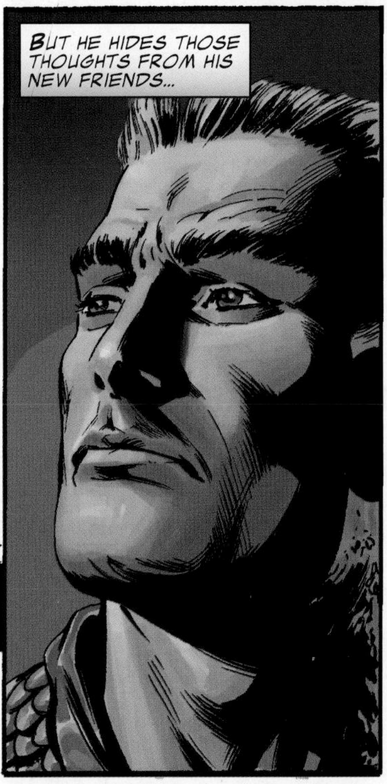
BUT HE HIDES THOSE THOUGHTS FROM HIS NEW FRIENDS...

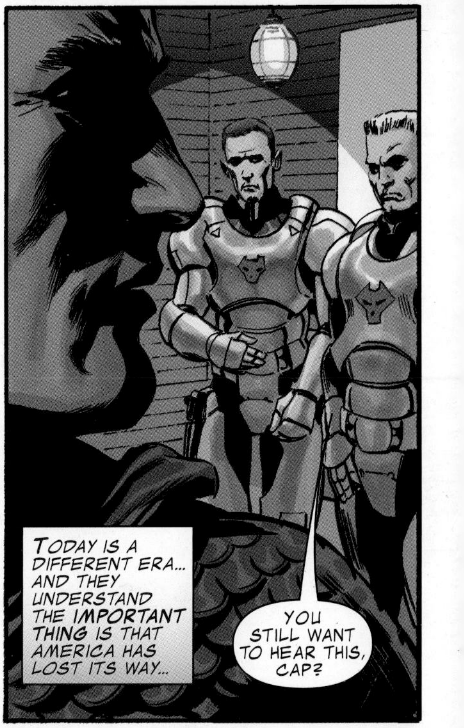
TODAY IS A DIFFERENT ERA... AND THEY UNDERSTAND THE IMPORTANT THING IS THAT AMERICA HAS LOST ITS WAY...
YOU STILL WANT TO HEAR THIS, CAP?

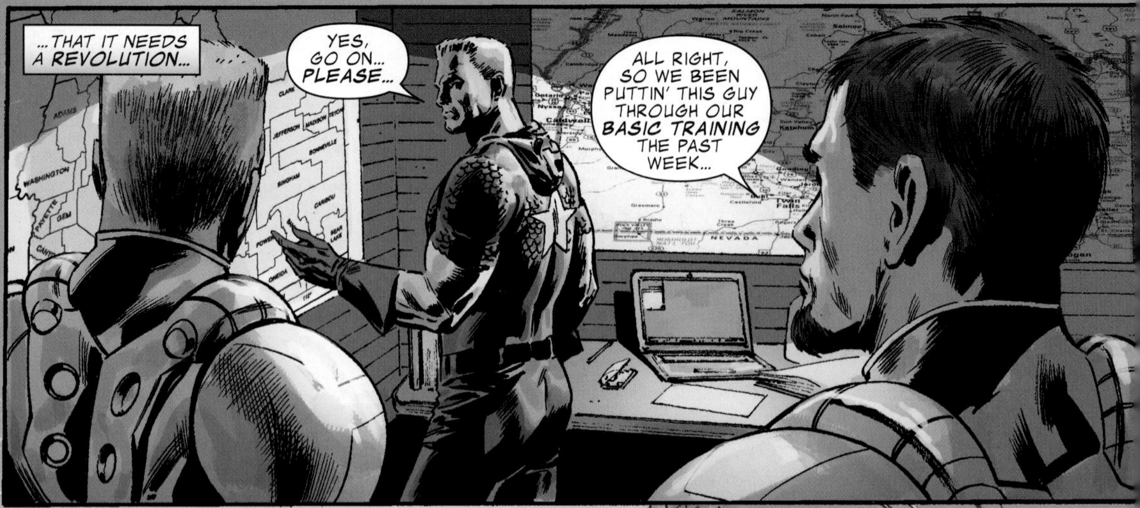
...THAT IT NEEDS A REVOLUTION...
YES, GO ON... PLEASE...
ALL RIGHT, SO WE BEEN PUTTIN' THIS GUY THROUGH OUR BASIC TRAINING THE PAST WEEK...

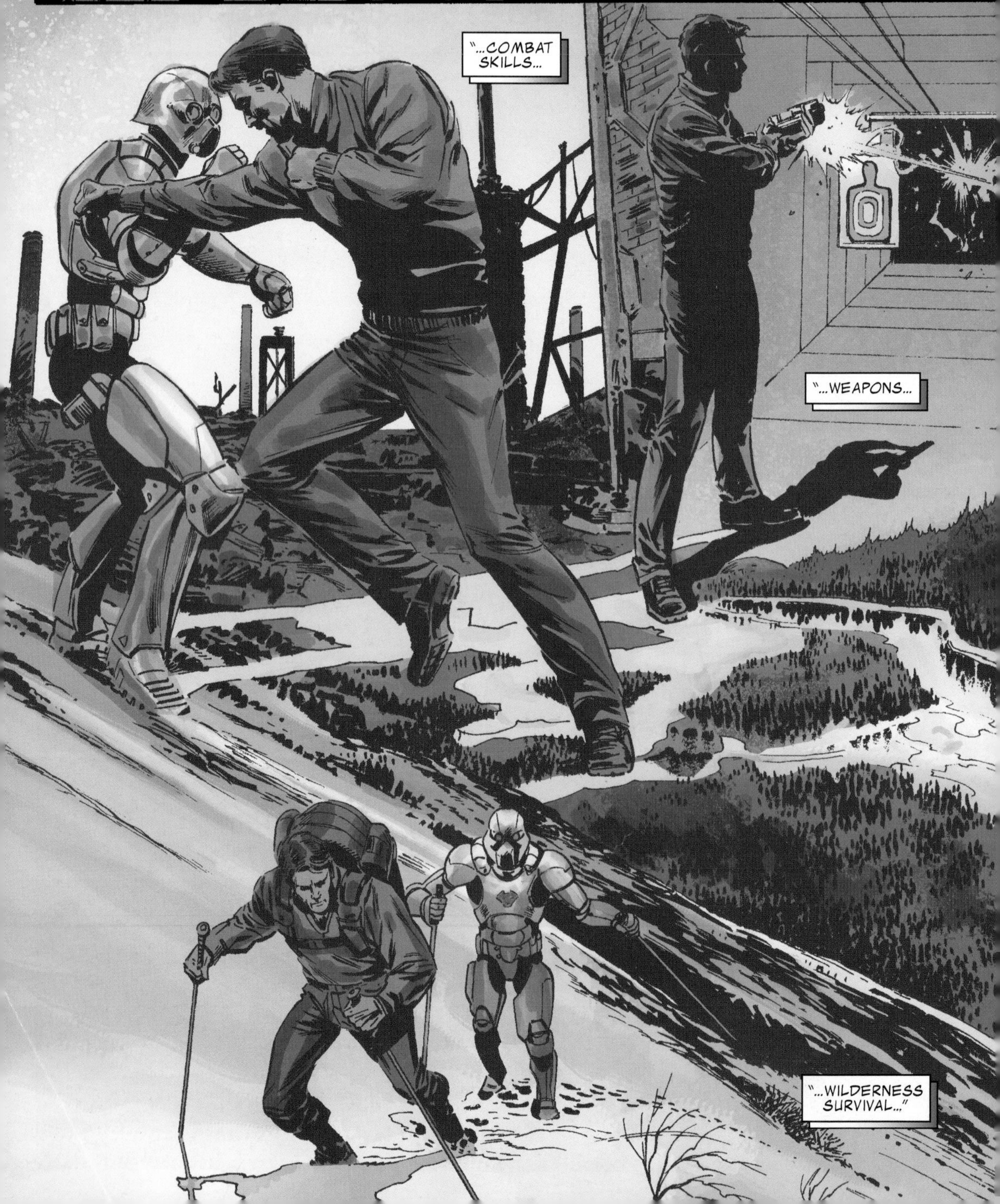
"...COMBAT SKILLS...
"...WEAPONS...
"...WILDERNESS SURVIVAL..."

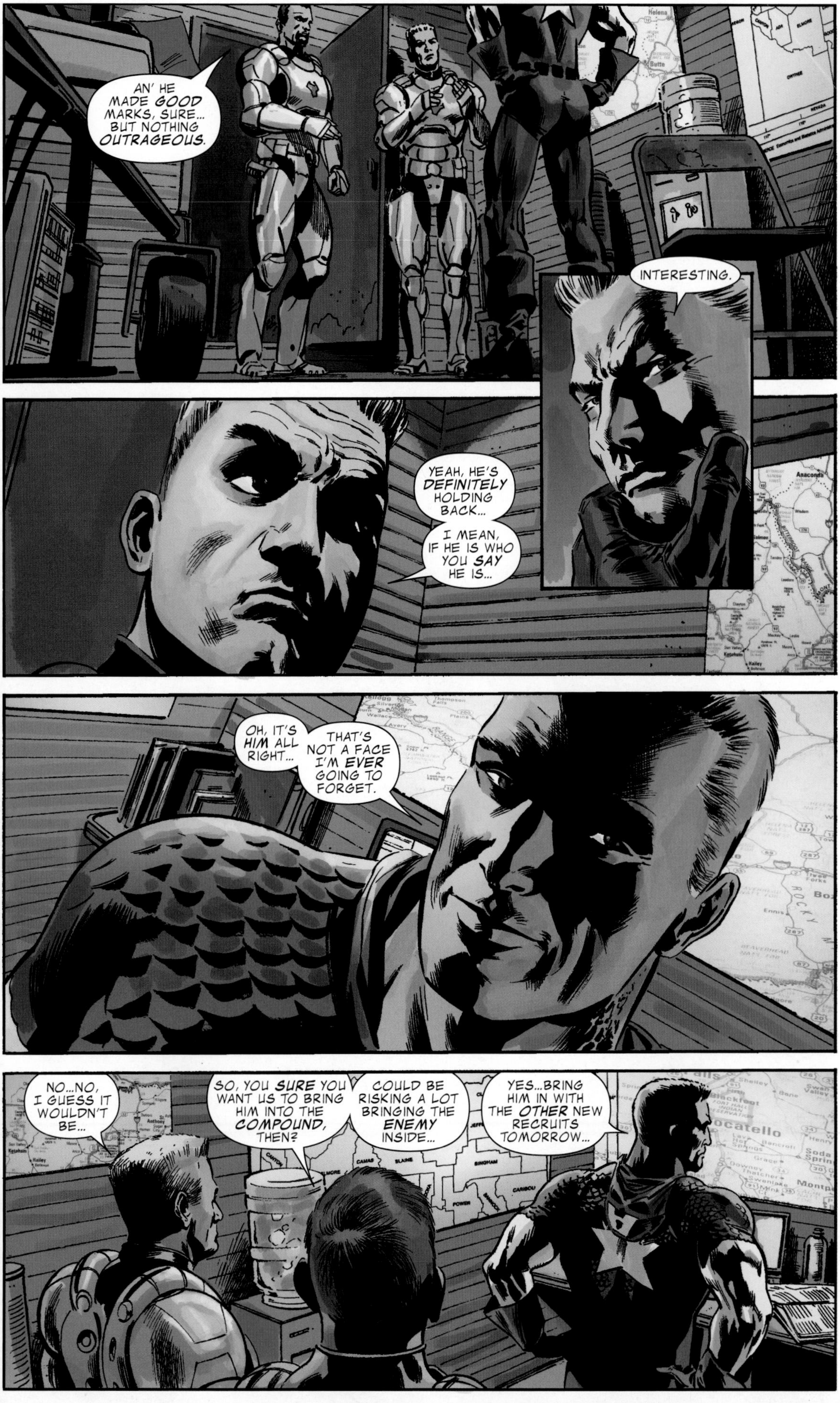

AN' HE MADE GOOD MARKS, SURE... BUT NOTHING OUTRAGEOUS.
INTERESTING.
YEAH, HE'S DEFINITELY HOLDING BACK...
I MEAN, IF HE IS WHO YOU SAY HE IS...
OH, IT'S HIM ALL RIGHT...
THAT'S NOT A FACE I'M EVER GOING TO FORGET.
NO...NO, I GUESS IT WOULDN'T BE...
SO, YOU SURE YOU WANT US TO BRING HIM INTO THE COMPOUND, THEN?
COULD BE RISKING A LOT BRINGING THE ENEMY INSIDE...
YES...BRING HIM IN WITH THE OTHER NEW RECRUITS TOMORROW...

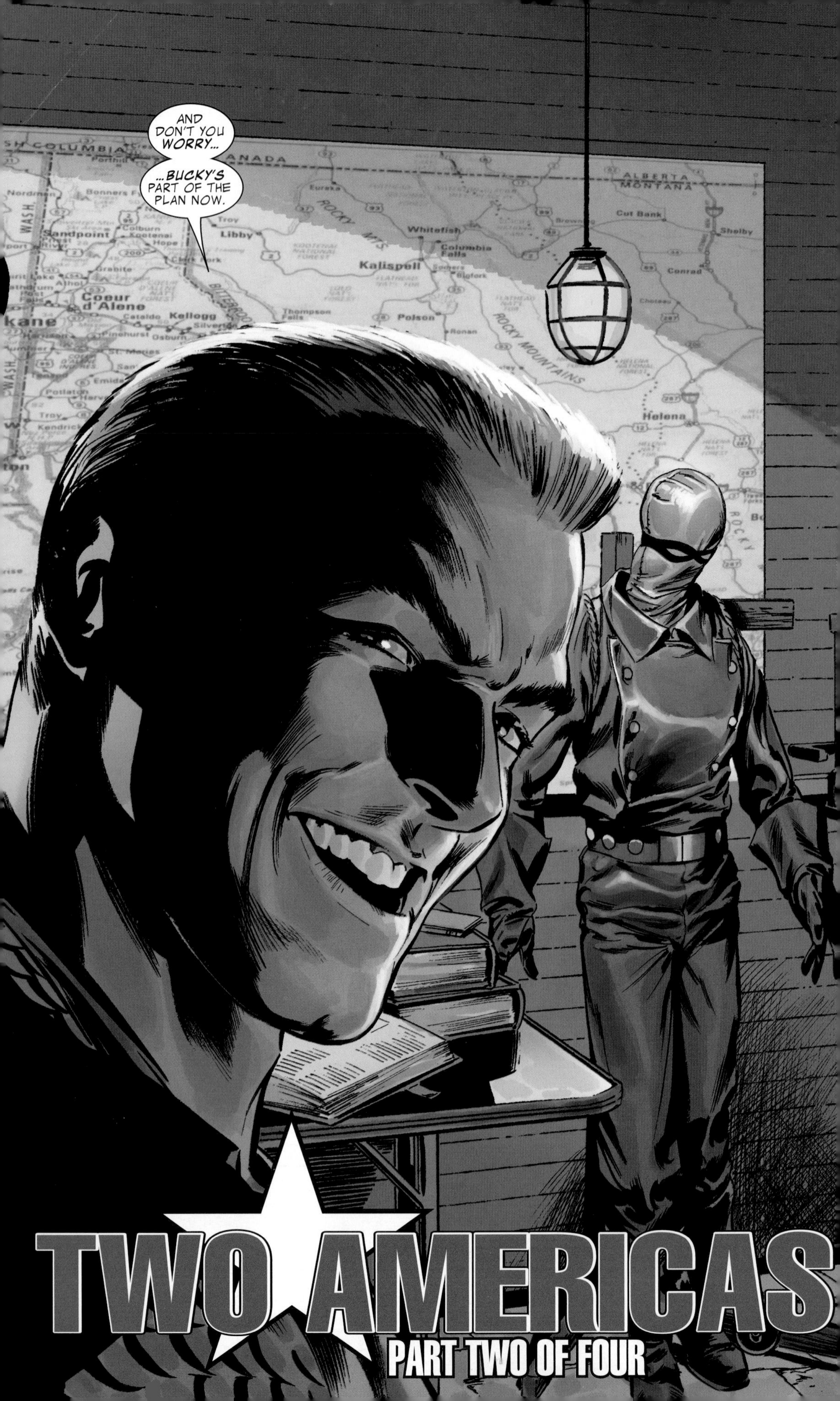
AND DON'T YOU WORRY...
...BUCKY'S PART OF THE PLAN NOW.
TWO AMERICAS
PART TWO OF FOUR

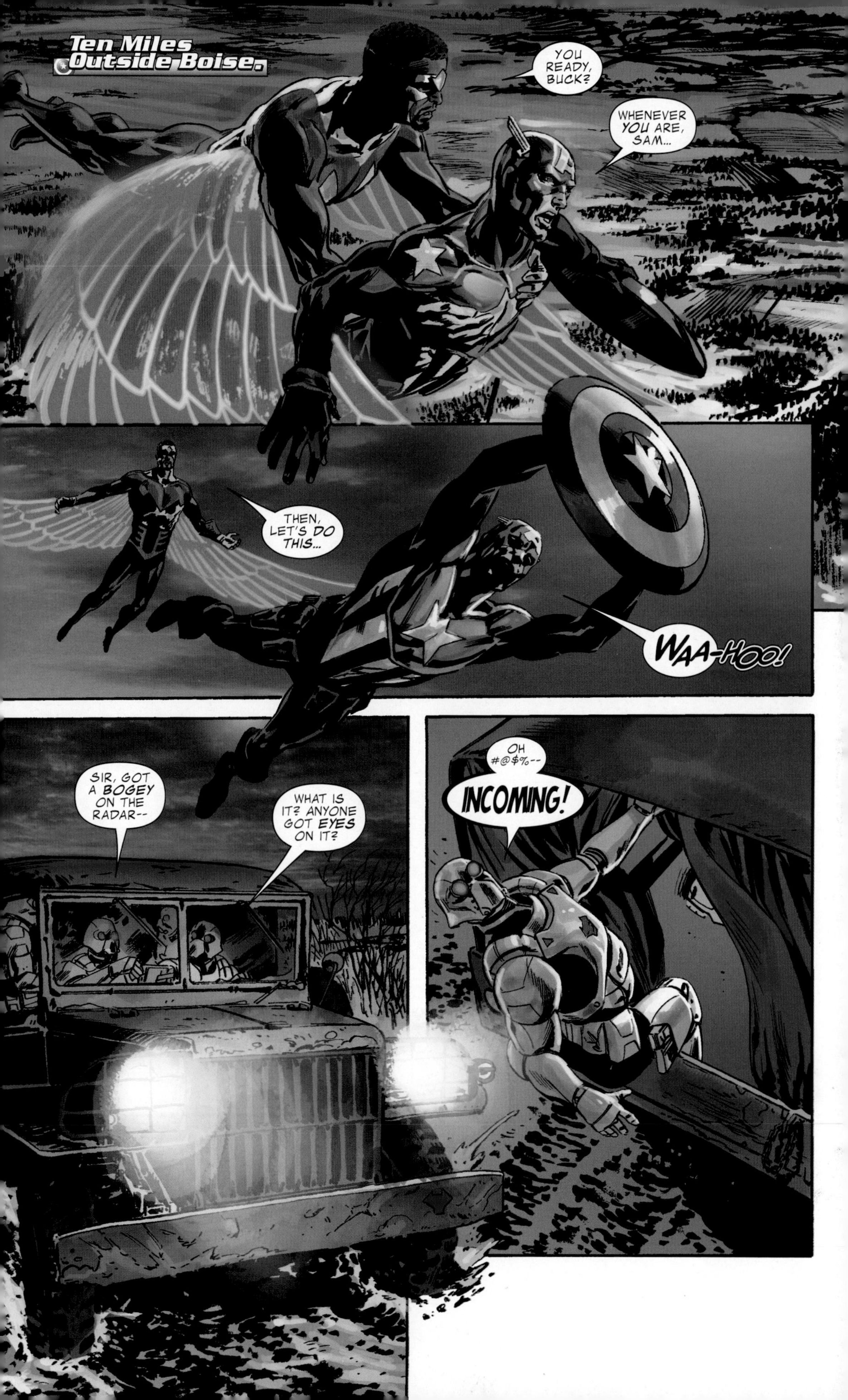
Ten Miles Outside Boise.
YOU READY, BUCK?
WHENEVER YOU ARE, SAM...
THEN, LET'S DO THIS...
WAA-HOO!
SIR, GOT A BOGEY ON THE RADAR--
WHAT IS IT? ANYONE GOT EYES ON IT?
OH #@$%--
INCOMING!

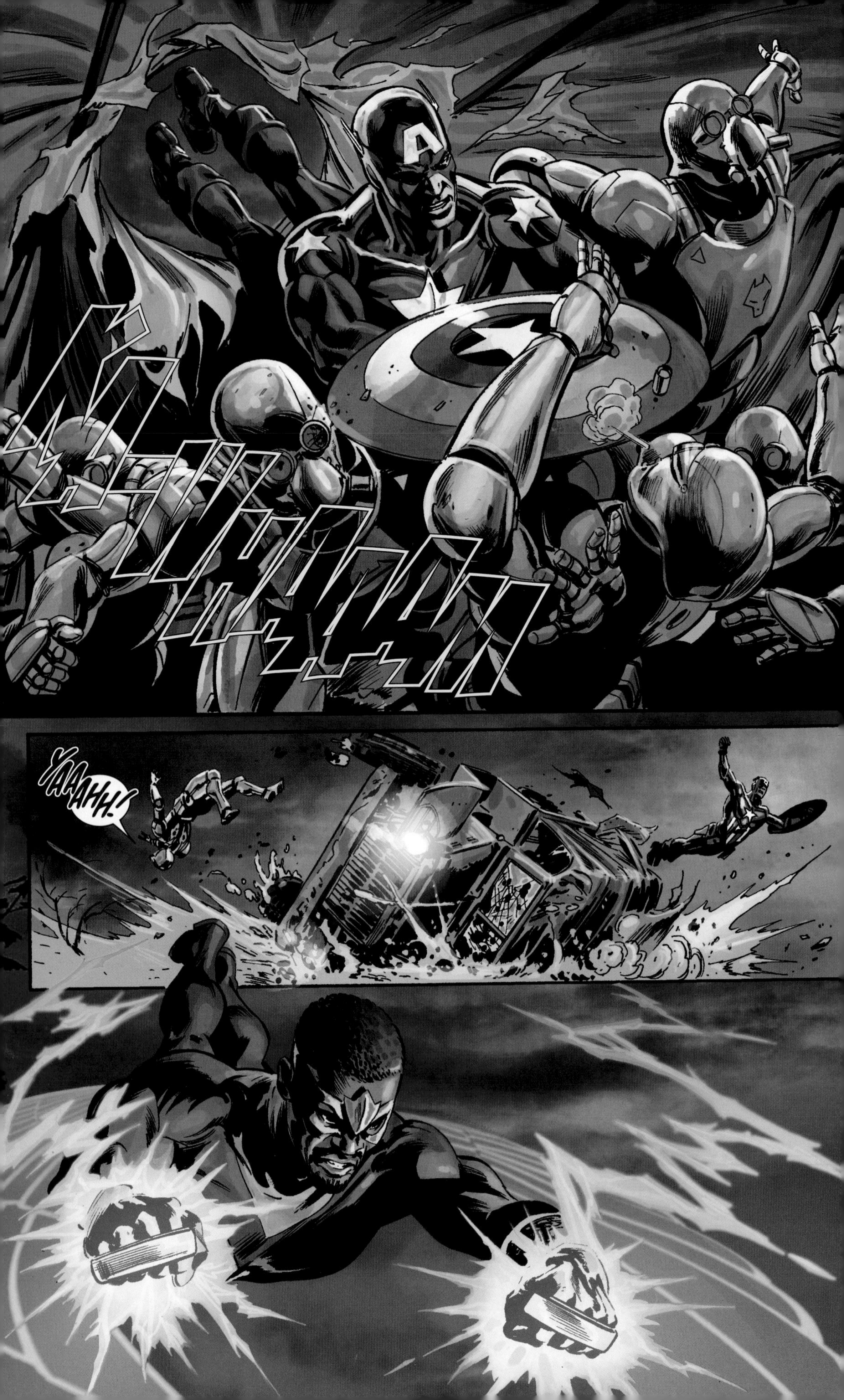
YAAAHH!

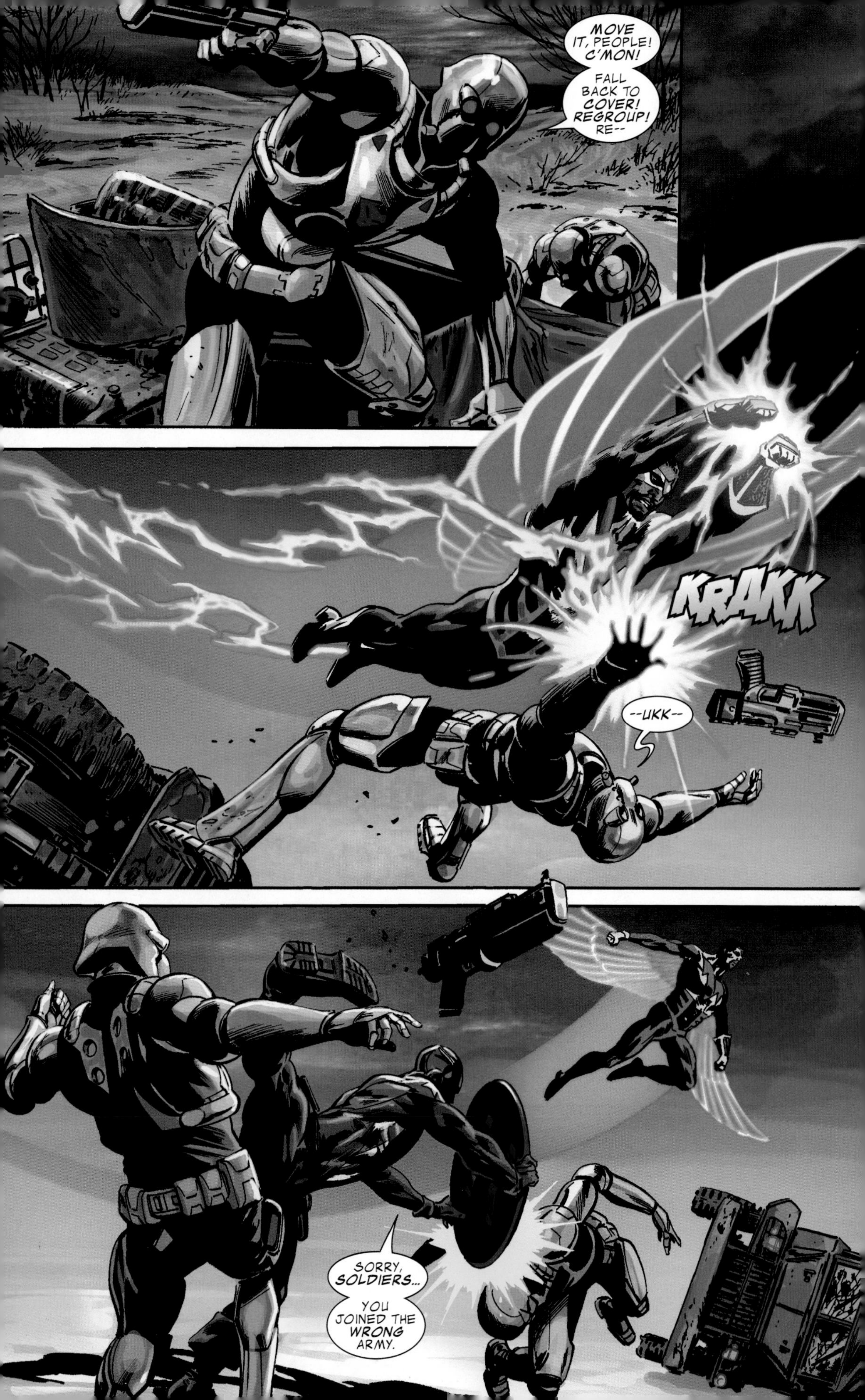
MOVE IT, PEOPLE! C'MON!
FALL BACK TO COVER! REGROUP! RE--
KRAKK
--UKK--
SORRY, SOLDIERS...
YOU JOINED THE WRONG ARMY.

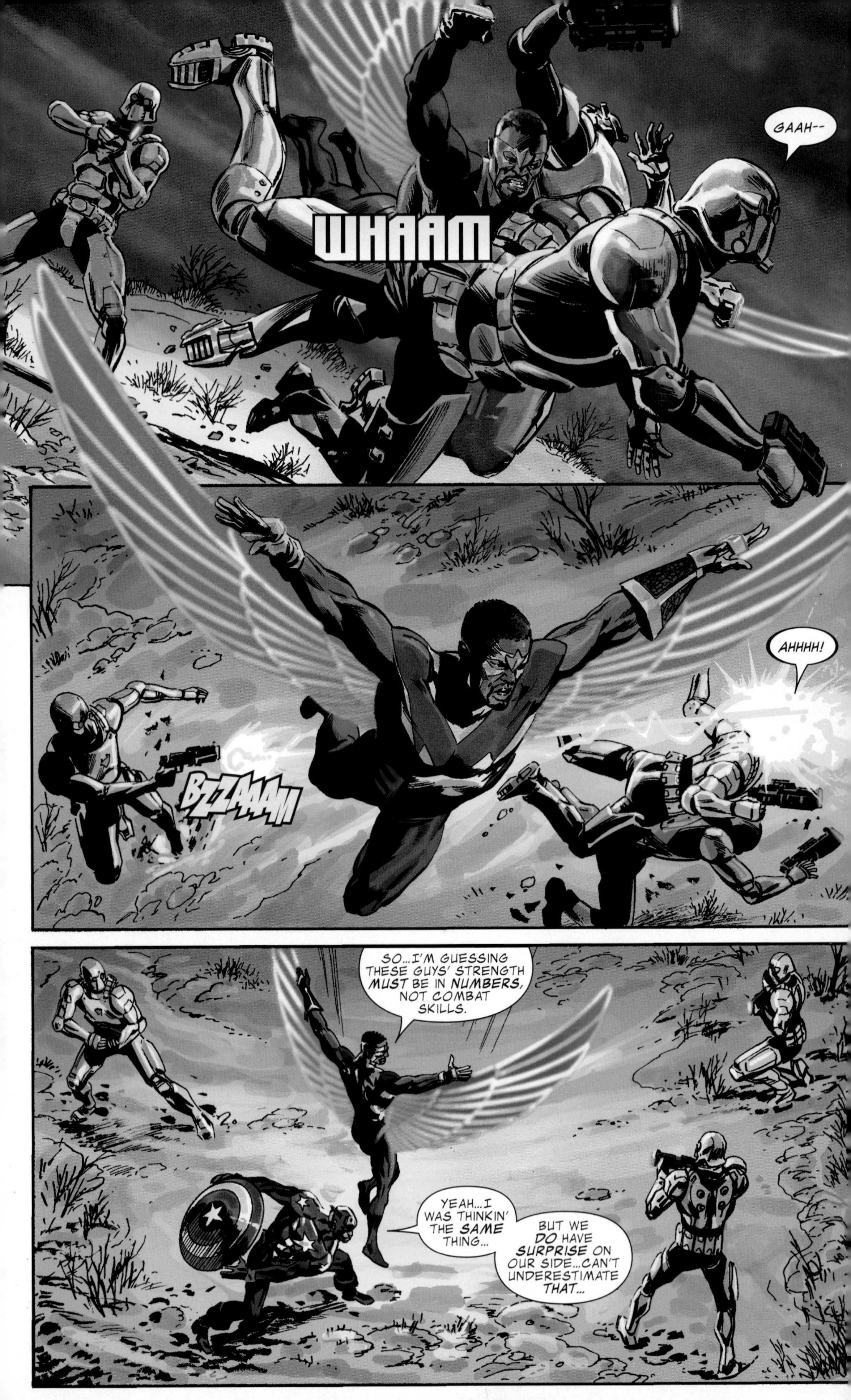
GAAH--
WHAAM
AHHHH!
BZZAAAM
SO...I'M GUESSING THESE GUYS' STRENGTH MUST BE IN NUMBERS, NOT COMBAT SKILLS.
YEAH...I WAS THINKIN' THE SAME THING...
BUT WE DO HAVE SURPRISE ON OUR SIDE...CAN'T UNDERESTIMATE THAT...

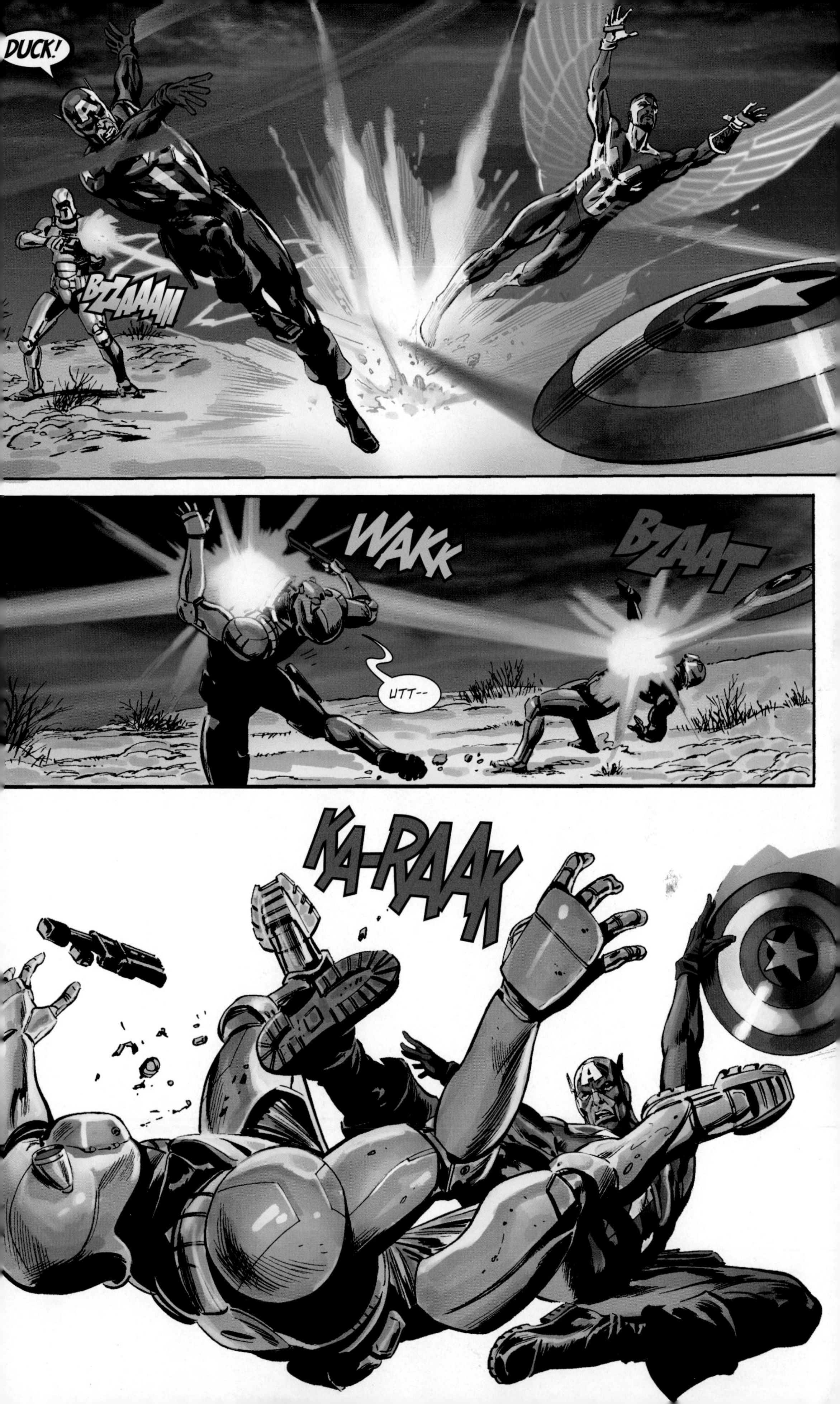
DUCK!
BZZAAAM
WAKK
BZAAT
UTT--
KA-RAAK

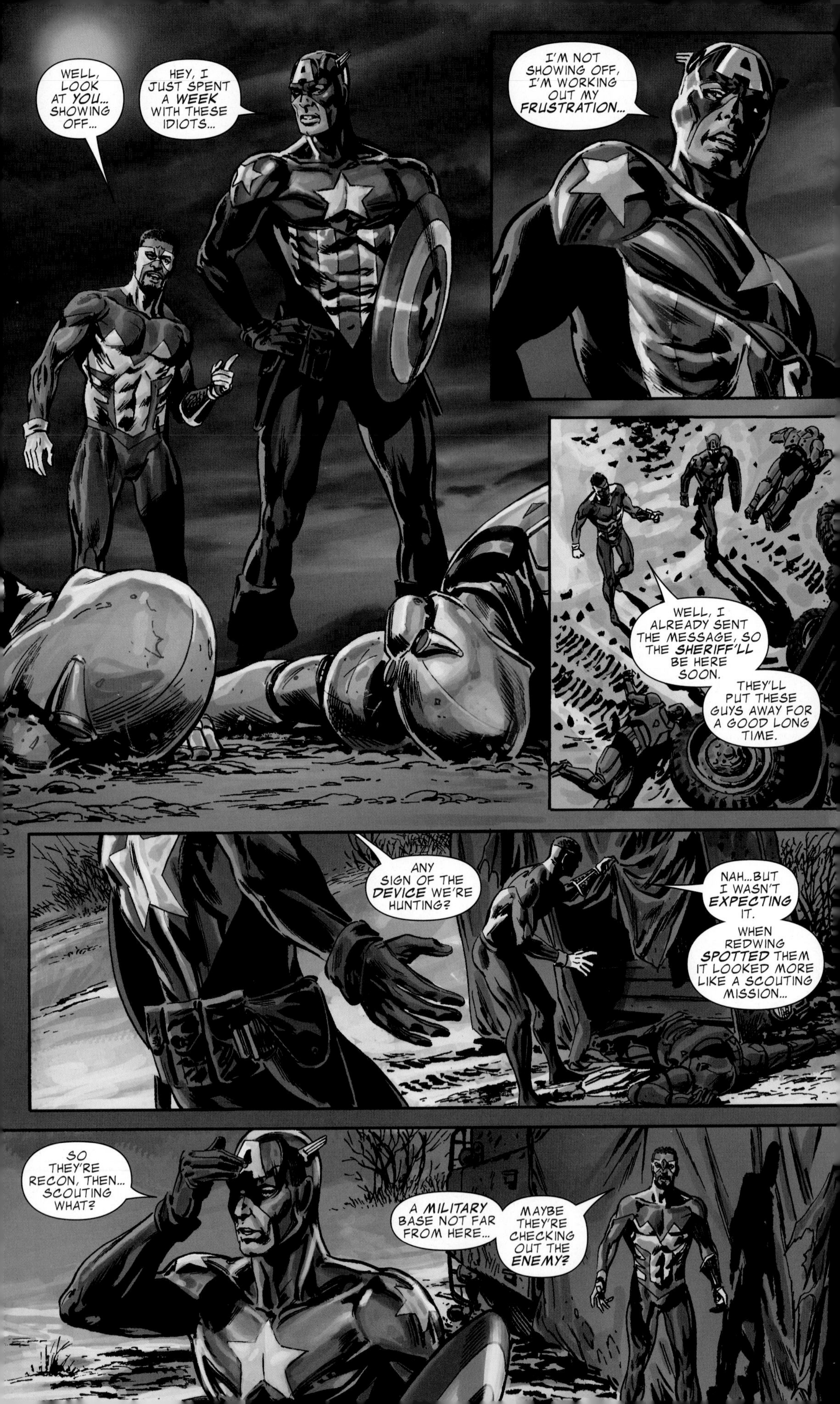

WELL, LOOK AT YOU... SHOWING OFF...
HEY, I JUST SPENT A WEEK WITH THESE IDIOTS...
I'M NOT SHOWING OFF, I'M WORKING OUT MY FRUSTRATION...
WELL, I ALREADY SENT THE MESSAGE, SO THE SHERIFF'LL BE HERE SOON.
THEY'LL PUT THESE GUYS AWAY FOR A GOOD LONG TIME.
ANY SIGN OF THE DEVICE WE'RE HUNTING?
NAH...BUT I WASN'T EXPECTING IT.
WHEN REDWING SPOTTED THEM IT LOOKED MORE LIKE A SCOUTING MISSION...
SO THEY'RE RECON, THEN... SCOUTING WHAT?
A MILITARY BASE NOT FAR FROM HERE...
MAYBE THEY'RE CHECKING OUT THE ENEMY?

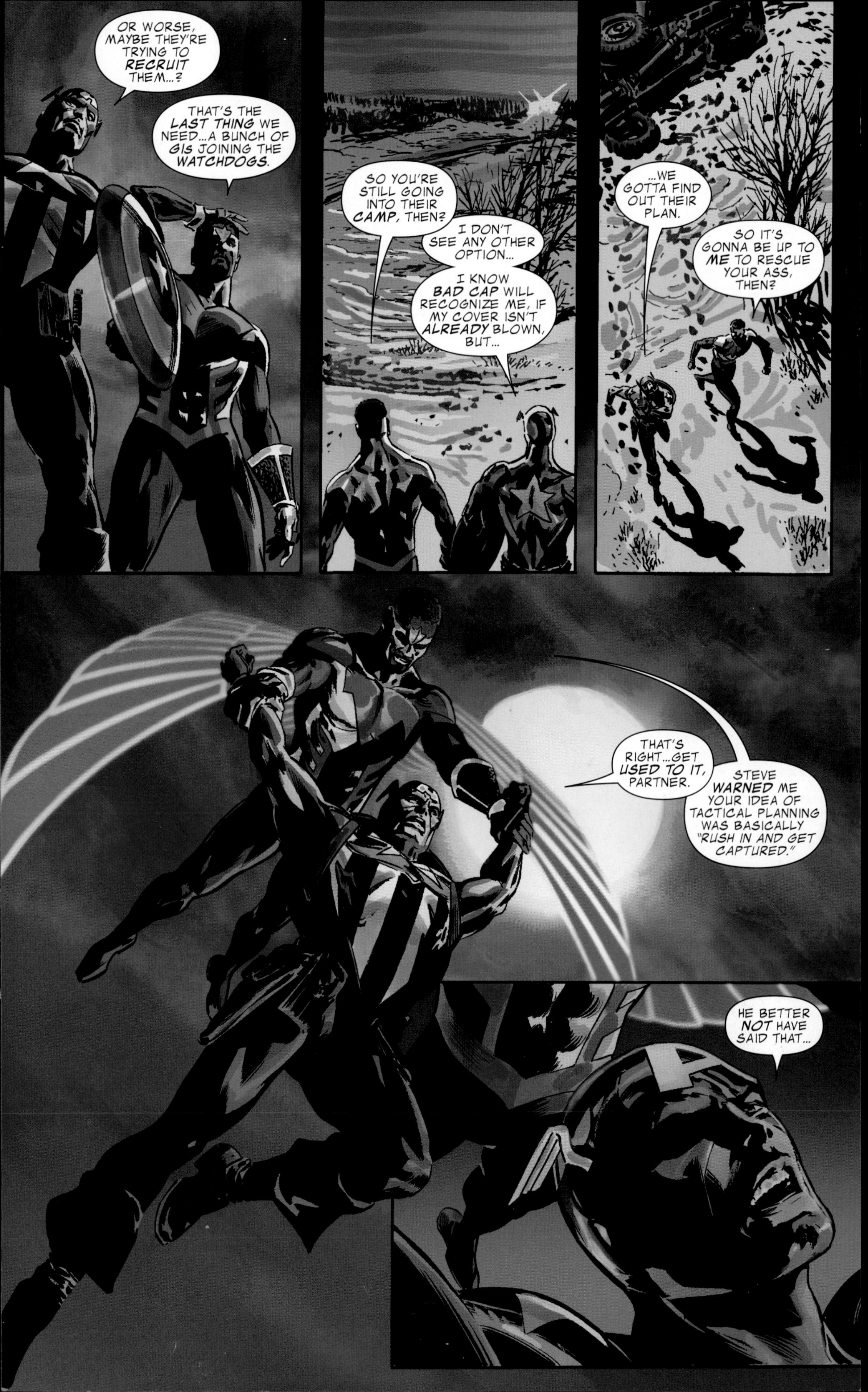
OR WORSE, MAYBE THEY'RE TRYING TO RECRUIT THEM...?
THAT'S THE LAST THING WE NEED...A BUNCH OF GIS JOINING THE WATCHDOGS.
SO YOU'RE STILL GOING INTO THEIR CAMP, THEN?
I DON'T SEE ANY OTHER OPTION...
I KNOW BAD CAP WILL RECOGNIZE ME, IF MY COVER ISN'T ALREADY BLOWN, BUT...
...WE GOTTA FIND OUT THEIR PLAN.
SO IT'S GONNA BE UP TO ME TO RESCUE YOUR ASS, THEN?
THAT'S RIGHT...GET USED TO IT, PARTNER.
STEVE WARNED ME YOUR IDEA OF TACTICAL PLANNING WAS BASICALLY "RUSH IN AND GET CAPTURED."
HE BETTER NOT HAVE SAID THAT...

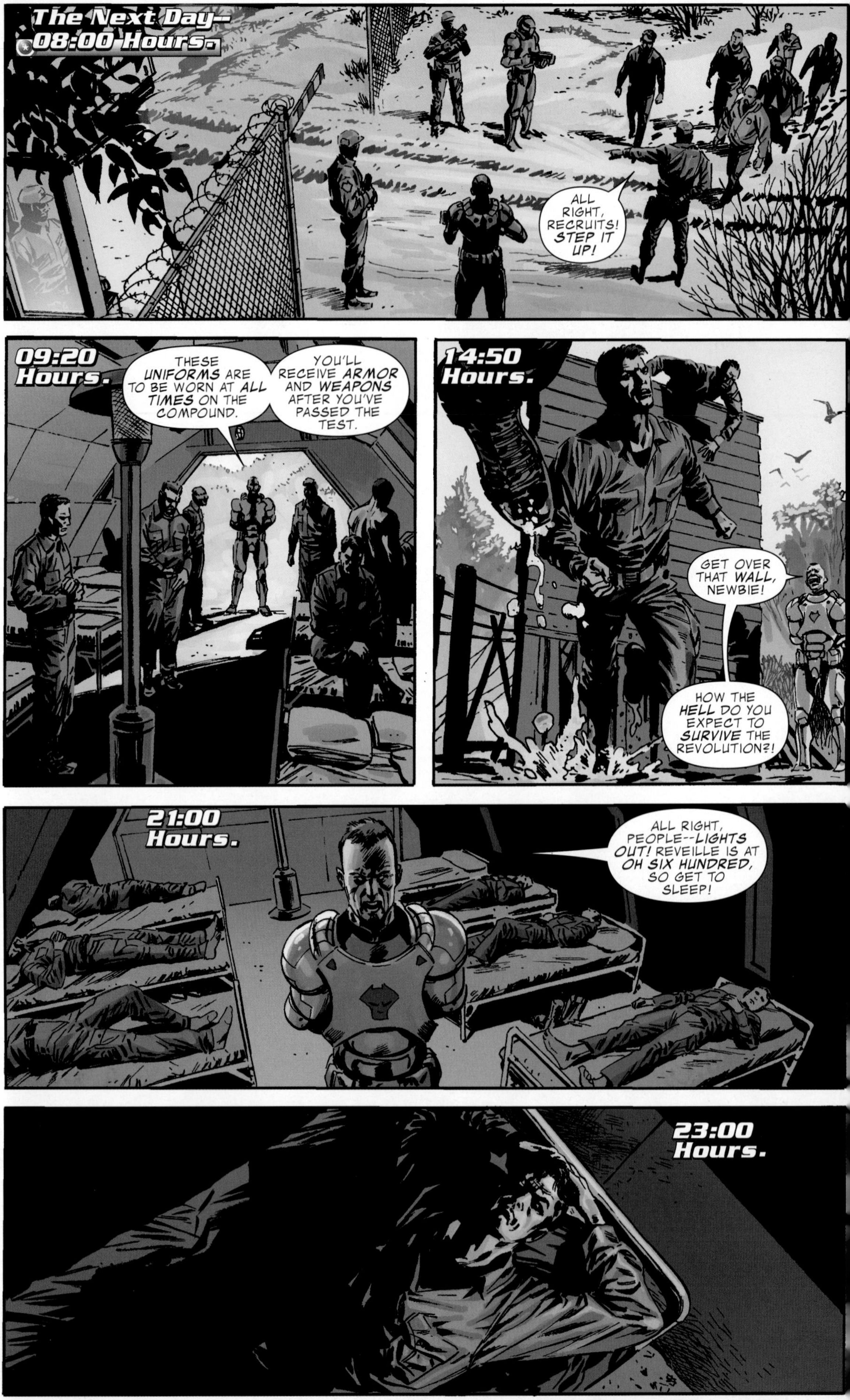
The Next Day--
08:00 Hours.
ALL RIGHT, RECRUITS! STEP IT UP!
09:20 Hours.
THESE UNIFORMS ARE TO BE WORN AT ALL TIMES ON THE COMPOUND.
YOU'LL RECEIVE ARMOR AND WEAPONS AFTER YOU'VE PASSED THE TEST.
14:50 Hours.
GET OVER THAT WALL, NEWBIE!
HOW THE HELL DO YOU EXPECT TO SURVIVE THE REVOLUTION?!
21:00 Hours.
ALL RIGHT, PEOPLE--LIGHTS OUT! REVEILLE IS AT OH SIX HUNDRED, SO GET TO SLEEP!
23:00 Hours.

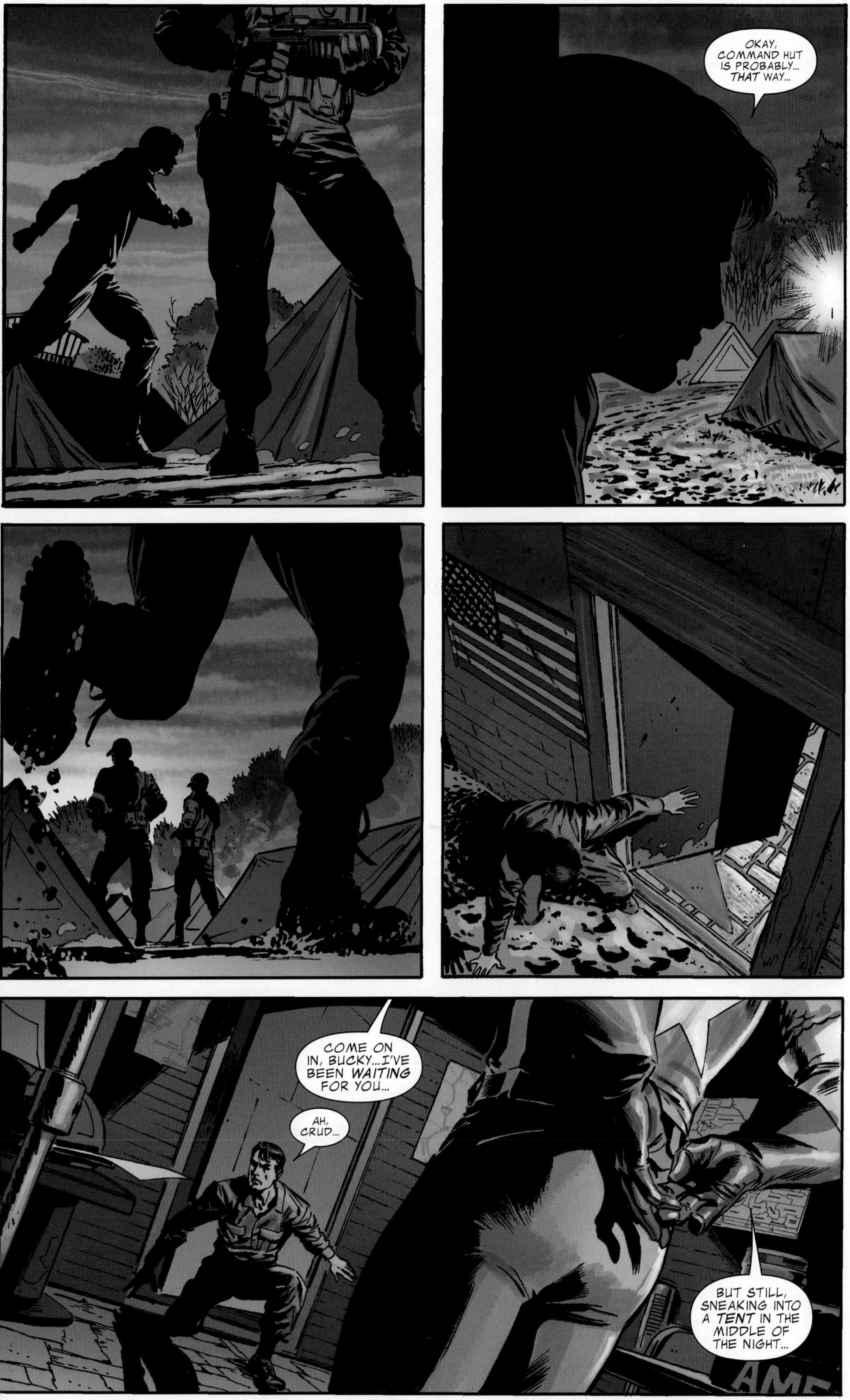
OKAY, COMMAND HUT IS PROBABLY... THAT WAY...
COME ON IN, BUCKY...I'VE BEEN WAITING FOR YOU...
AH, CRUD...
BUT STILL, SNEAKING INTO A TENT IN THE MIDDLE OF THE NIGHT...

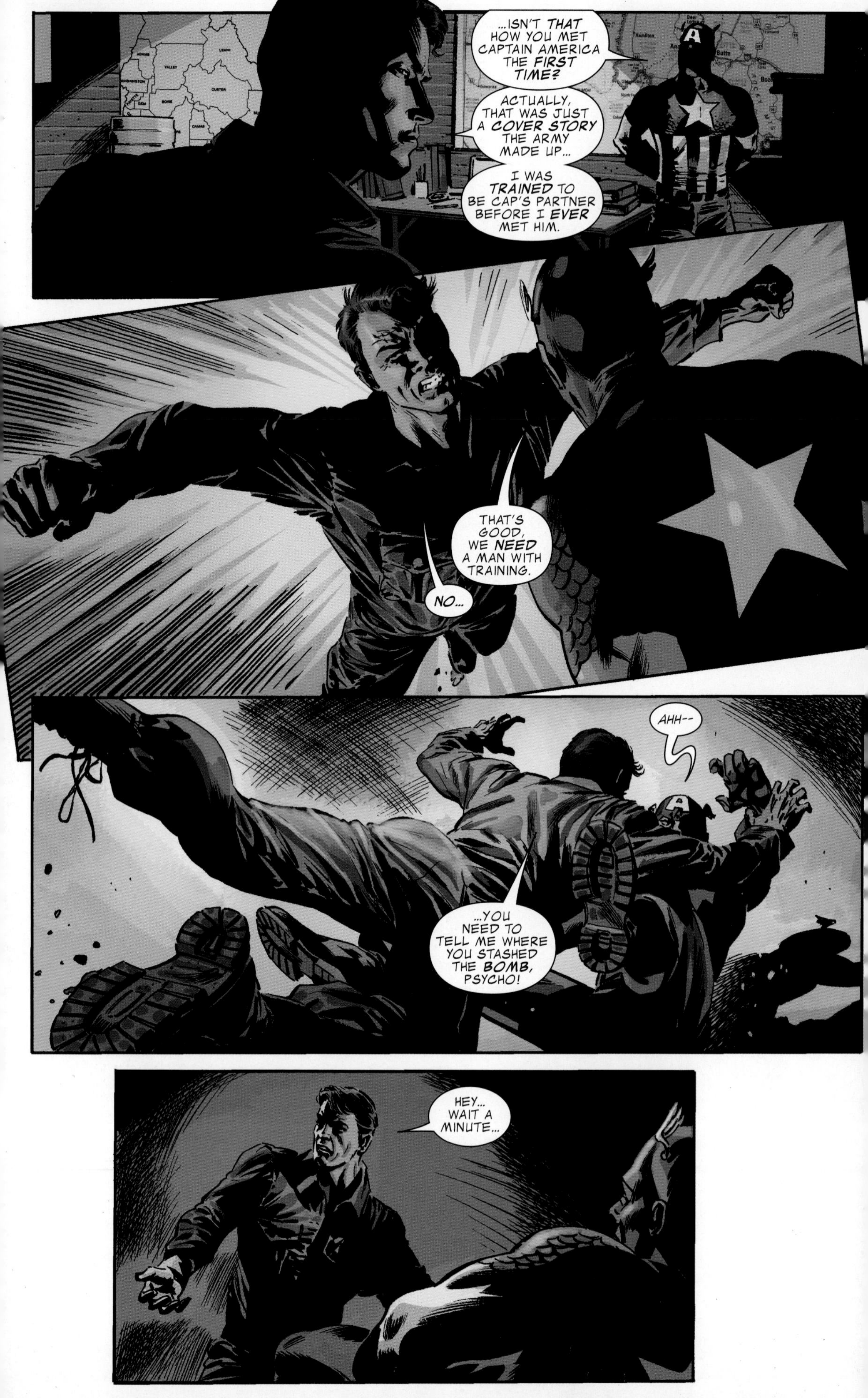
...ISN'T THAT HOW YOU MET CAPTAIN AMERICA THE FIRST TIME?
ACTUALLY, THAT WAS JUST A COVER STORY THE ARMY MADE UP...
I WAS TRAINED TO BE CAP'S PARTNER BEFORE I EVER MET HIM.
THAT'S GOOD, WE NEED A MAN WITH TRAINING.
NO...
AHH--
...YOU NEED TO TELL ME WHERE YOU STASHED THE BOMB, PSYCHO!
HEY... WAIT A MINUTE...

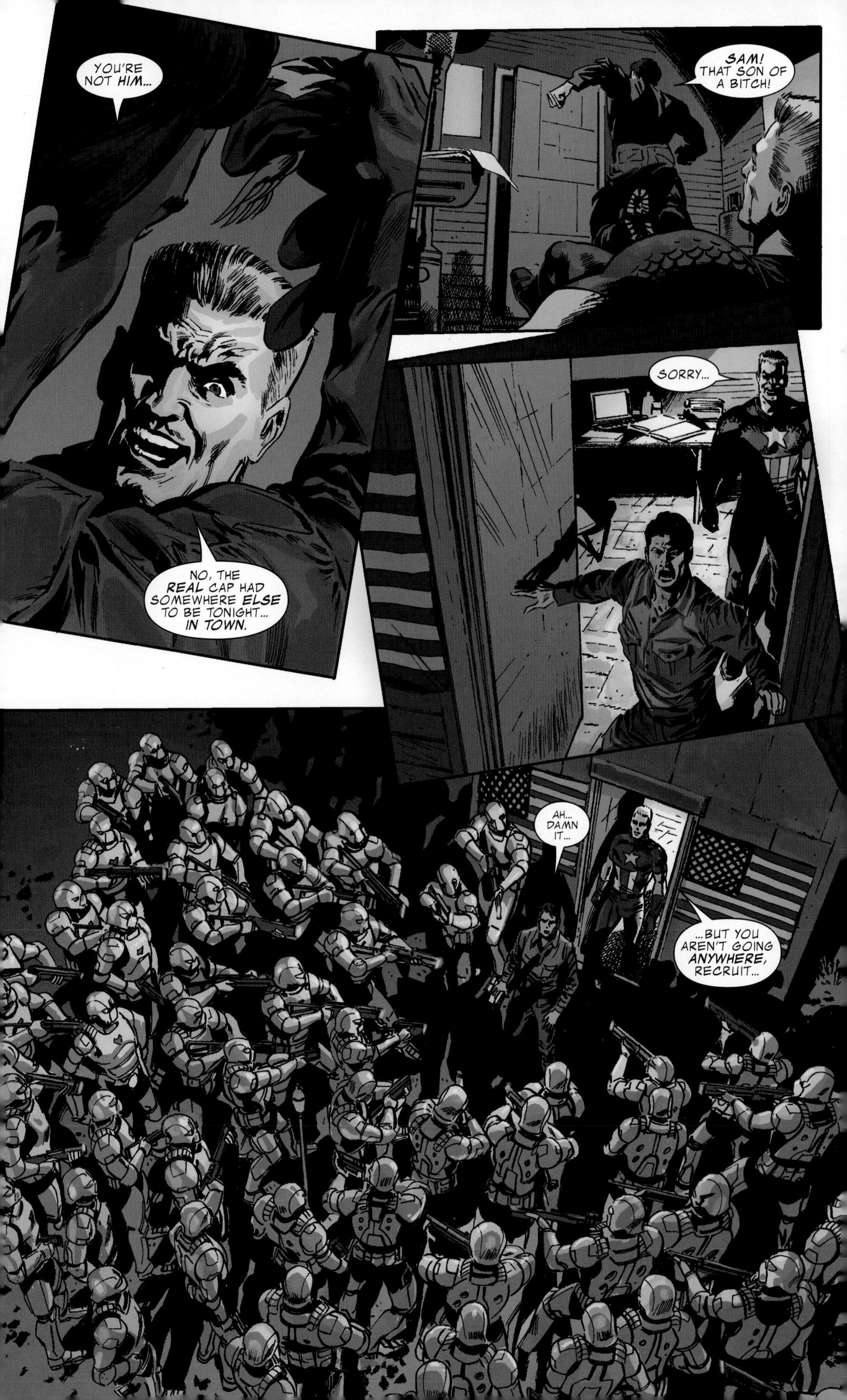
YOU'RE NOT HIM...
SAM! THAT SON OF A BITCH!
NO, THE REAL CAP HAD SOMEWHERE ELSE TO BE TONIGHT... IN TOWN.
SORRY...
AH... DAMN IT...
...BUT YOU AREN'T GOING ANYWHERE, RECRUIT...

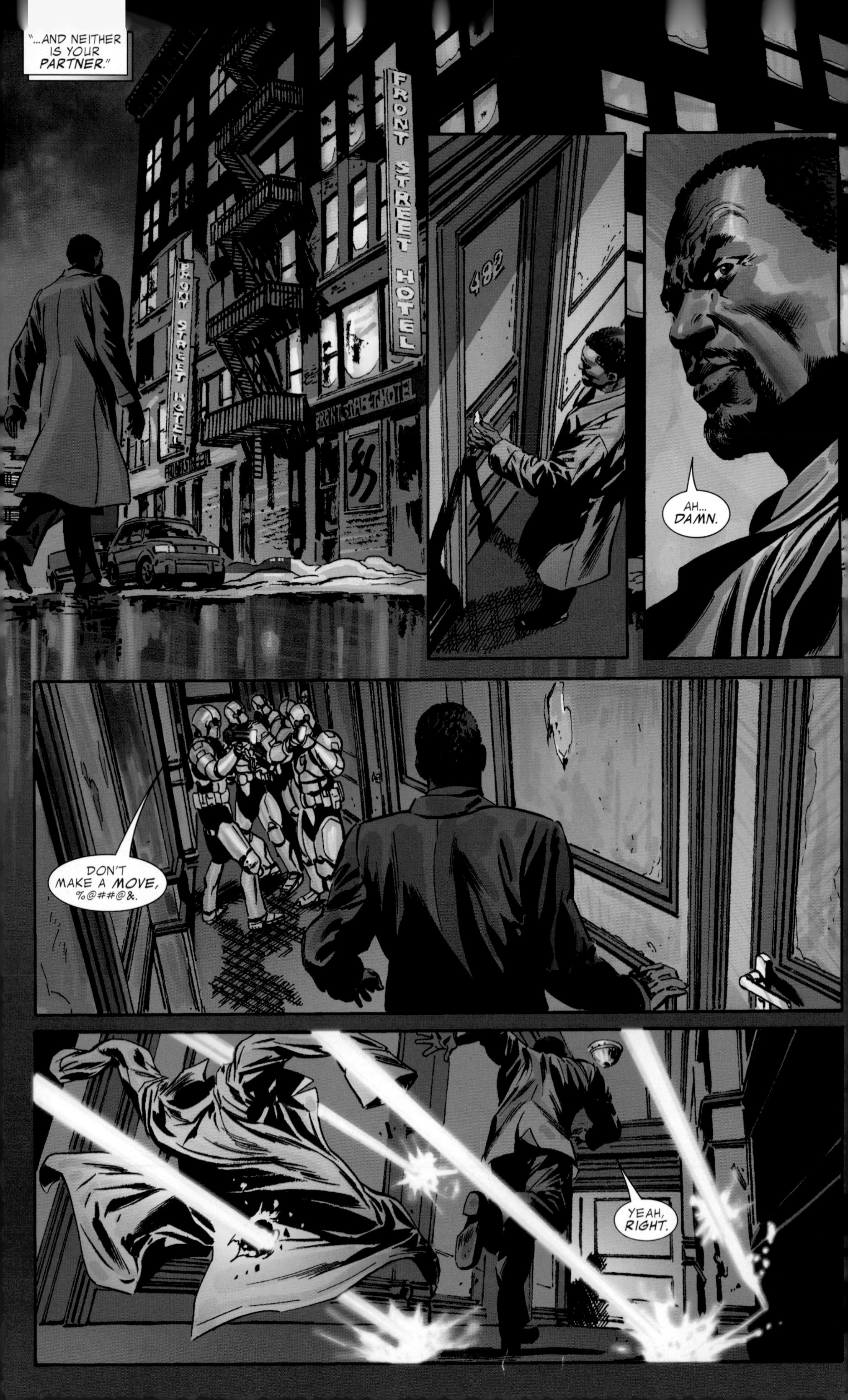
"...AND NEITHER IS YOUR PARTNER."
FRONT STREET HOTEL
FRONT STREET HOTEL
482
AH... DAMN.
DON'T MAKE A MOVE, %@##@&.
YEAH, RIGHT.

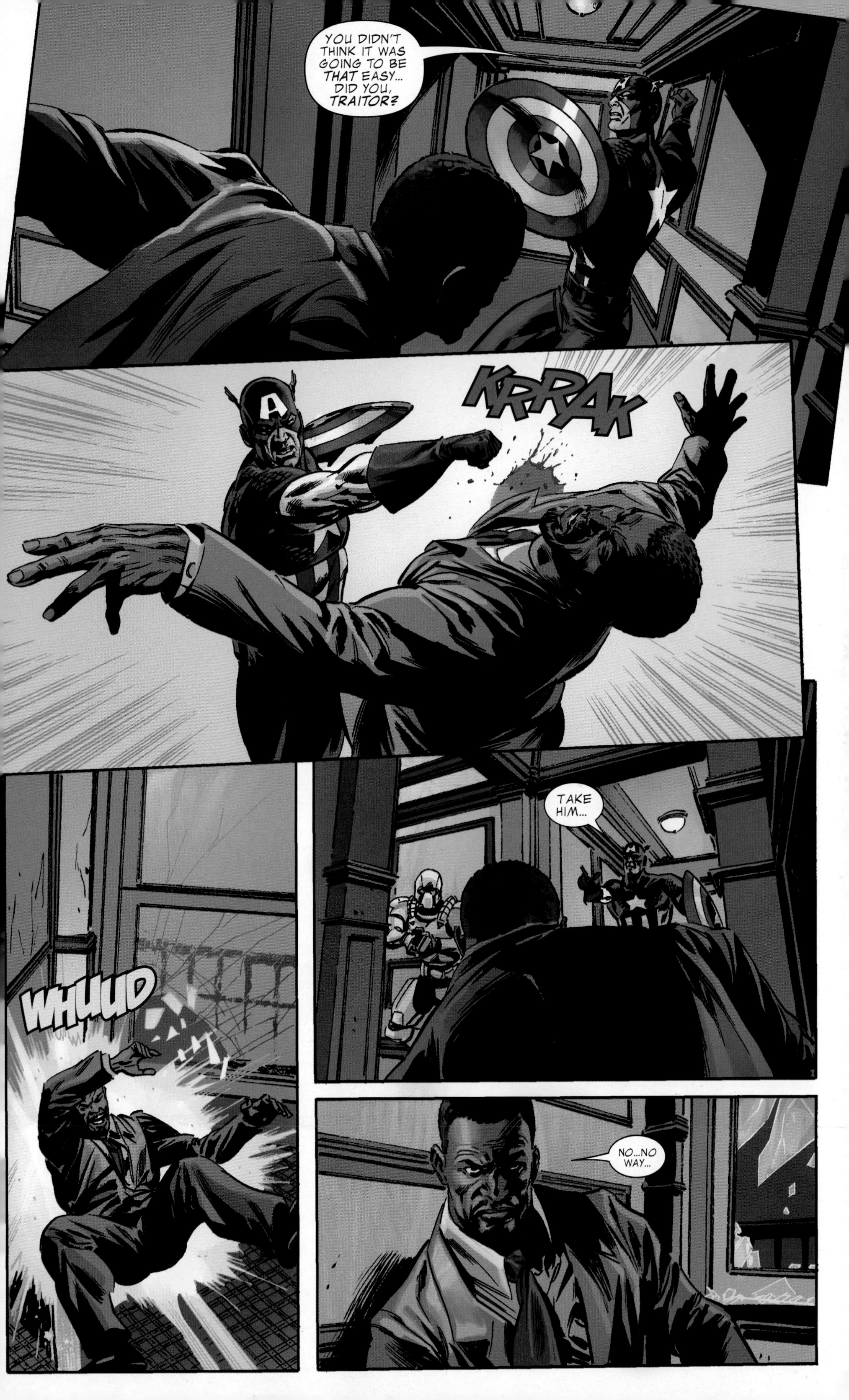
YOU DIDN'T THINK IT WAS GOING TO BE THAT EASY... DID YOU, TRAITOR?
KRRAK
WHUUD
TAKE HIM...
NO...NO WAY...

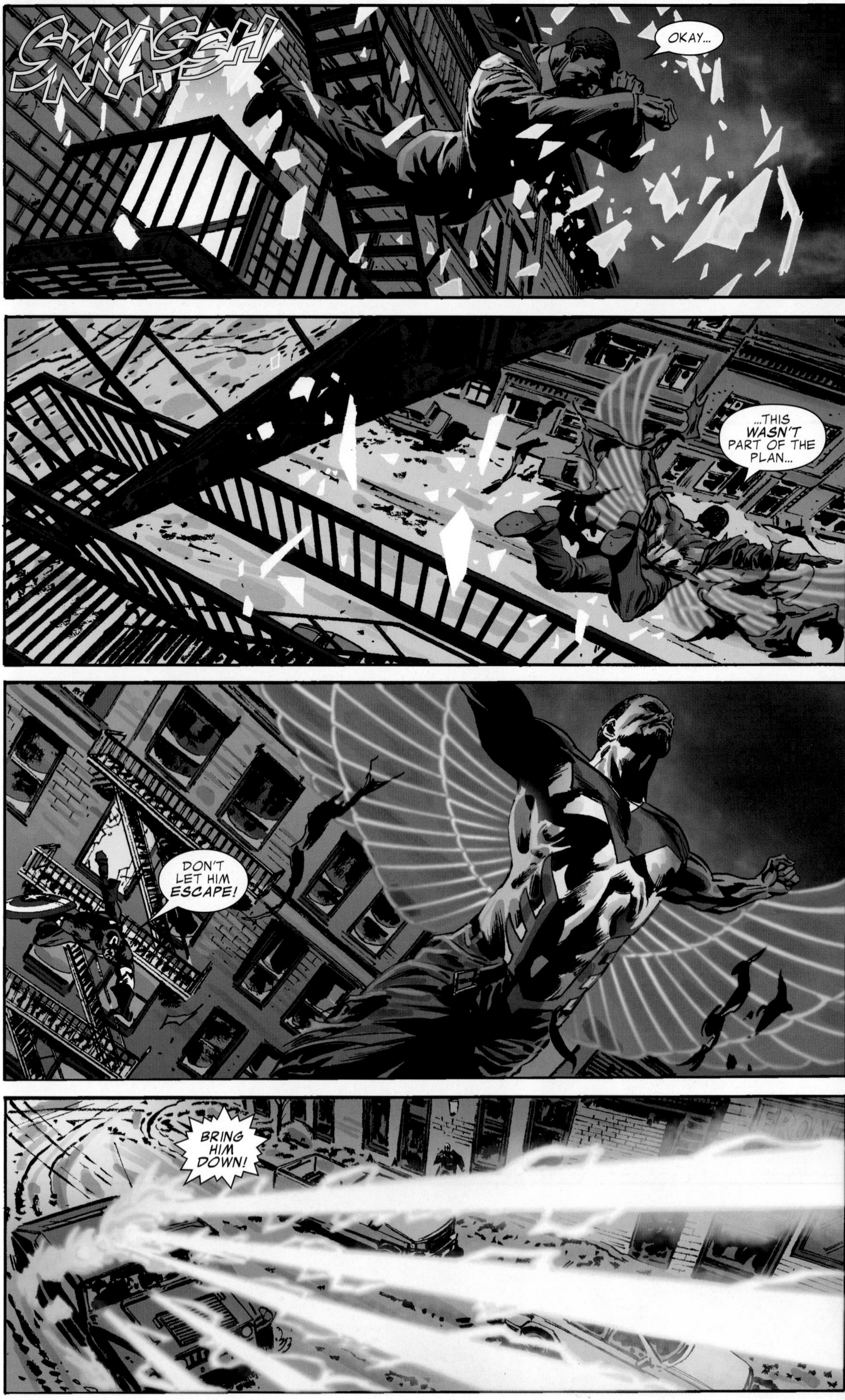

SKKASSH
OKAY...
...THIS WASN'T PART OF THE PLAN...
DON'T LET HIM ESCAPE!
BRING HIM DOWN!

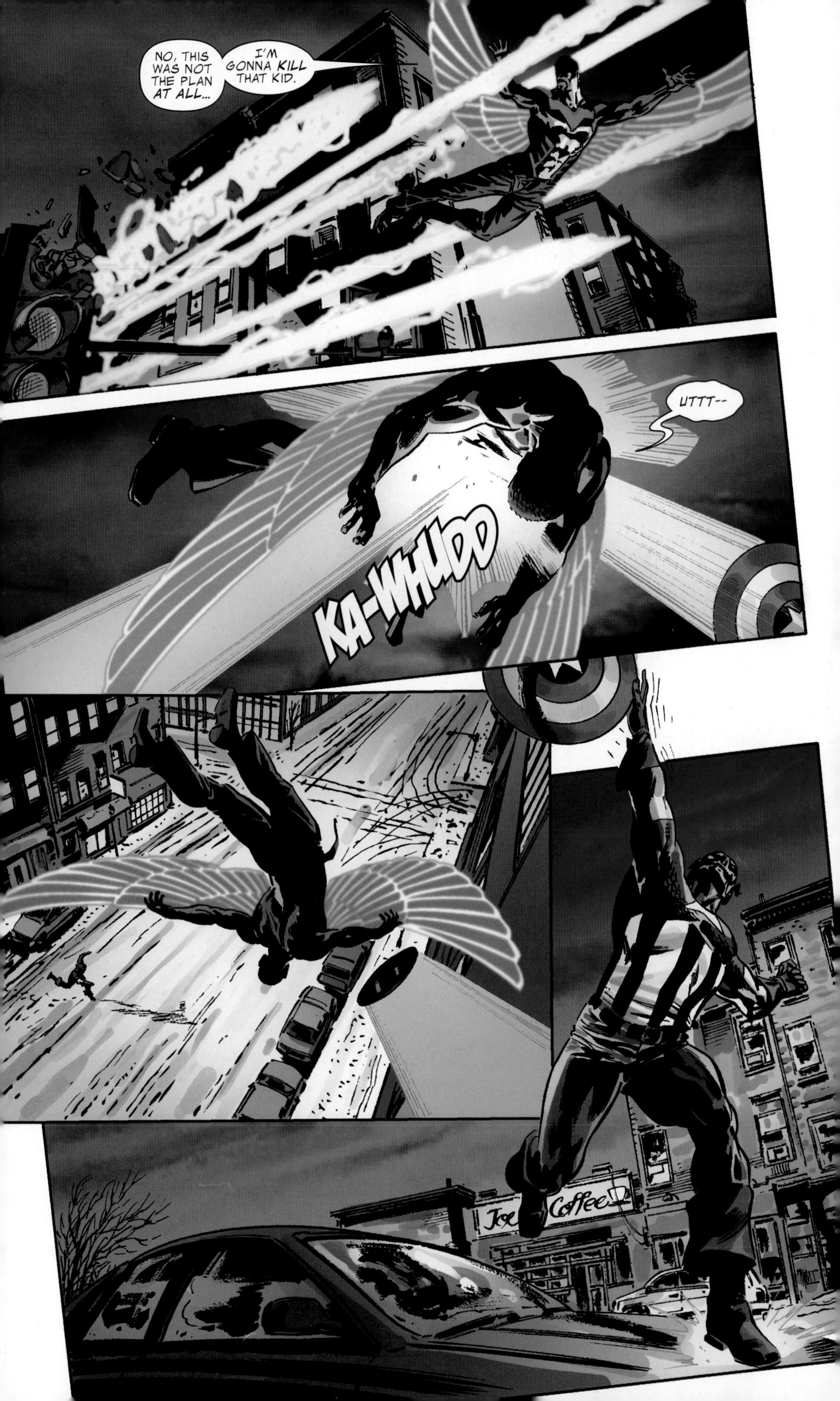
NO, THIS WAS NOT THE PLAN AT ALL...
I'M GONNA KILL THAT KID.
UTTT--
KA-WHUDD
Joe Coffee

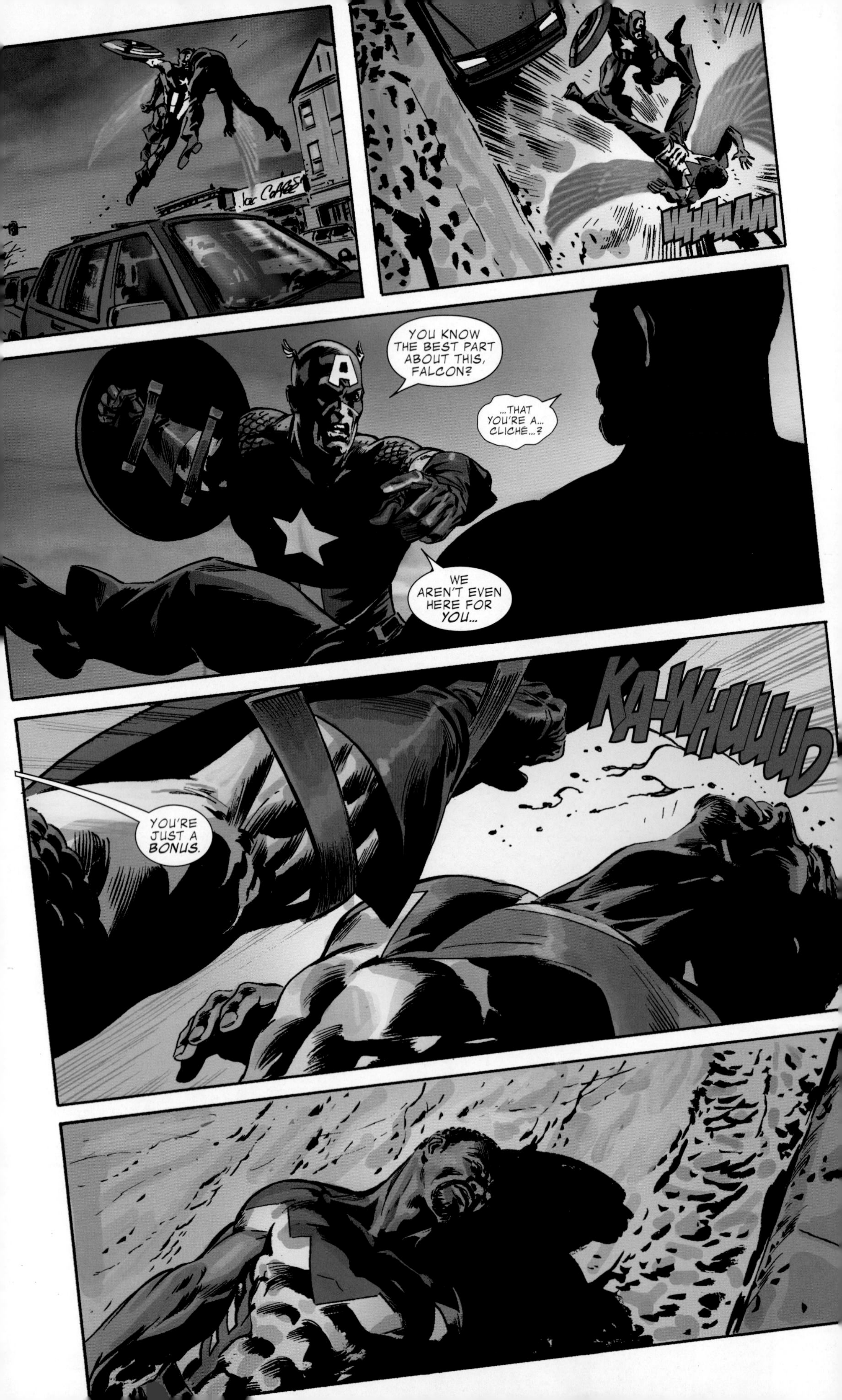

WHAAAM
YOU KNOW THE BEST PART ABOUT THIS, FALCON?
...THAT YOU'RE A... CLICHÉ...?
WE AREN'T EVEN HERE FOR YOU...
KA-WHUUUD
YOU'RE JUST A BONUS.

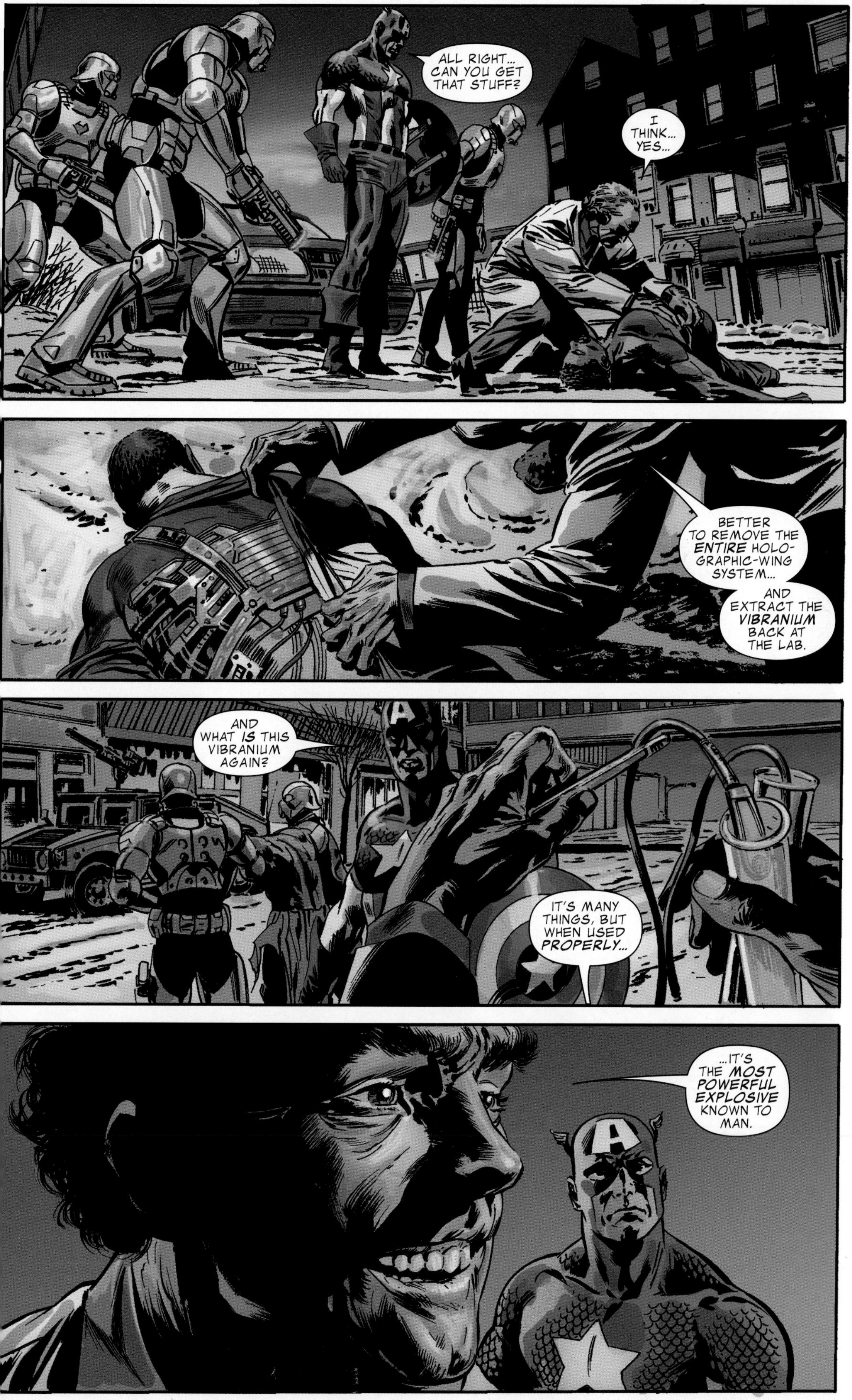
ALL RIGHT... CAN YOU GET THAT STUFF?
I THINK... YES...
BETTER TO REMOVE THE ENTIRE HOLO-GRAPHIC-WING SYSTEM...
AND EXTRACT THE VIBRANIUM BACK AT THE LAB.
AND WHAT IS THIS VIBRANIUM AGAIN?
IT'S MANY THINGS, BUT WHEN USED PROPERLY...
...IT'S THE MOST POWERFUL EXPLOSIVE KNOWN TO MAN.

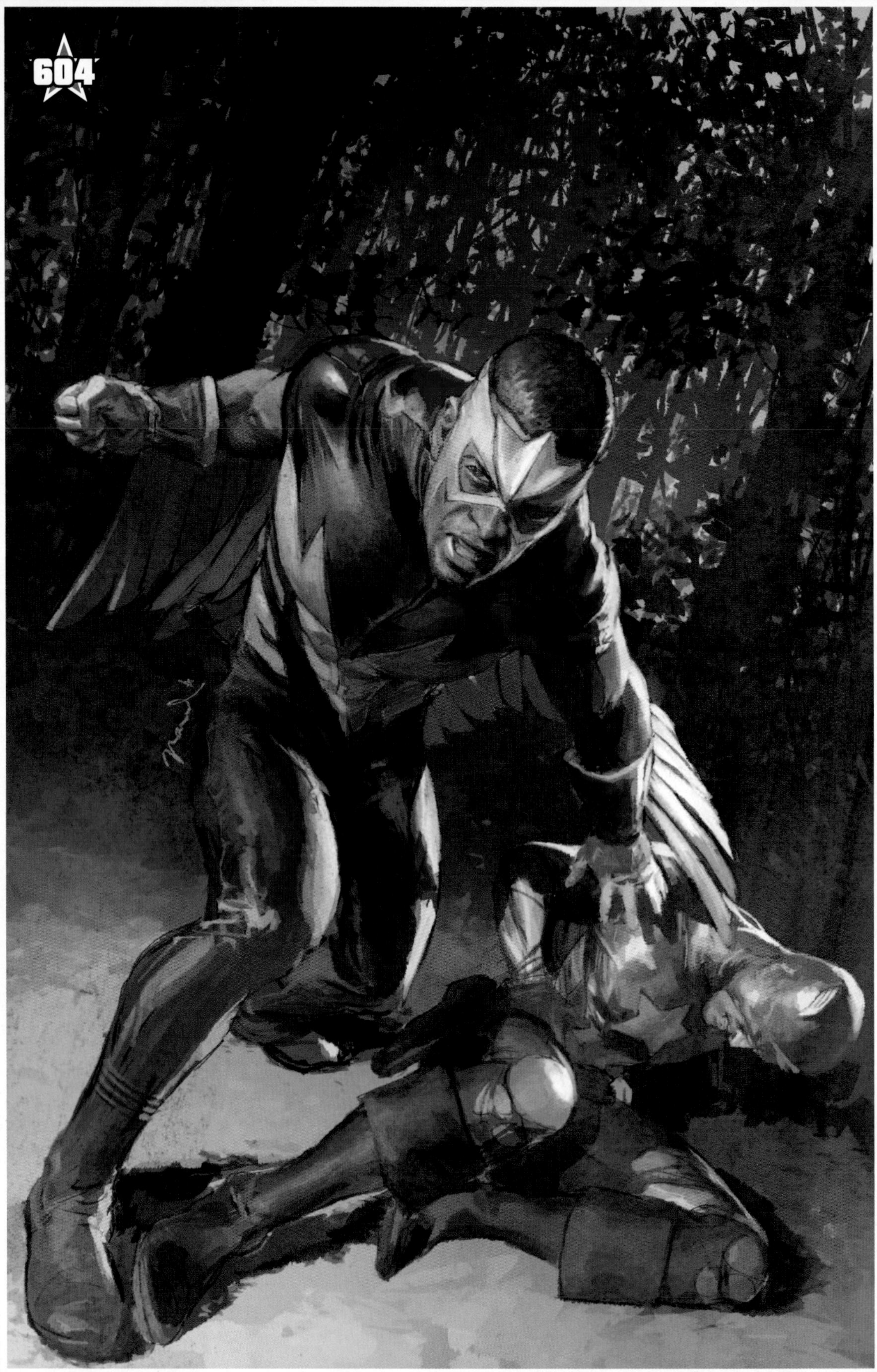
604

TWO AMERICAS PART 4

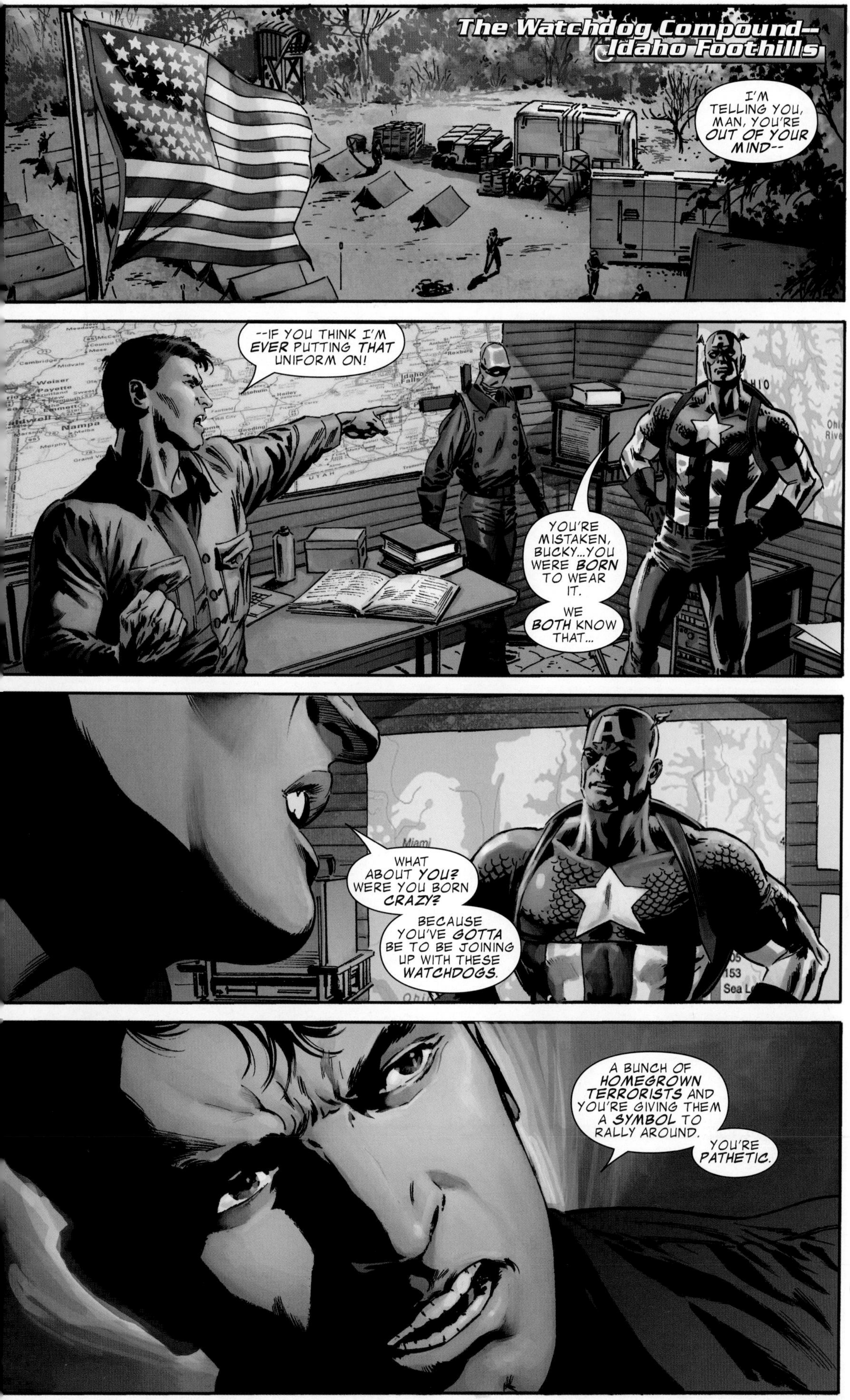
The Watchdog Compound--
Idaho Foothills
I'M TELLING YOU, MAN, YOU'RE OUT OF YOUR MIND--
--IF YOU THINK I'M EVER PUTTING THAT UNIFORM ON!
YOU'RE MISTAKEN, BUCKY...YOU WERE BORN TO WEAR IT.
WE BOTH KNOW THAT...
WHAT ABOUT YOU? WERE YOU BORN CRAZY?
BECAUSE YOU'VE GOTTA BE TO BE JOINING UP WITH THESE WATCHDOGS.
A BUNCH OF HOMEGROWN TERRORISTS AND YOU'RE GIVING THEM A SYMBOL TO RALLY AROUND.
YOU'RE PATHETIC.

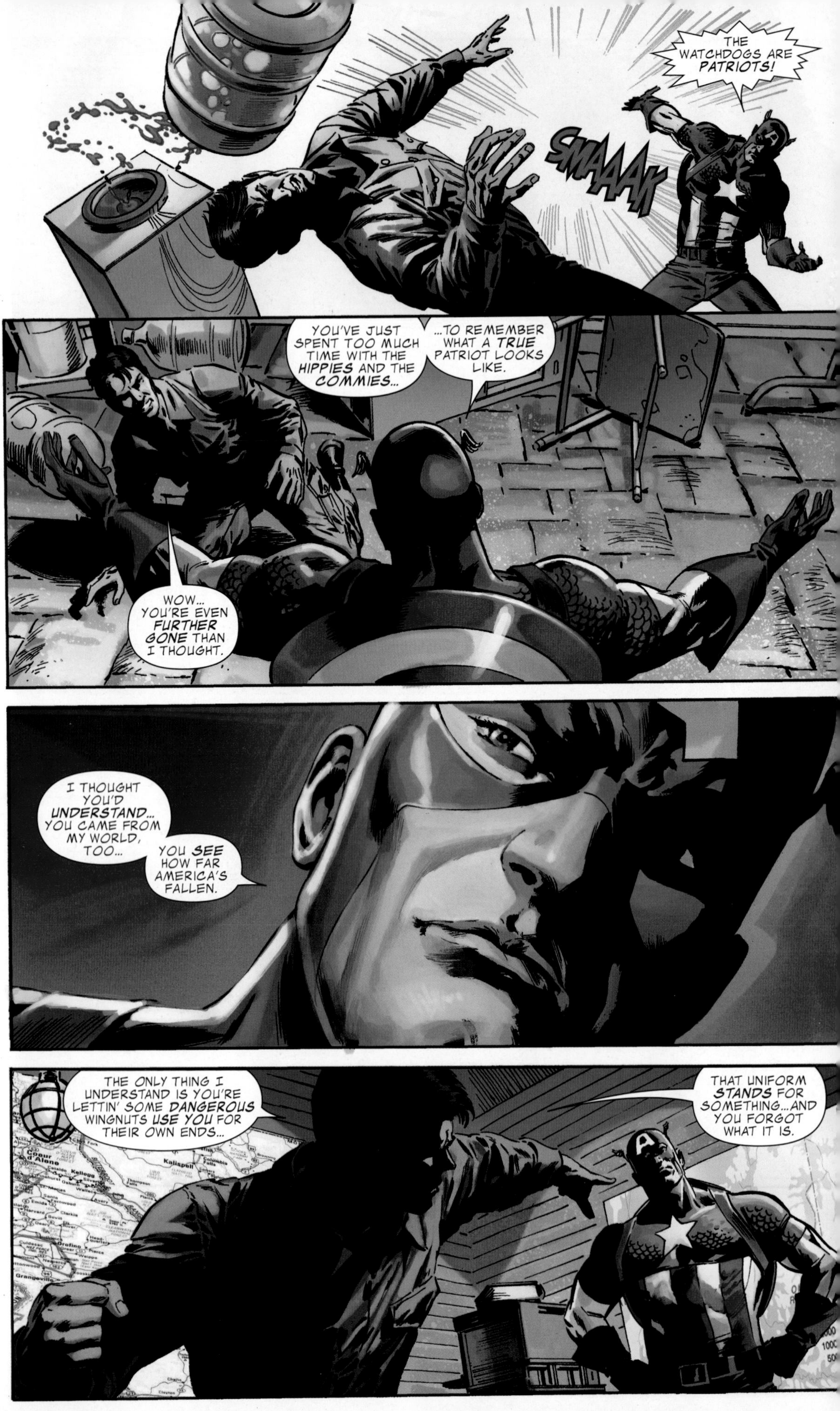
THE WATCHDOGS ARE PATRIOTS!
SMAAAK
YOU'VE JUST SPENT TOO MUCH TIME WITH THE HIPPIES AND THE COMMIES...
...TO REMEMBER WHAT A TRUE PATRIOT LOOKS LIKE.
WOW... YOU'RE EVEN FURTHER GONE THAN I THOUGHT.
I THOUGHT YOU'D UNDERSTAND... YOU CAME FROM MY WORLD, TOO...
YOU SEE HOW FAR AMERICA'S FALLEN.
THE ONLY THING I UNDERSTAND IS YOU'RE LETTIN' SOME DANGEROUS WINGNUTS USE YOU FOR THEIR OWN ENDS...
THAT UNIFORM STANDS FOR SOMETHING...AND YOU FORGOT WHAT IT IS.

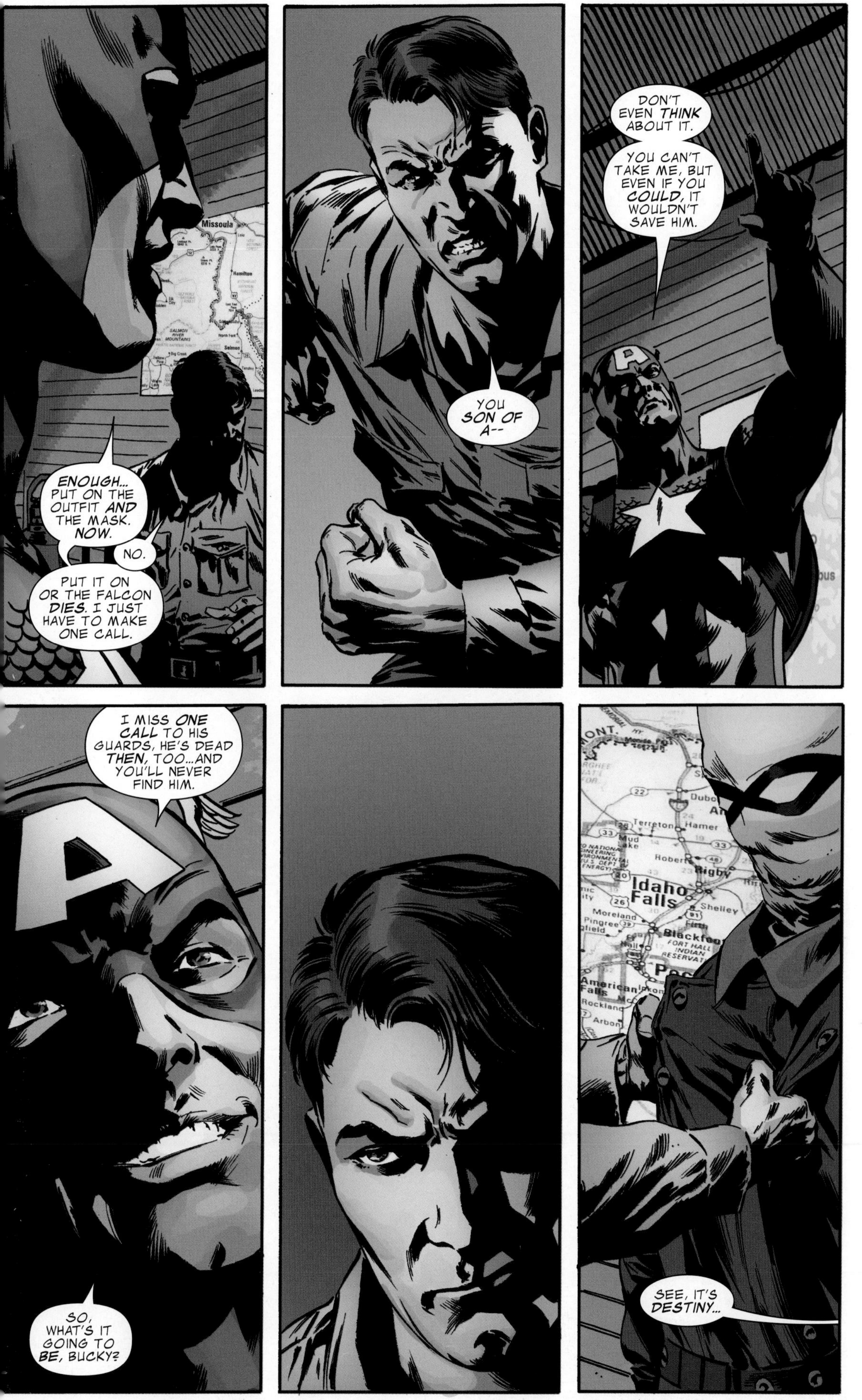
ENOUGH... PUT ON THE OUTFIT AND THE MASK. NOW.
NO.
PUT IT ON OR THE FALCON DIES. I JUST HAVE TO MAKE ONE CALL.
YOU SON OF A--
DON'T EVEN THINK ABOUT IT.
YOU CAN'T TAKE ME, BUT EVEN IF YOU COULD, IT WOULDN'T SAVE HIM.
I MISS ONE CALL TO HIS GUARDS, HE'S DEAD THEN, TOO...AND YOU'LL NEVER FIND HIM.
SO, WHAT'S IT GOING TO BE, BUCKY?
SEE, IT'S DESTINY...

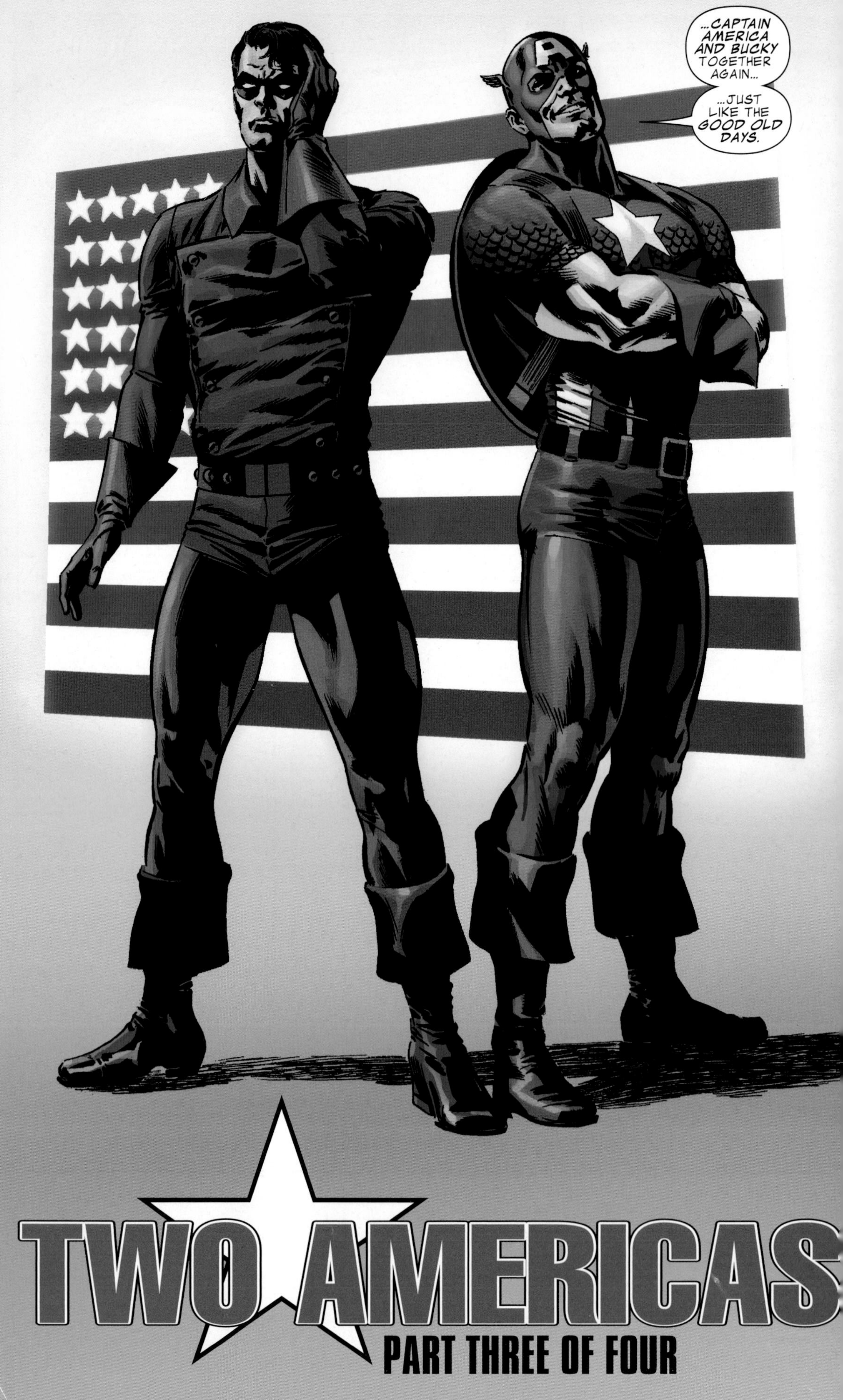
...CAPTAIN AMERICA AND BUCKY TOGETHER AGAIN...
...JUST LIKE THE GOOD OLD DAYS.
TWO AMERICAS
PART THREE OF FOUR

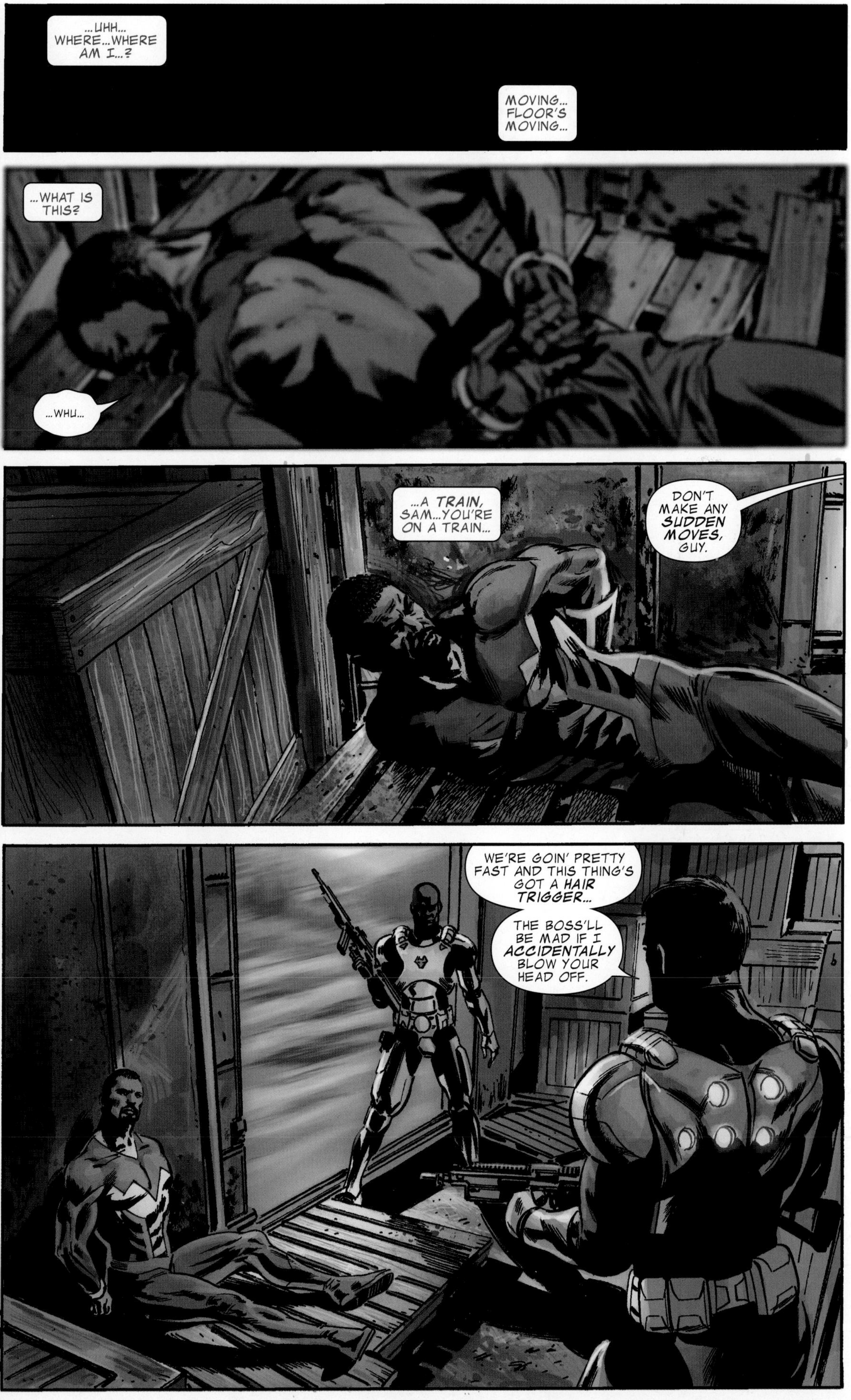
...UHH... WHERE...WHERE AM I...?
MOVING... FLOOR'S MOVING...
...WHAT IS THIS?
...WHU...
...A TRAIN, SAM...YOU'RE ON A TRAIN...
DON'T MAKE ANY SUDDEN MOVES, GUY.
WE'RE GOIN' PRETTY FAST AND THIS THING'S GOT A HAIR TRIGGER...
THE BOSS'LL BE MAD IF I ACCIDENTALLY BLOW YOUR HEAD OFF.

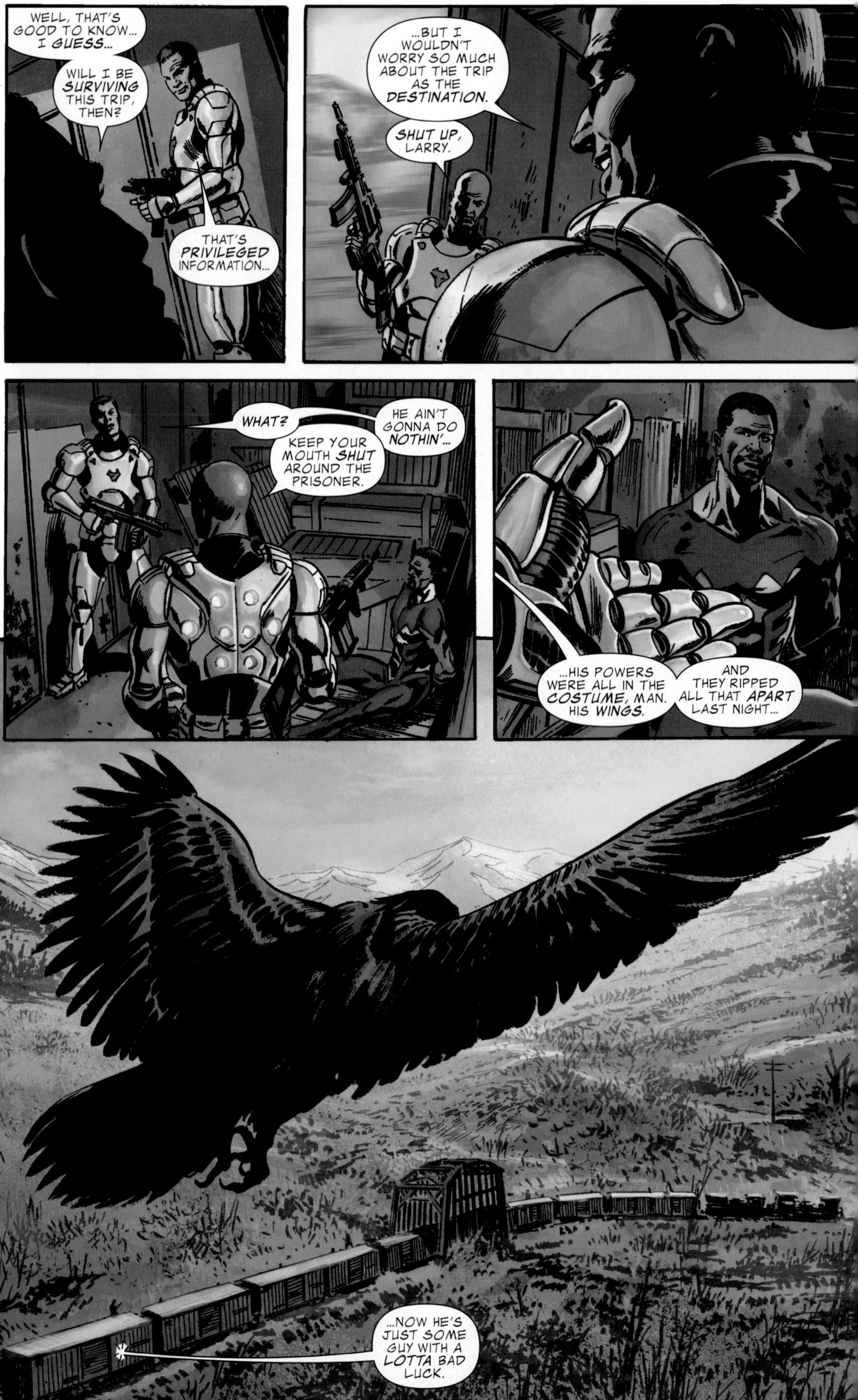
WELL, THAT'S GOOD TO KNOW... I GUESS...
WILL I BE SURVIVING THIS TRIP, THEN?
THAT'S PRIVILEGED INFORMATION...
...BUT I WOULDN'T WORRY SO MUCH ABOUT THE TRIP AS THE DESTINATION.
SHUT UP, LARRY.
WHAT?
KEEP YOUR MOUTH SHUT AROUND THE PRISONER.
HE AIN'T GONNA DO NOTHIN'...
...HIS POWERS WERE ALL IN THE COSTUME, MAN. HIS WINGS.
AND THEY RIPPED ALL THAT APART LAST NIGHT...
...NOW HE'S JUST SOME GUY WITH A LOTTA BAD LUCK.

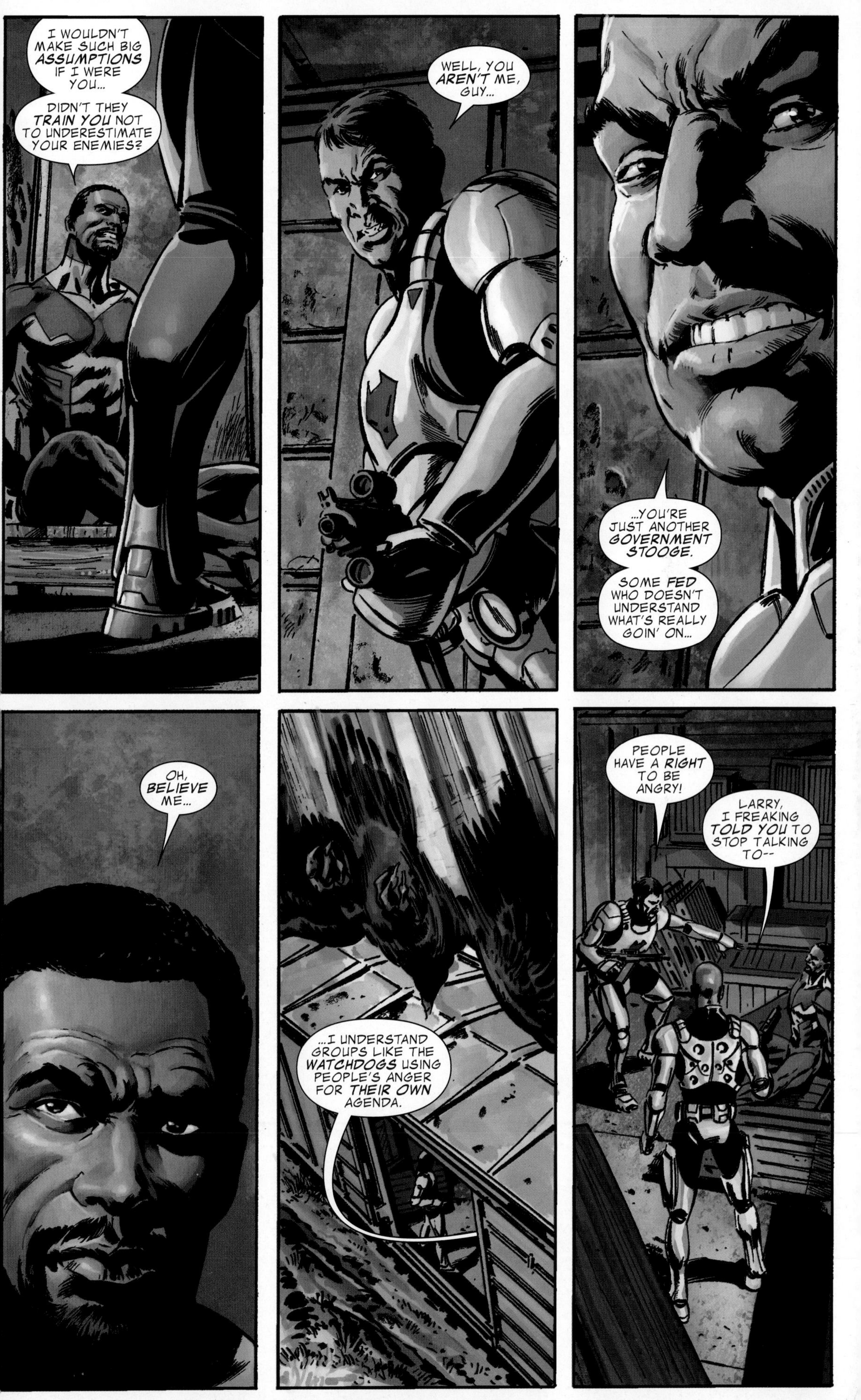
I WOULDN'T MAKE SUCH BIG ASSUMPTIONS IF I WERE YOU...
DIDN'T THEY TRAIN YOU NOT TO UNDERESTIMATE YOUR ENEMIES?
WELL, YOU AREN'T ME, GUY...
...YOU'RE JUST ANOTHER GOVERNMENT STOOGE.
SOME FED WHO DOESN'T UNDERSTAND WHAT'S REALLY GOIN' ON...
OH, BELIEVE ME...
...I UNDERSTAND GROUPS LIKE THE WATCHDOGS USING PEOPLE'S ANGER FOR THEIR OWN AGENDA.
PEOPLE HAVE A RIGHT TO BE ANGRY!
LARRY, I FREAKING TOLD YOU TO STOP TALKING TO--

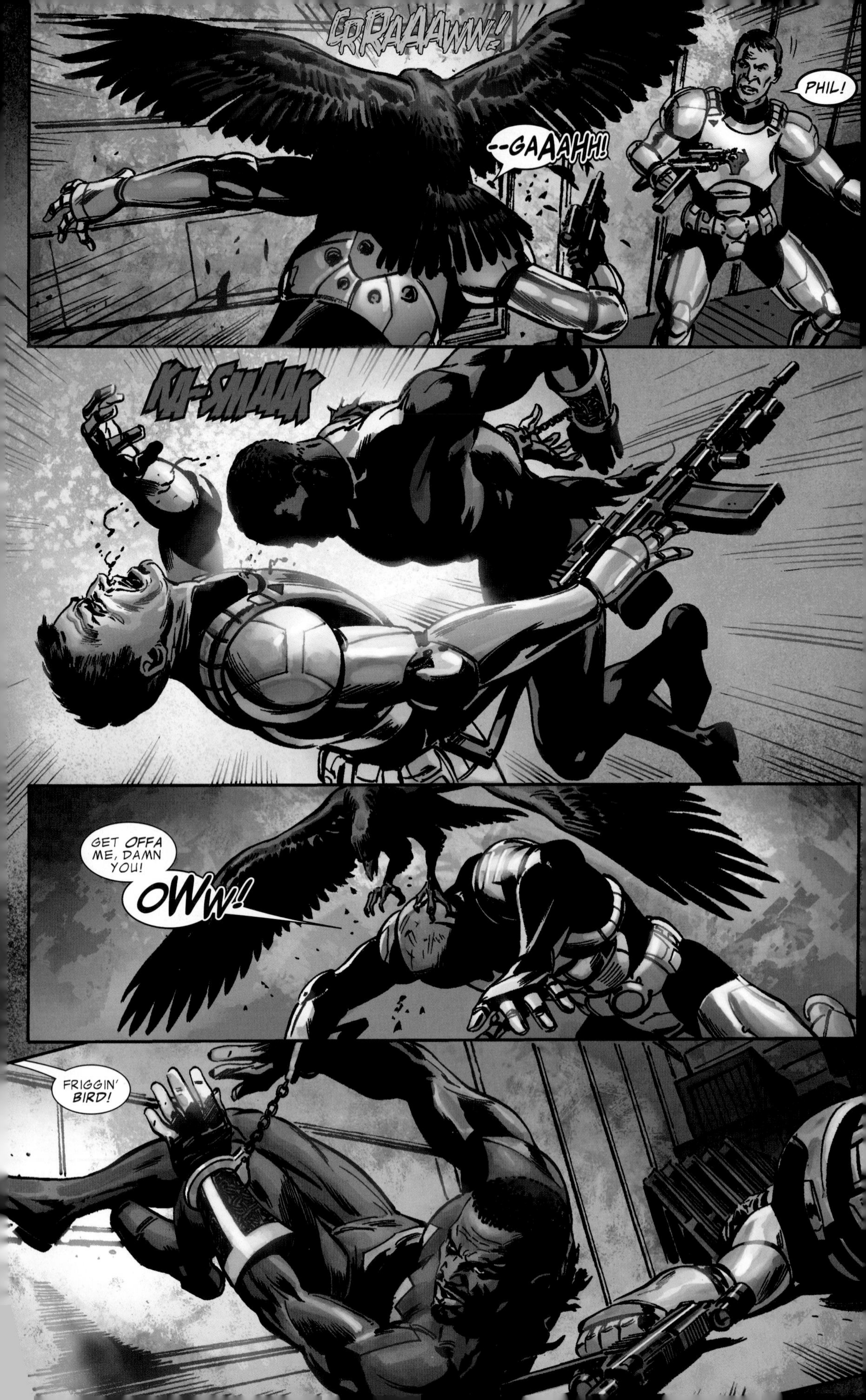
CRRAAAWW!
PHIL!
--GAAAHH!
KA-SMAAK
GET OFFA ME, DAMN YOU!
OWW!
FRIGGIN' BIRD!

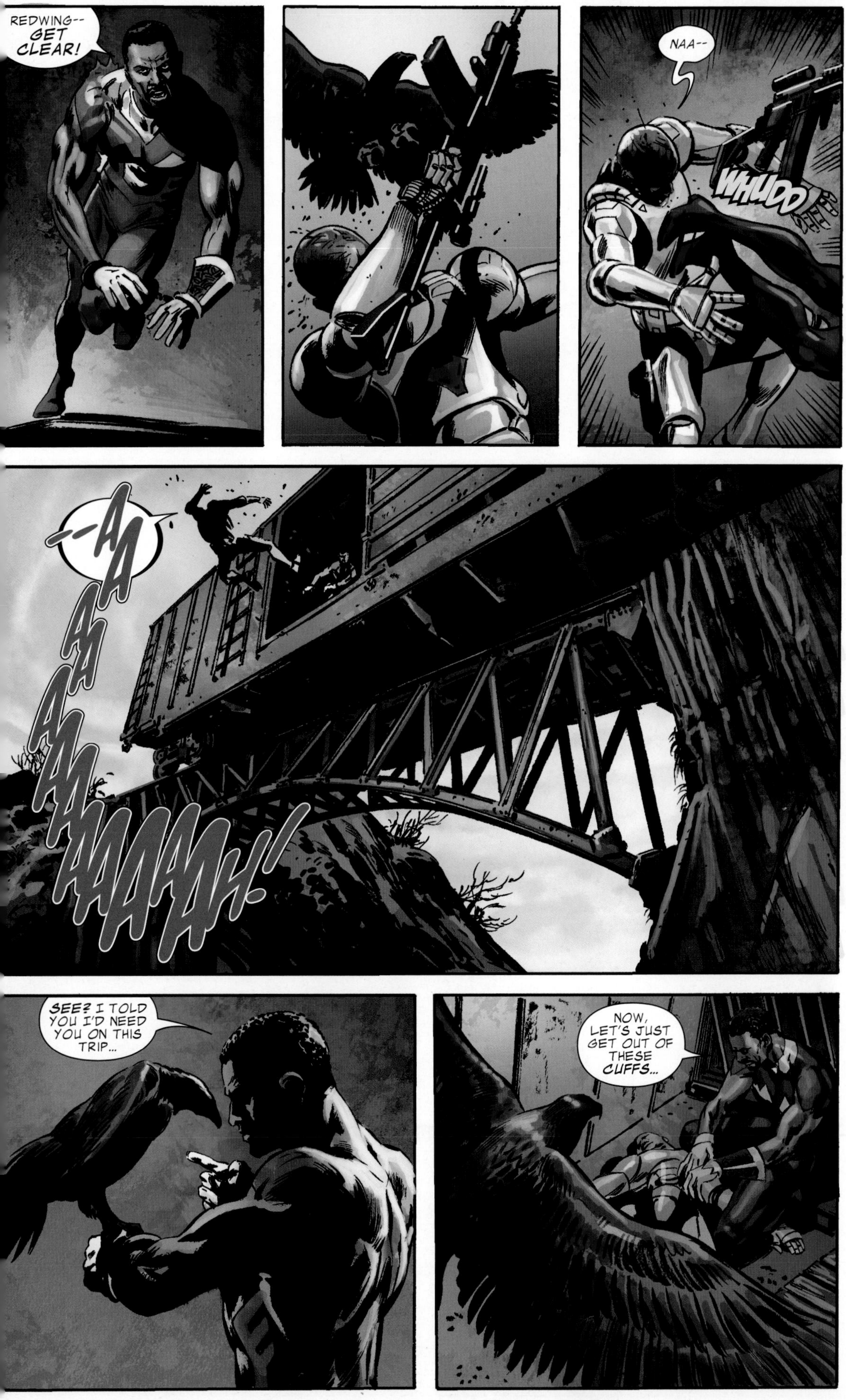
REDWING-- GET CLEAR!
NAA--
WHUDD
--AAAAAAAAAAAAAAAAH!
SEE? I TOLD YOU I'D NEED YOU ON THIS TRIP...
NOW, LET'S JUST GET OUT OF THESE CUFFS...

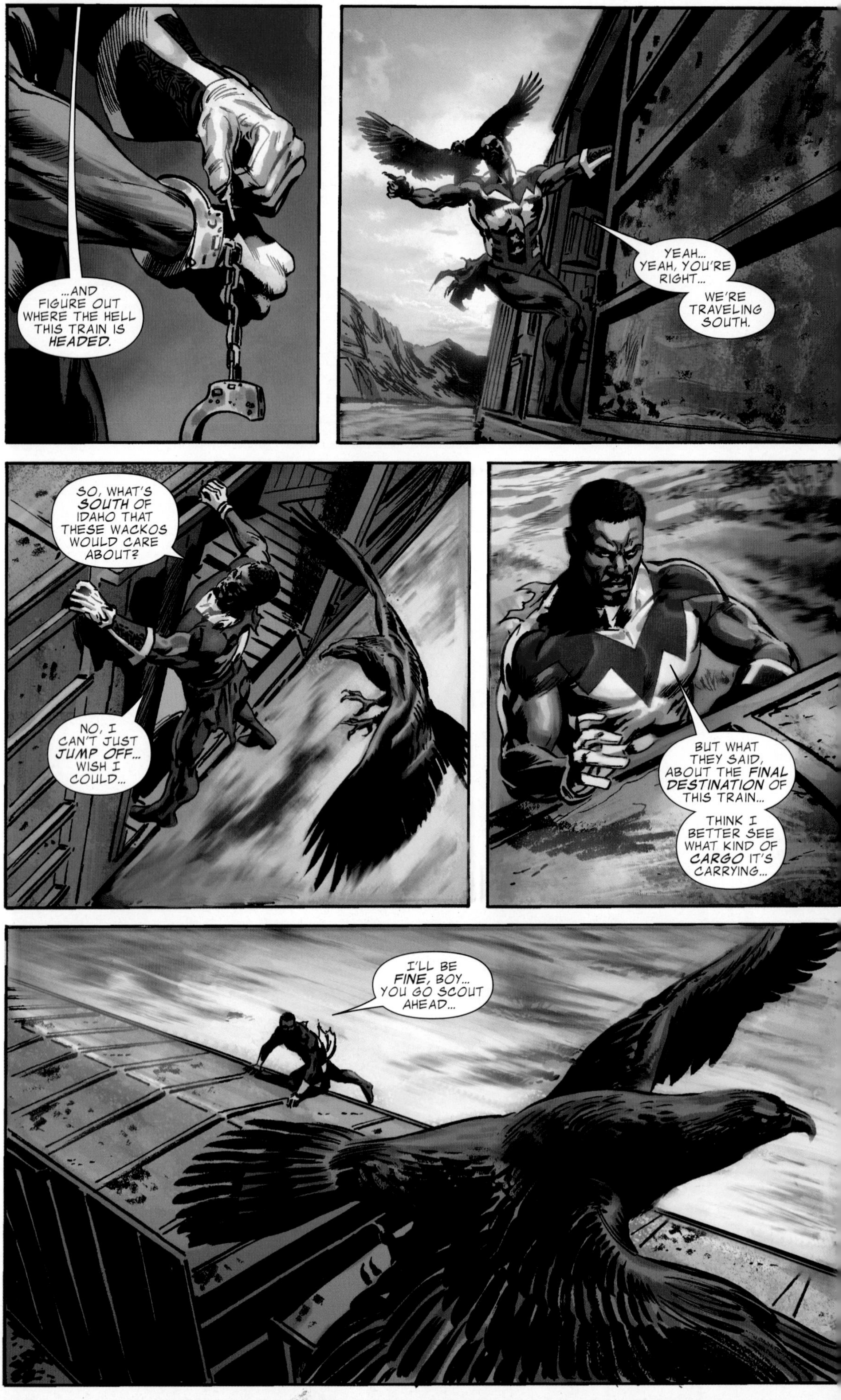
...AND FIGURE OUT WHERE THE HELL THIS TRAIN IS HEADED.
YEAH... YEAH, YOU'RE RIGHT...
WE'RE TRAVELING SOUTH.
SO, WHAT'S SOUTH OF IDAHO THAT THESE WACKOS WOULD CARE ABOUT?
NO, I CAN'T JUST JUMP OFF... WISH I COULD...
BUT WHAT THEY SAID, ABOUT THE FINAL DESTINATION OF THIS TRAIN...
THINK I BETTER SEE WHAT KIND OF CARGO IT'S CARRYING...
I'LL BE FINE, BOY... YOU GO SCOUT AHEAD...

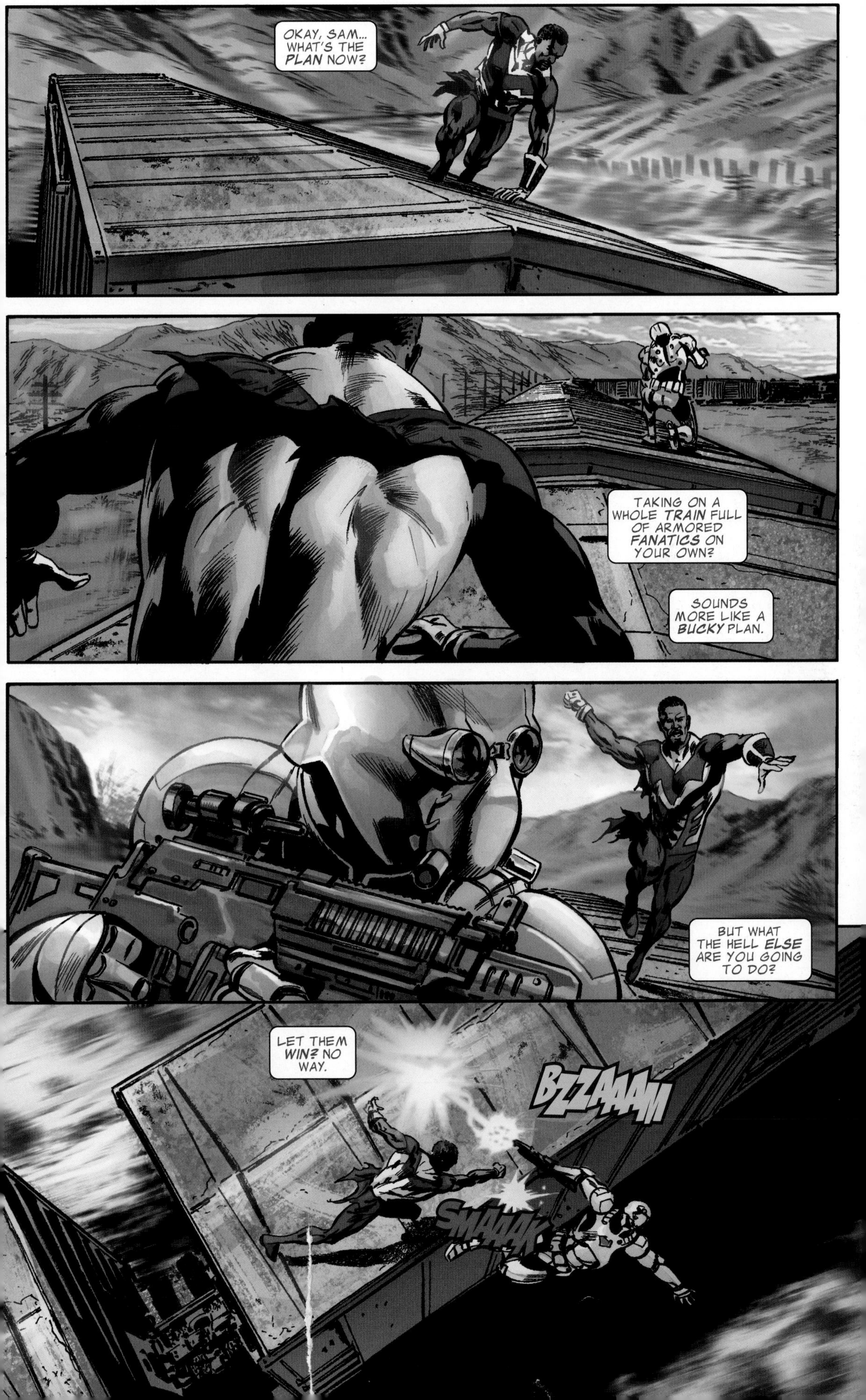
OKAY, SAM... WHAT'S THE PLAN NOW?
TAKING ON A WHOLE TRAIN FULL OF ARMORED FANATICS ON YOUR OWN?
SOUNDS MORE LIKE A BUCKY PLAN.
BUT WHAT THE HELL ELSE ARE YOU GOING TO DO?
LET THEM WIN? NO WAY.
BZZAAAM
SMAAAK

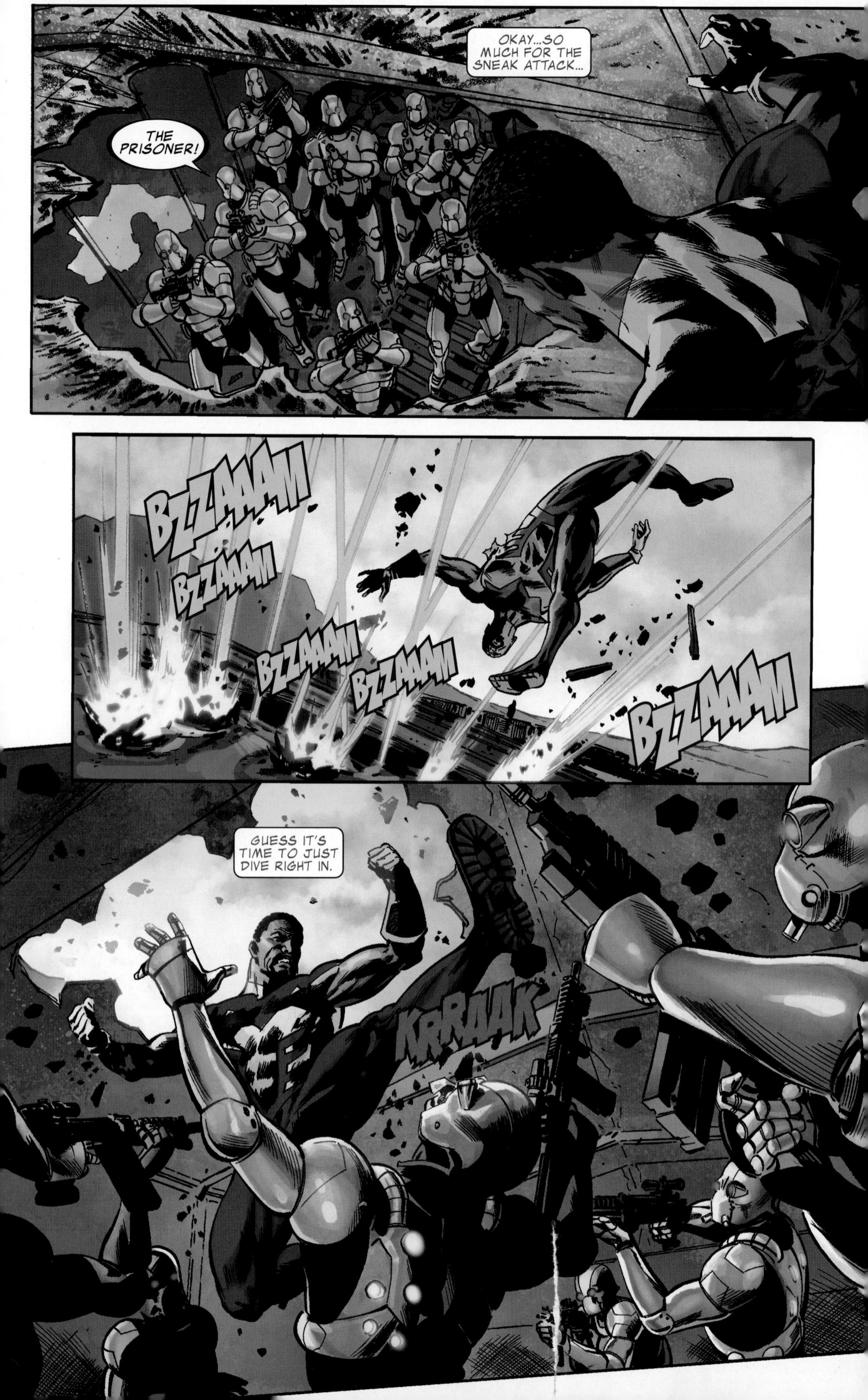
OKAY...SO MUCH FOR THE SNEAK ATTACK...
THE PRISONER!
BZZAAAM
BZZAAAM
BZZAAAM
BZZAAAM
BZZAAAM
GUESS IT'S TIME TO JUST DIVE RIGHT IN.
KRRAAK

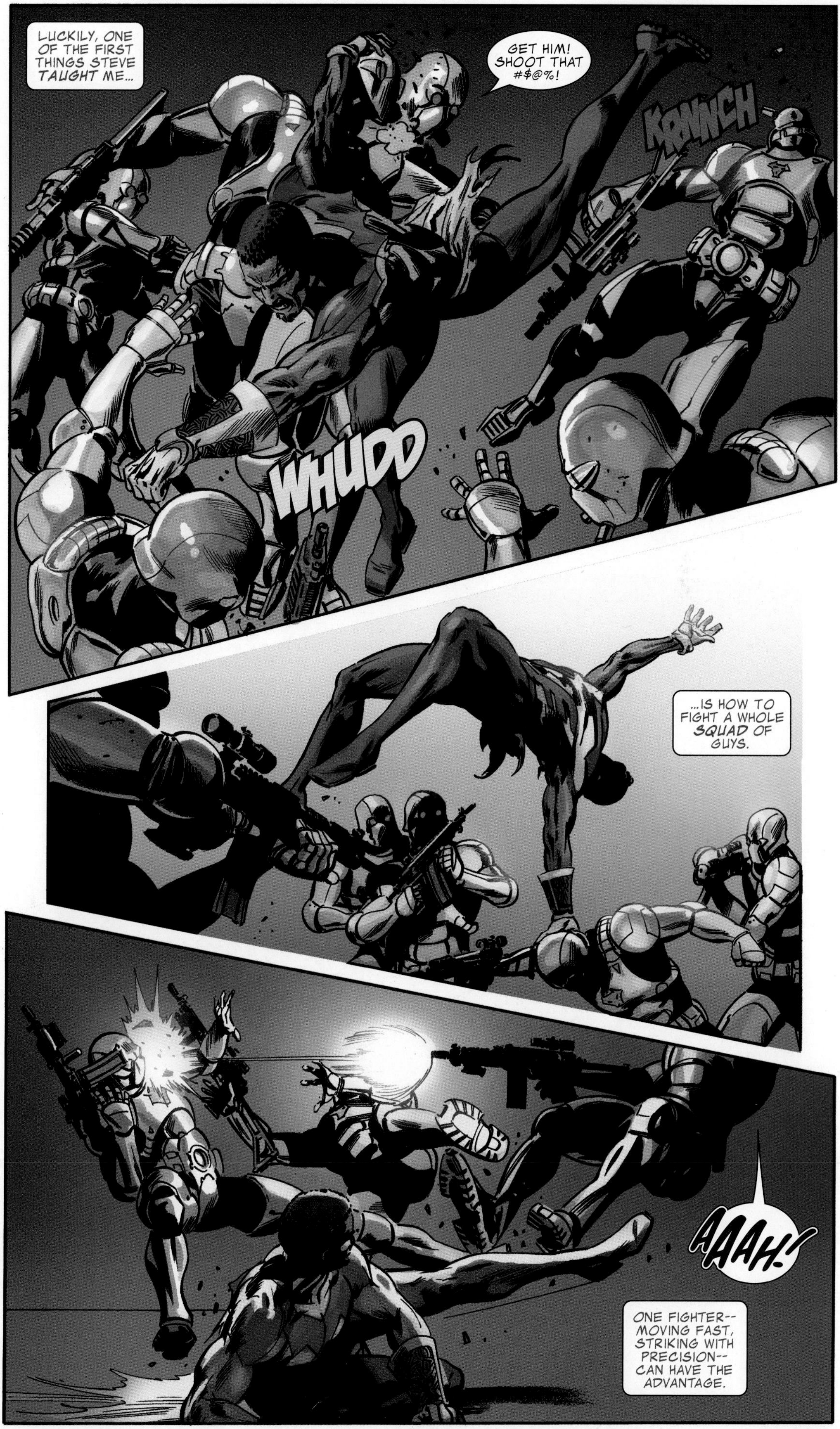
LUCKILY, ONE OF THE FIRST THINGS STEVE TAUGHT ME...
GET HIM! SHOOT THAT #$@%!
KRNNCH
WHUDD
...IS HOW TO FIGHT A WHOLE SQUAD OF GUYS.
AAAH!
ONE FIGHTER-- MOVING FAST, STRIKING WITH PRECISION-- CAN HAVE THE ADVANTAGE.

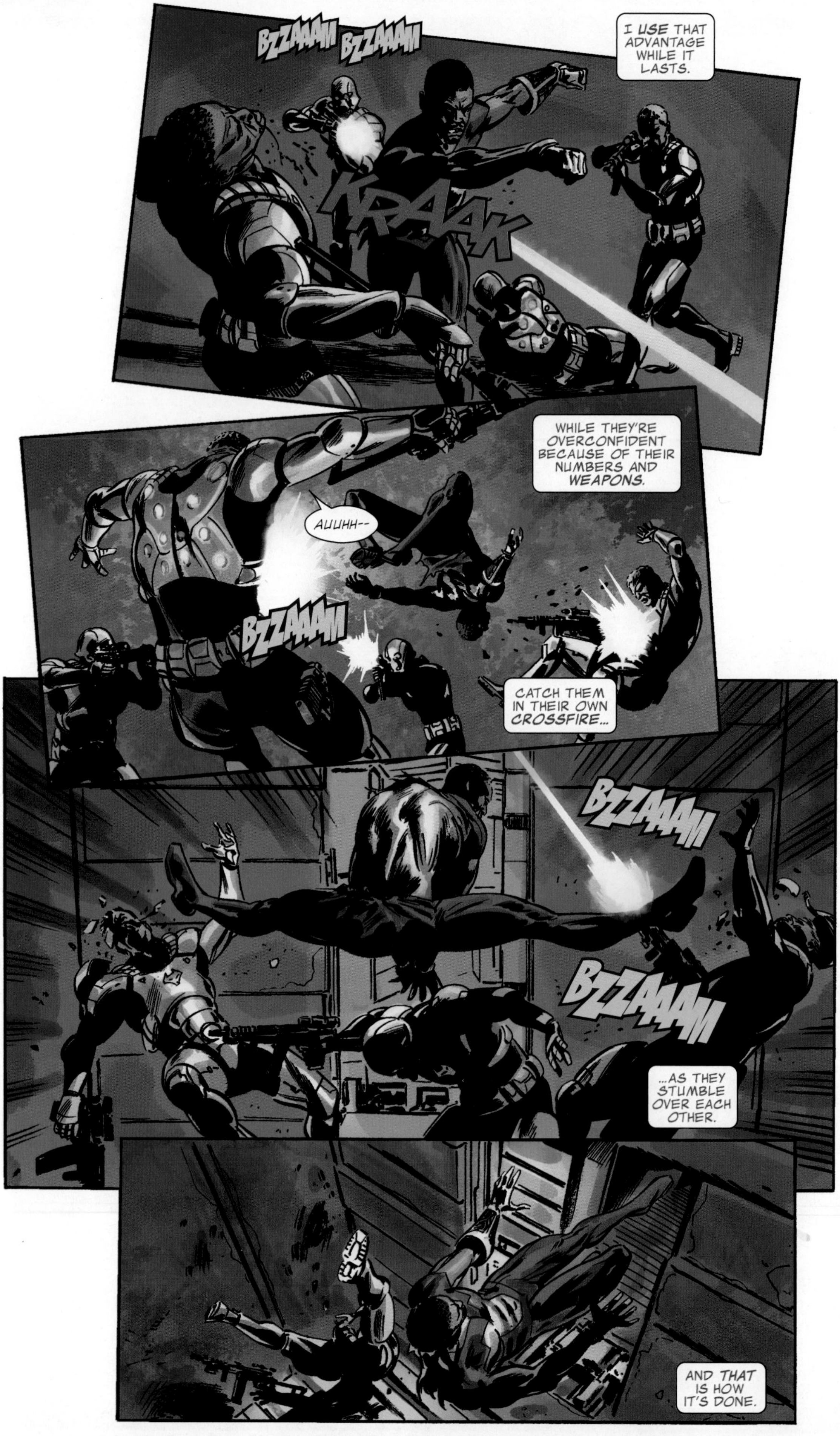
BZZAAAM BZZAAAM
I USE THAT ADVANTAGE WHILE IT LASTS.
KRAAK
WHILE THEY'RE OVERCONFIDENT BECAUSE OF THEIR NUMBERS AND WEAPONS.
AUUHH--
BZZAAAM
CATCH THEM IN THEIR OWN CROSSFIRE...
BZZAAAM
BZZAAAM
...AS THEY STUMBLE OVER EACH OTHER.
AND THAT IS HOW IT'S DONE.

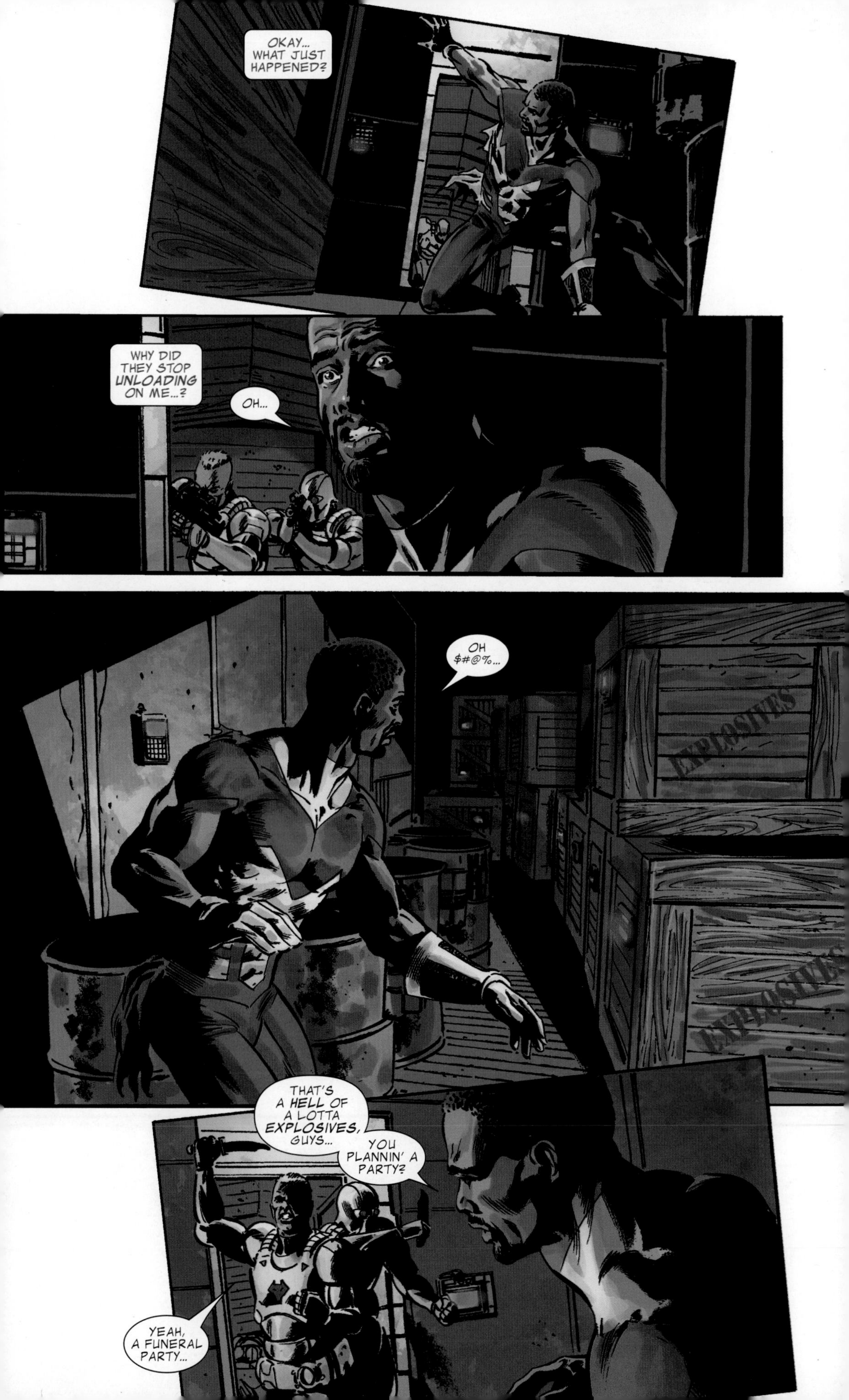
OKAY... WHAT JUST HAPPENED?
WHY DID THEY STOP UNLOADING ON ME...?
OH...
OH $#@%...
EXPLOSIVES
EXPLOSIVES
THAT'S A HELL OF A LOTTA EXPLOSIVES, GUYS...
YOU PLANNIN' A PARTY?
YEAH, A FUNERAL PARTY...

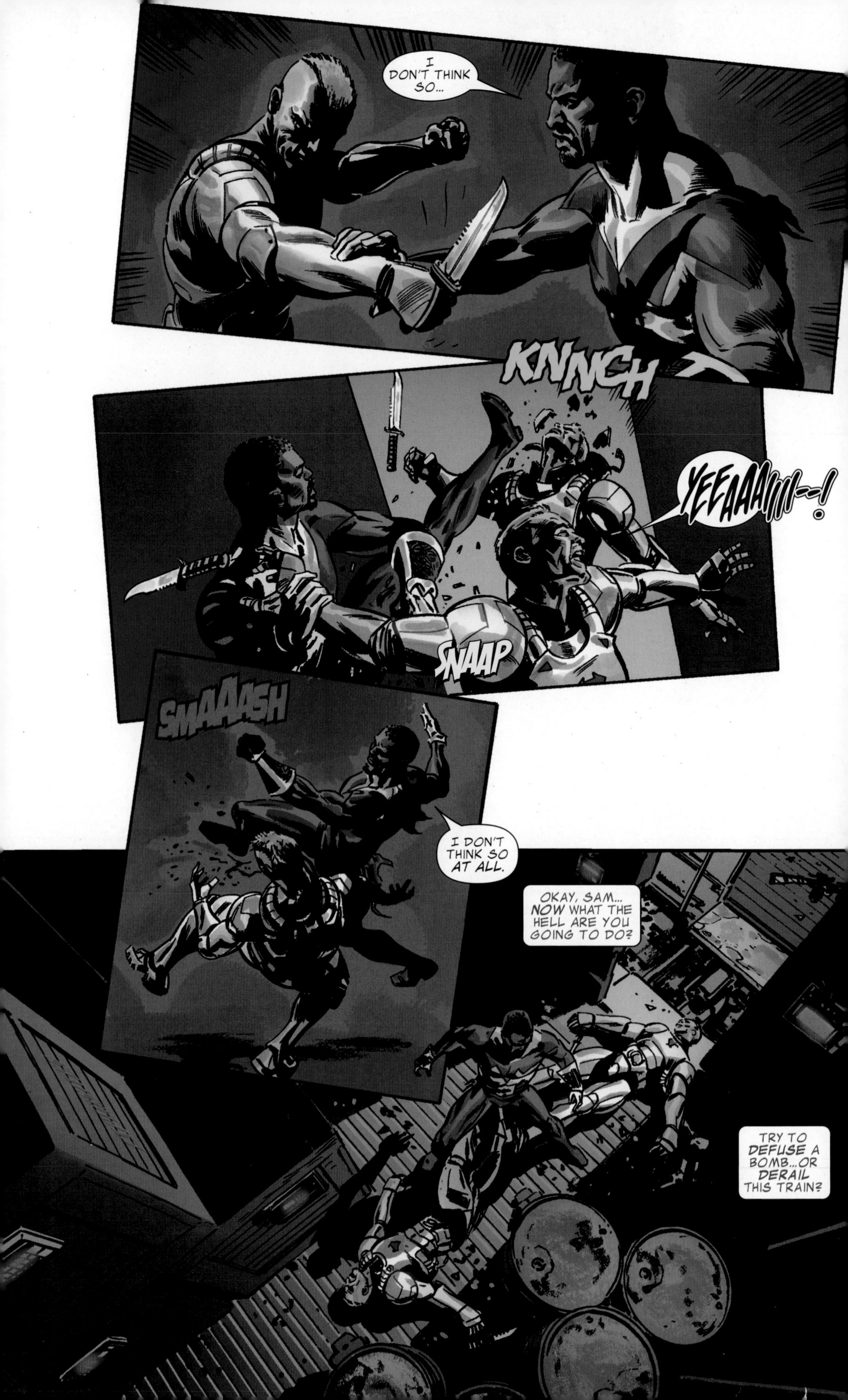
I DON'T THINK SO...
KNNCH
YEEAAAIIIII--!
SNAAP
SMAAASH
I DON'T THINK SO AT ALL.
OKAY, SAM... NOW WHAT THE HELL ARE YOU GOING TO DO?
TRY TO DEFUSE A BOMB...OR DERAIL THIS TRAIN?

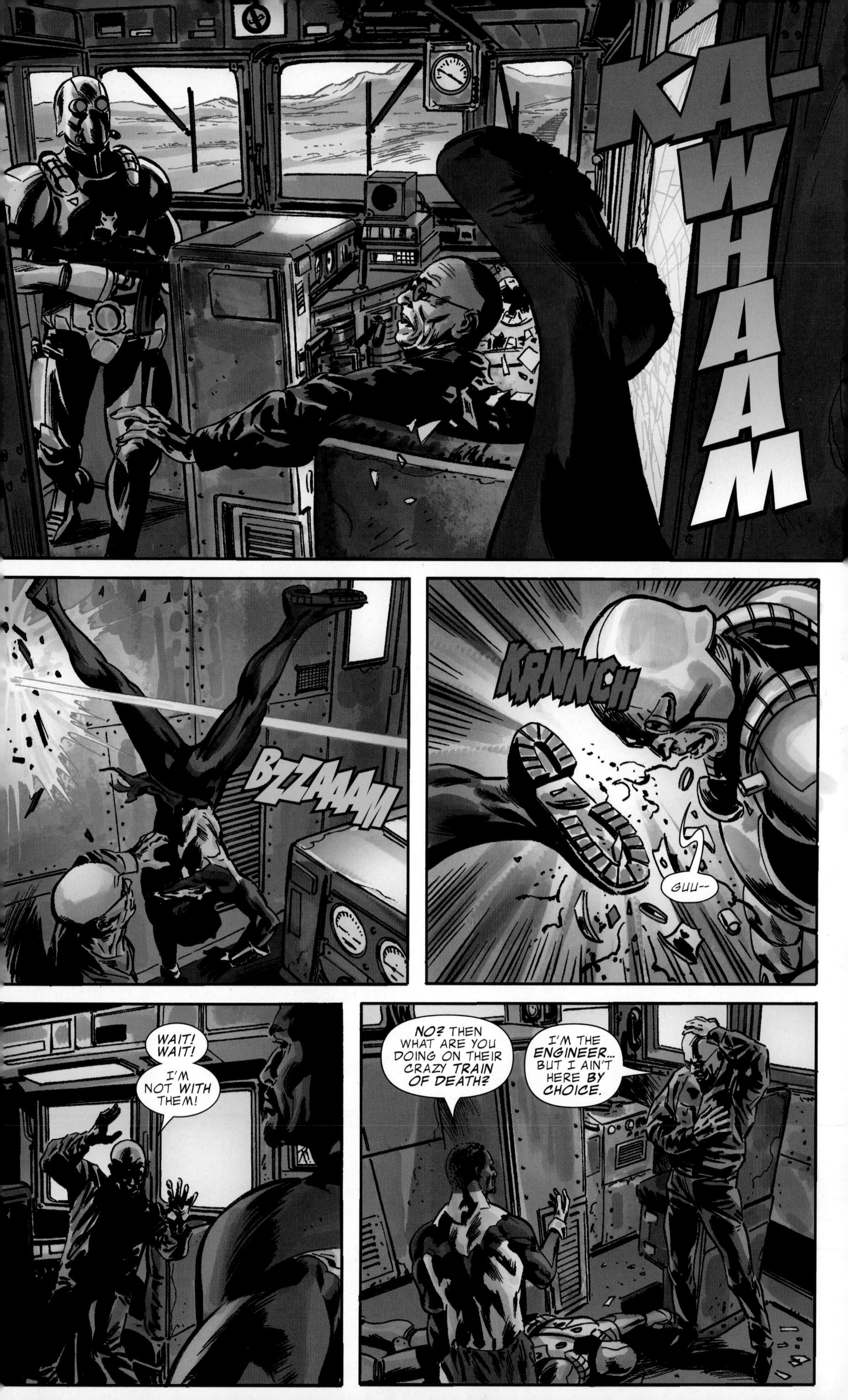
KA-WHAAM
BZZAAAM
KRNNCH
GUU--
WAIT! WAIT!
I'M NOT WITH THEM!
NO? THEN WHAT ARE YOU DOING ON THEIR CRAZY TRAIN OF DEATH?
I'M THE ENGINEER... BUT I AIN'T HERE BY CHOICE.

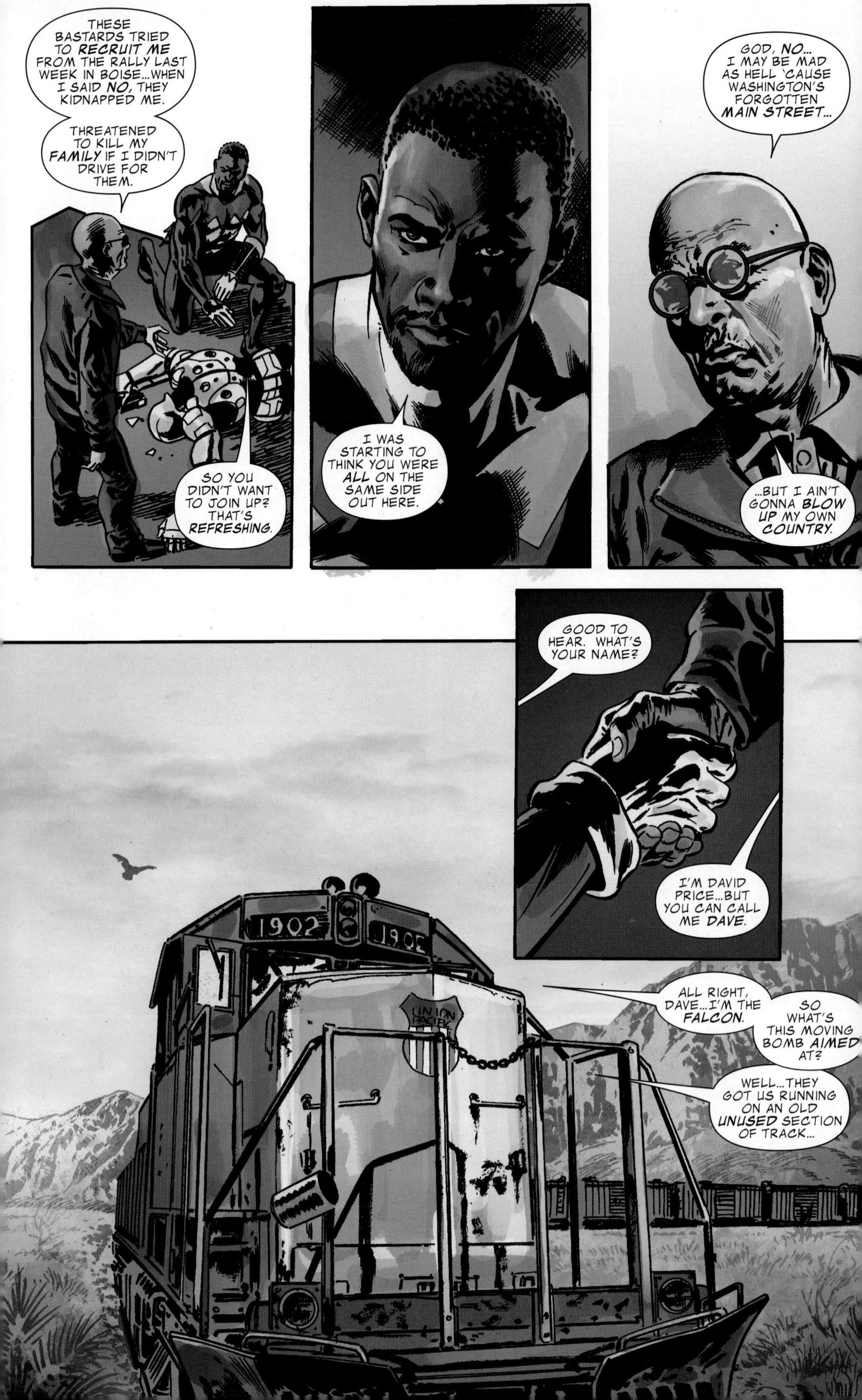
THESE BASTARDS TRIED TO RECRUIT ME FROM THE RALLY LAST WEEK IN BOISE...WHEN I SAID NO, THEY KIDNAPPED ME.
THREATENED TO KILL MY FAMILY IF I DIDN'T DRIVE FOR THEM.
SO YOU DIDN'T WANT TO JOIN UP? THAT'S REFRESHING.
I WAS STARTING TO THINK YOU WERE ALL ON THE SAME SIDE OUT HERE.
GOD, NO... I MAY BE MAD AS HELL 'CAUSE WASHINGTON'S FORGOTTEN MAIN STREET...
...BUT I AIN'T GONNA BLOW UP MY OWN COUNTRY.
GOOD TO HEAR. WHAT'S YOUR NAME?
I'M DAVID PRICE...BUT YOU CAN CALL ME DAVE.
1902
UNION PACIFIC
ALL RIGHT, DAVE...I'M THE FALCON.
SO WHAT'S THIS MOVING BOMB AIMED AT?
WELL...THEY GOT US RUNNING ON AN OLD UNUSED SECTION OF TRACK...

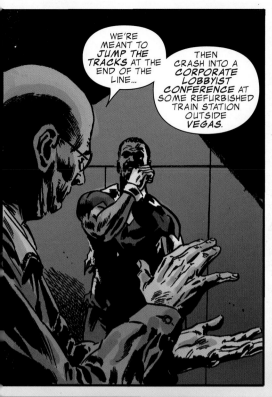

WE'RE MEANT TO *JUMP THE TRACKS* AT THE END OF THE LINE...

THEN CRASH INTO A *CORPORATE LOBBYIST CONFERENCE* AT SOME REFURBISHED TRAIN STATION OUTSIDE VEGAS.

I'M NO FAN OF *LOBBYISTS*, BUT WE CAN'T LET 'EM GET BLOWN TO *SMITHEREENS*.

YEAH, I HEAR YOU...BUT THERE'S NO *STOPPING* THIS TRAIN...

THEY DESTROYED ALL THE BRAKES...BEST I CAN DO IS *SLOW US UP* TO TAKE THE CURVES...

CRAP.

THAT'S NOT GOOD.

NO, AN' SOMETHIN' *ELSE*...FROM THE WAY THEY WERE TALKIN' ABOUT IT...

SOUNDS LIKE BLOWIN' UP THIS *CONFERENCE* IS JUST A *DISTRACTION*...

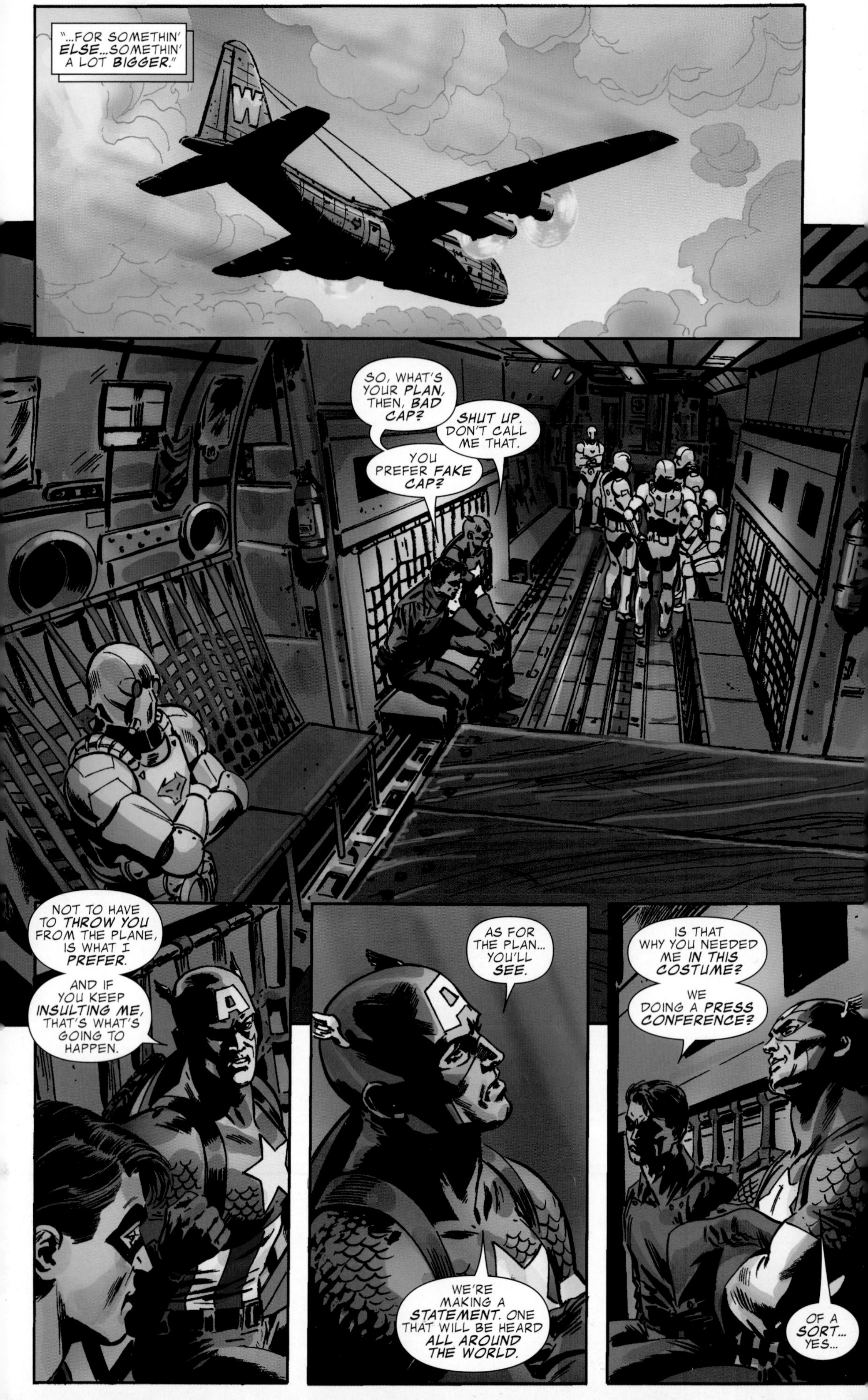
"...FOR SOMETHIN' ELSE...SOMETHIN' A LOT BIGGER."
SO, WHAT'S YOUR PLAN, THEN, BAD CAP?
SHUT UP. DON'T CALL ME THAT.
YOU PREFER FAKE CAP?
NOT TO HAVE TO THROW YOU FROM THE PLANE, IS WHAT I PREFER.
AND IF YOU KEEP INSULTING ME, THAT'S WHAT'S GOING TO HAPPEN.
AS FOR THE PLAN... YOU'LL SEE.
WE'RE MAKING A STATEMENT. ONE THAT WILL BE HEARD ALL AROUND THE WORLD.
IS THAT WHY YOU NEEDED ME IN THIS COSTUME?
WE DOING A PRESS CONFERENCE?
OF A SORT... YES...

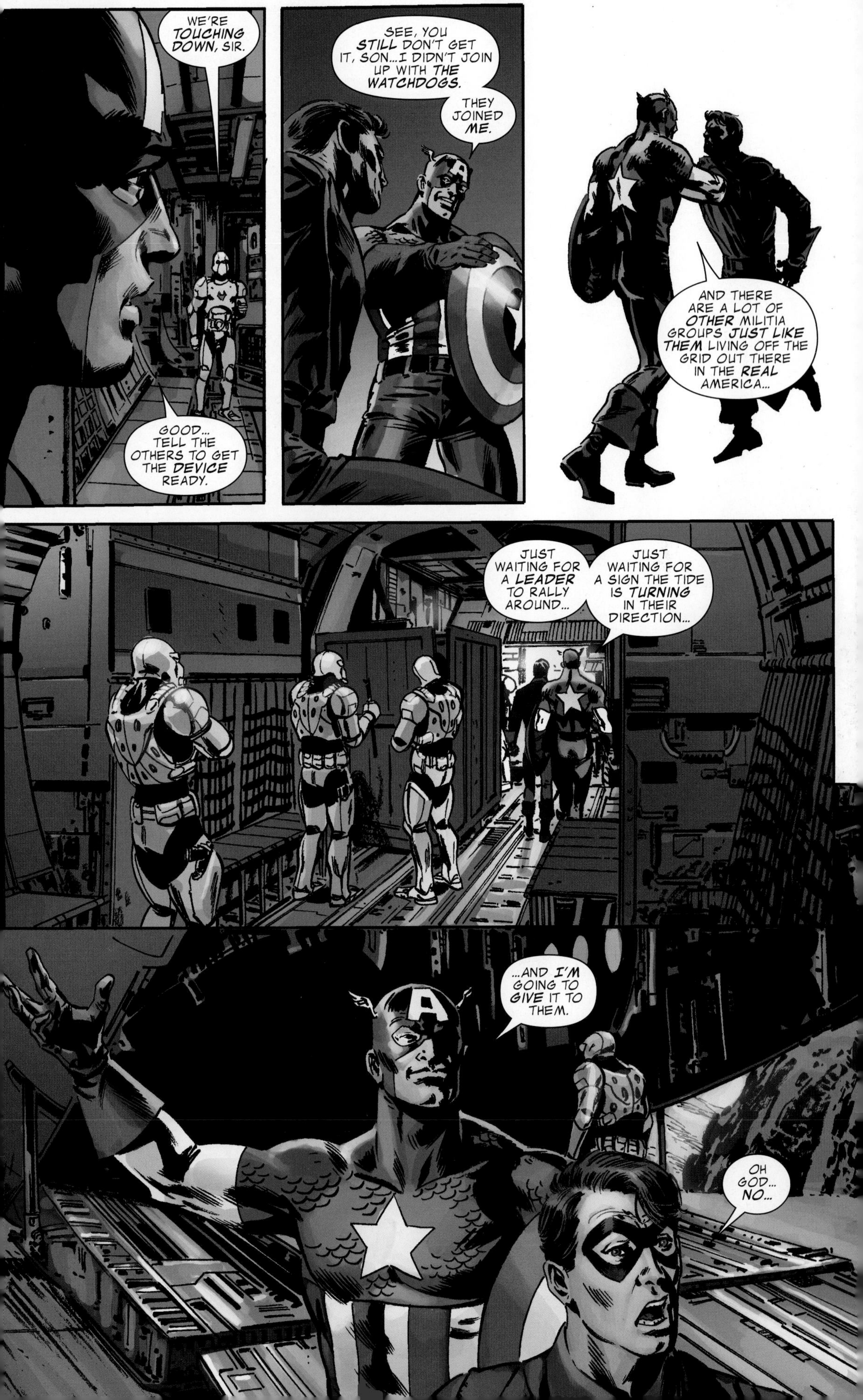
WE'RE TOUCHING DOWN, SIR.
GOOD... TELL THE OTHERS TO GET THE DEVICE READY.
SEE, YOU STILL DON'T GET IT, SON... I DIDN'T JOIN UP WITH THE WATCHDOGS.
THEY JOINED ME.
AND THERE ARE A LOT OF OTHER MILITIA GROUPS JUST LIKE THEM LIVING OFF THE GRID OUT THERE IN THE REAL AMERICA...
JUST WAITING FOR A LEADER TO RALLY AROUND...
JUST WAITING FOR A SIGN THE TIDE IS TURNING IN THEIR DIRECTION...
...AND I'M GOING TO GIVE IT TO THEM.
OH GOD... NO...

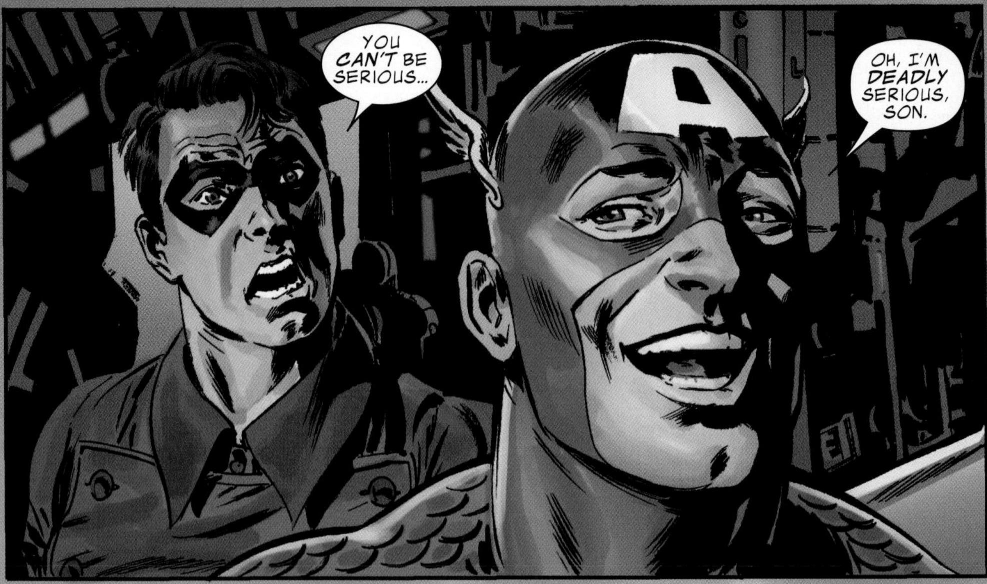
YOU CAN'T BE SERIOUS...
OH, I'M DEADLY SERIOUS, SON.

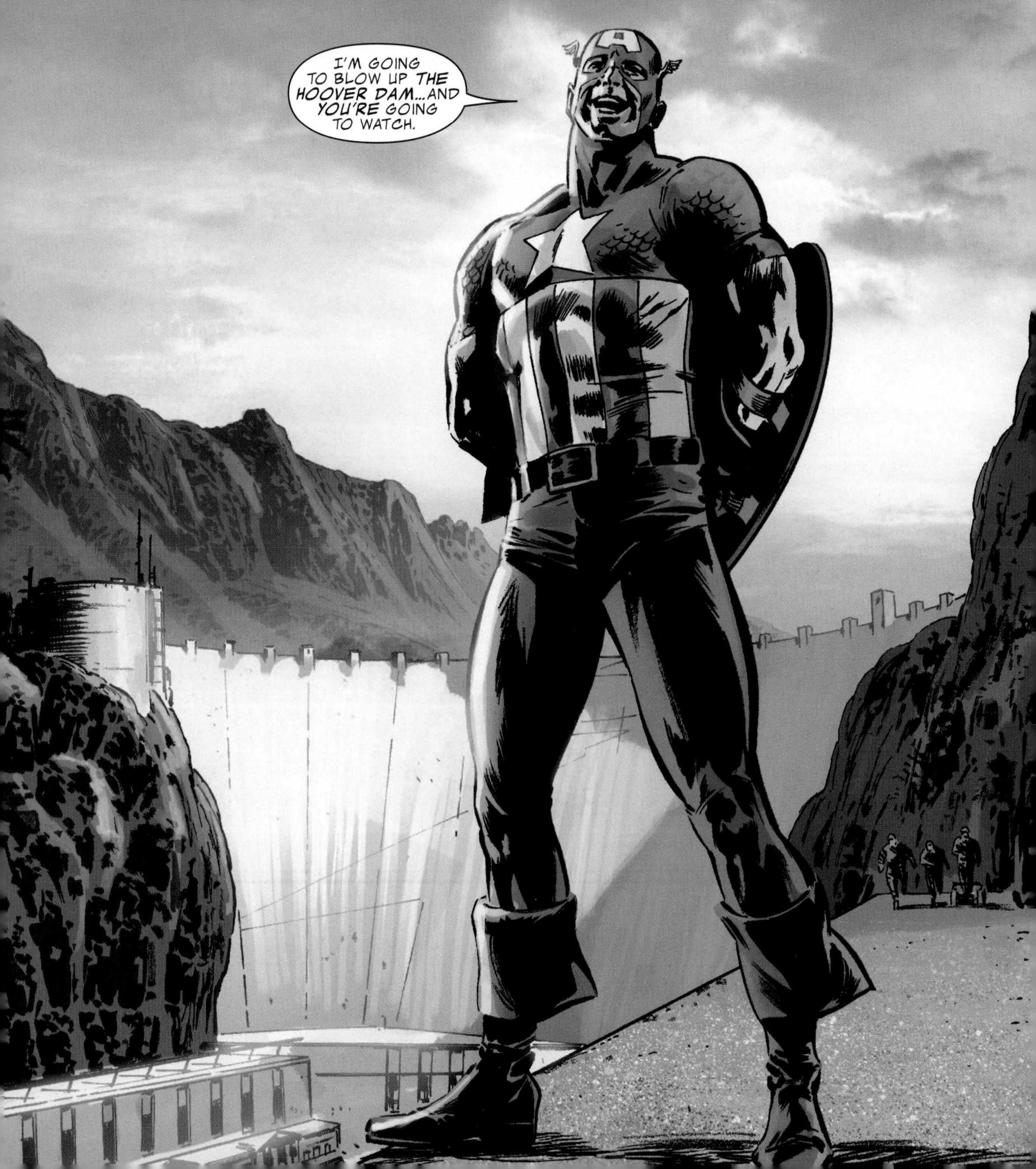
I'M GOING TO BLOW UP THE HOOVER DAM...AND YOU'RE GOING TO WATCH.

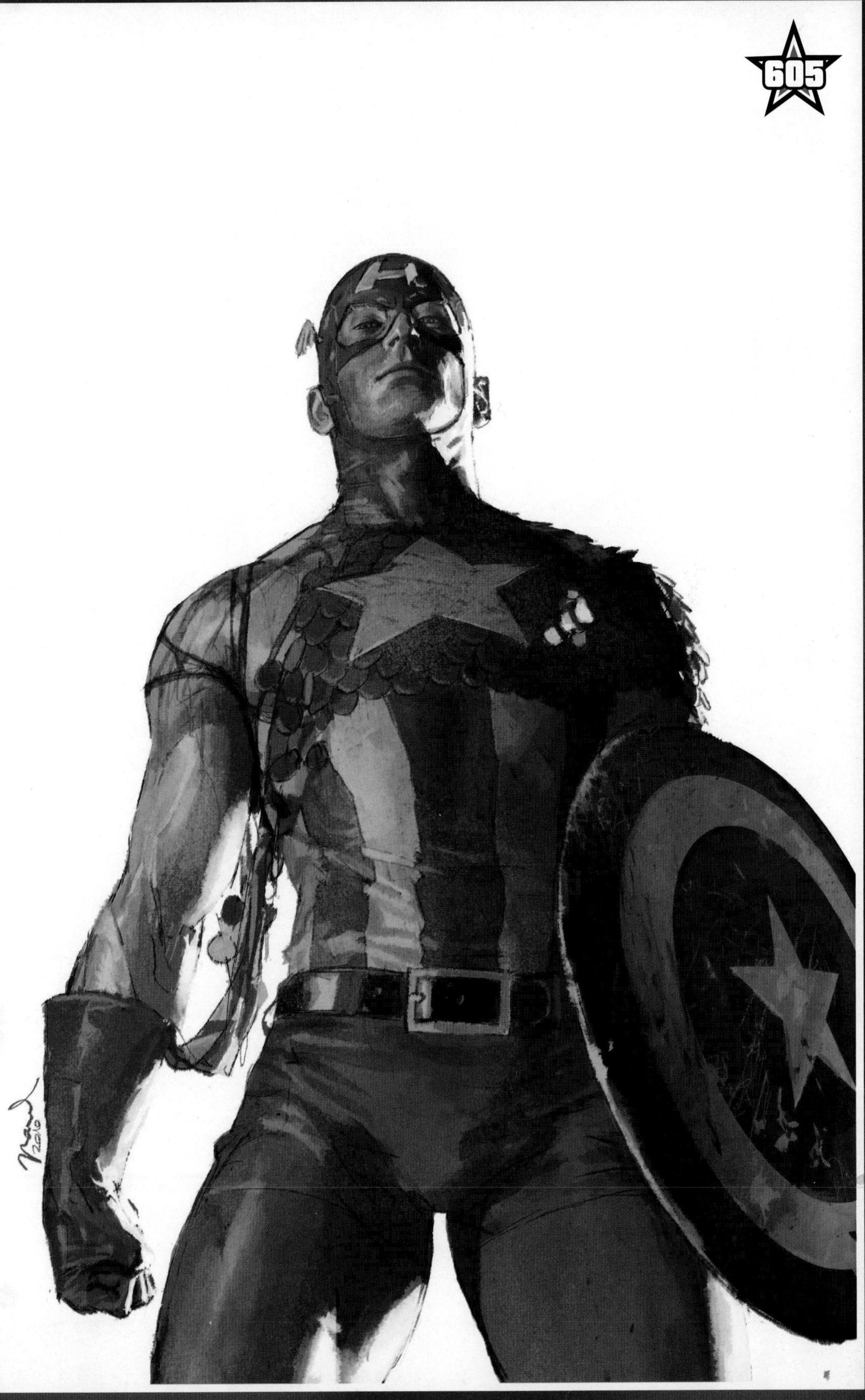
605

TWO AMERICAS CONCLUSION

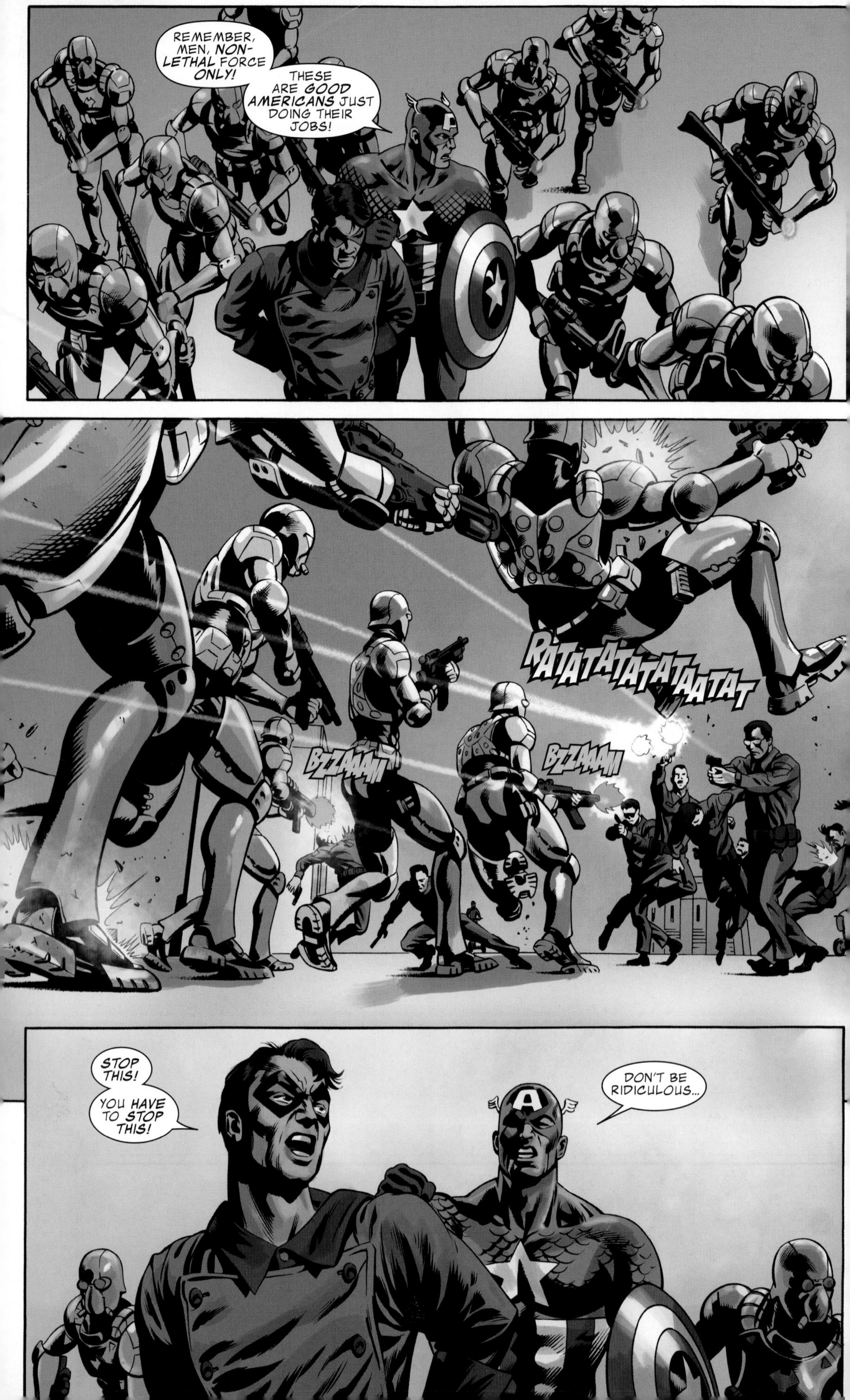
REMEMBER, MEN, NON-LETHAL FORCE ONLY!
THESE ARE GOOD AMERICANS JUST DOING THEIR JOBS!
RATATATATATATAATAT
BZZAAAM
BZZAAAM
STOP THIS!
YOU HAVE TO STOP THIS!
DON'T BE RIDICULOUS...

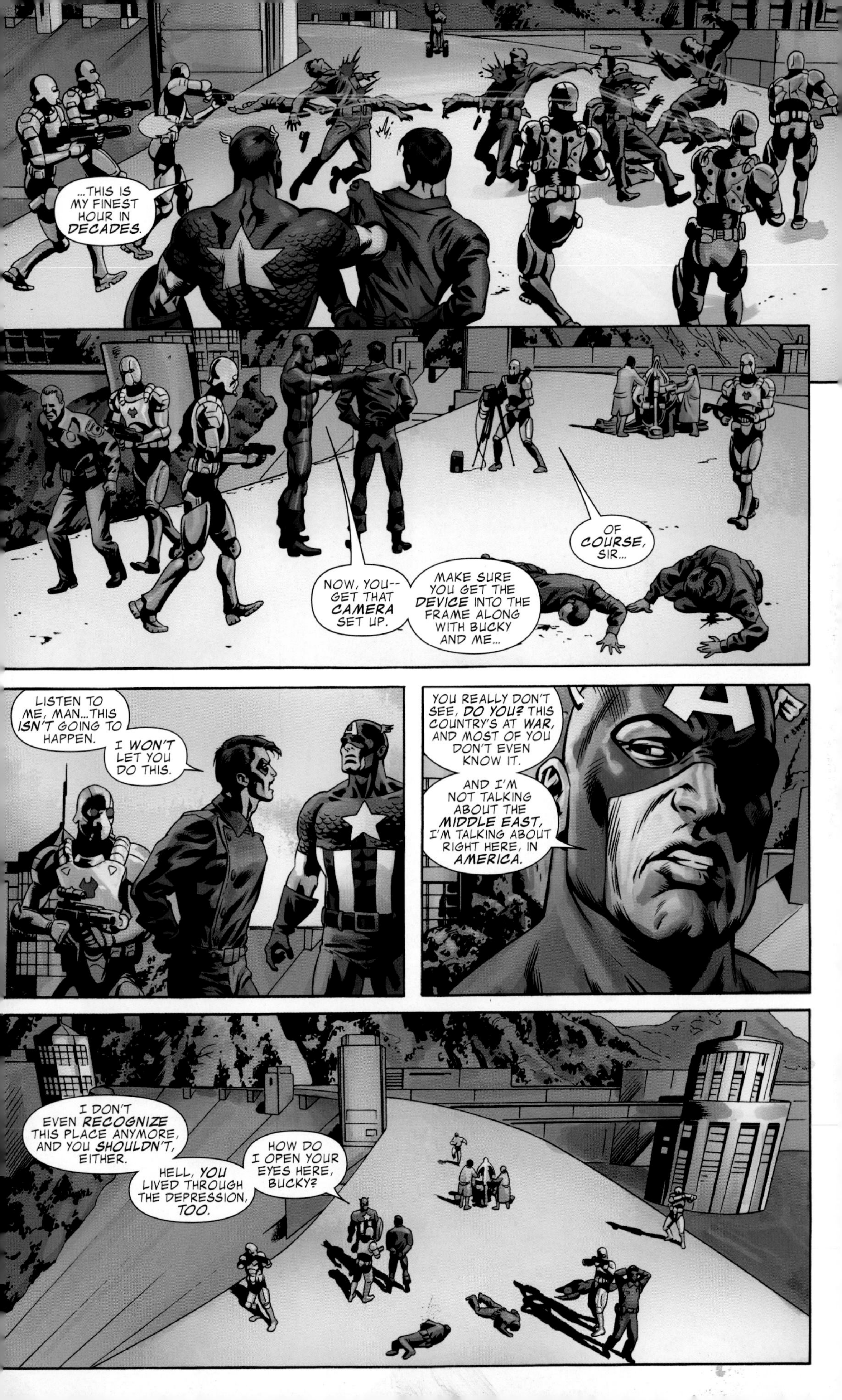
...THIS IS MY FINEST HOUR IN DECADES.
NOW, YOU-- GET THAT CAMERA SET UP.
MAKE SURE YOU GET THE DEVICE INTO THE FRAME ALONG WITH BUCKY AND ME...
OF COURSE, SIR...
LISTEN TO ME, MAN...THIS ISN'T GOING TO HAPPEN.
I WON'T LET YOU DO THIS.
YOU REALLY DON'T SEE, DO YOU? THIS COUNTRY'S AT WAR, AND MOST OF YOU DON'T EVEN KNOW IT.
AND I'M NOT TALKING ABOUT THE MIDDLE EAST, I'M TALKING ABOUT RIGHT HERE, IN AMERICA.
I DON'T EVEN RECOGNIZE THIS PLACE ANYMORE, AND YOU SHOULDN'T, EITHER.
HELL, YOU LIVED THROUGH THE DEPRESSION, TOO.
HOW DO I OPEN YOUR EYES HERE, BUCKY?

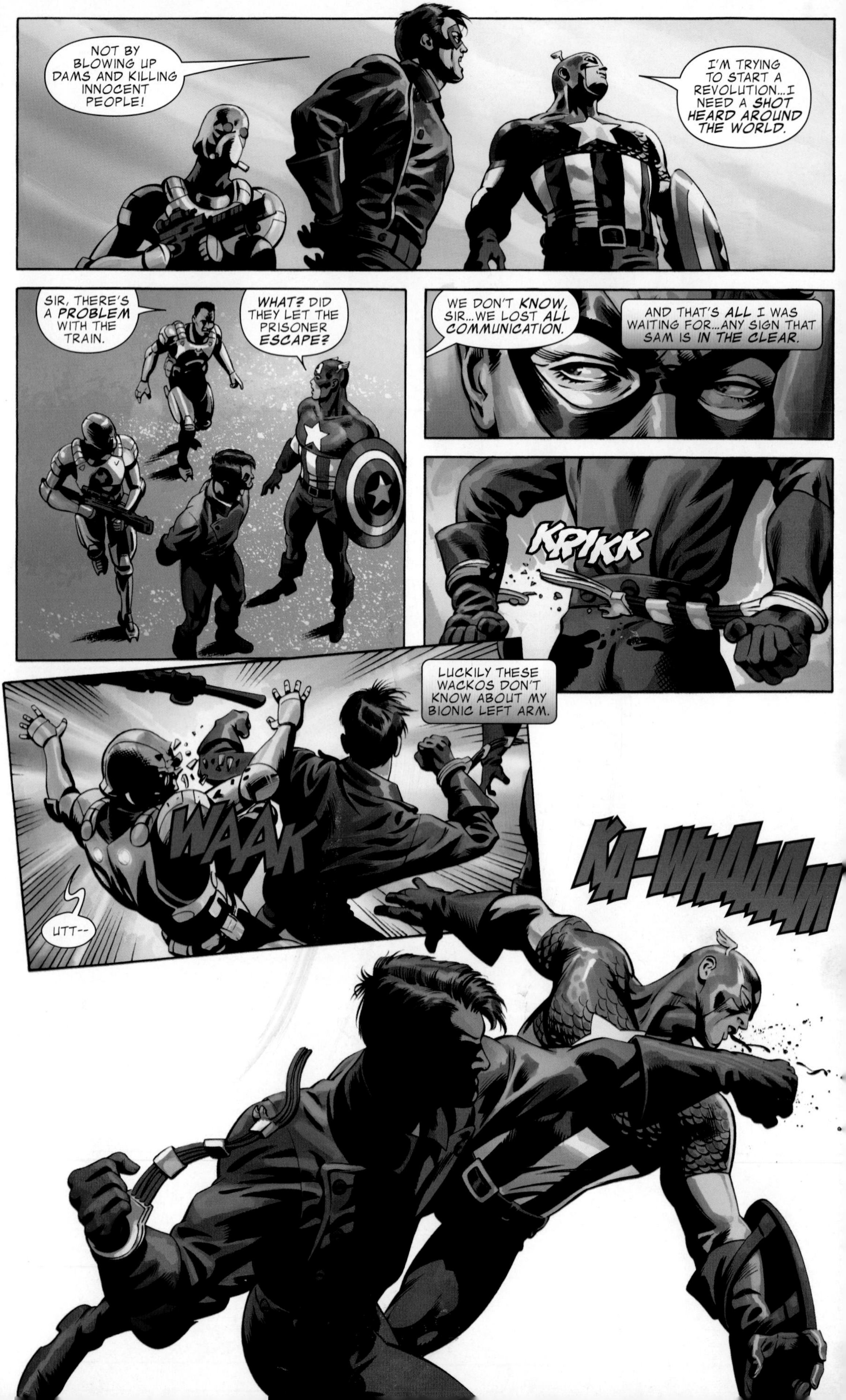
NOT BY BLOWING UP DAMS AND KILLING INNOCENT PEOPLE!
I'M TRYING TO START A REVOLUTION...I NEED A SHOT HEARD AROUND THE WORLD.
SIR, THERE'S A PROBLEM WITH THE TRAIN.
WHAT? DID THEY LET THE PRISONER ESCAPE?
WE DON'T KNOW, SIR...WE LOST ALL COMMUNICATION.
AND THAT'S ALL I WAS WAITING FOR...ANY SIGN THAT SAM IS IN THE CLEAR.
KRIKK
LUCKILY THESE WACKOS DON'T KNOW ABOUT MY BIONIC LEFT ARM.
WAAK
UTT--
KA-WHAAAAM

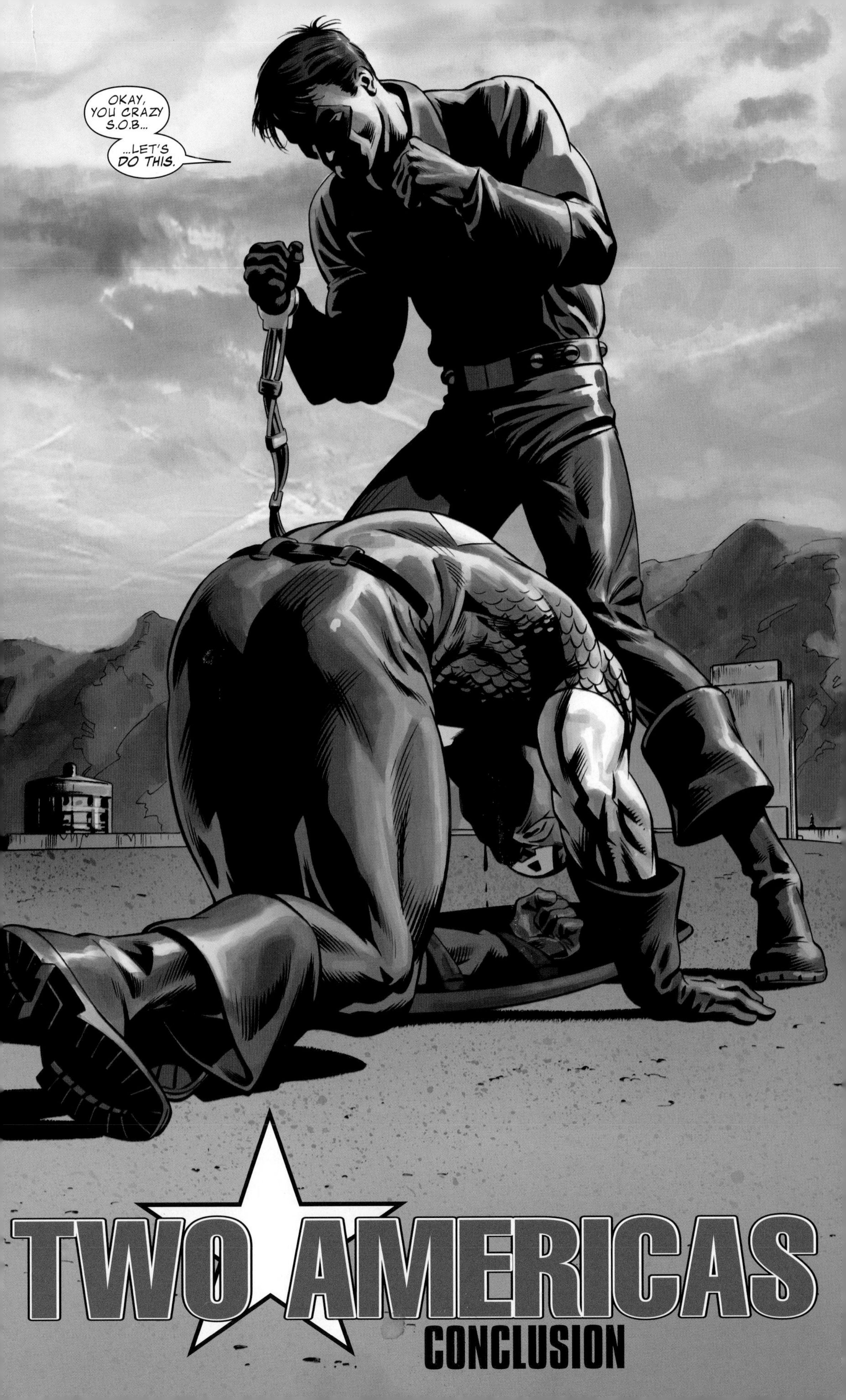
OKAY, YOU CRAZY S.O.B...
...LET'S DO THIS.
TWO AMERICAS
CONCLUSION

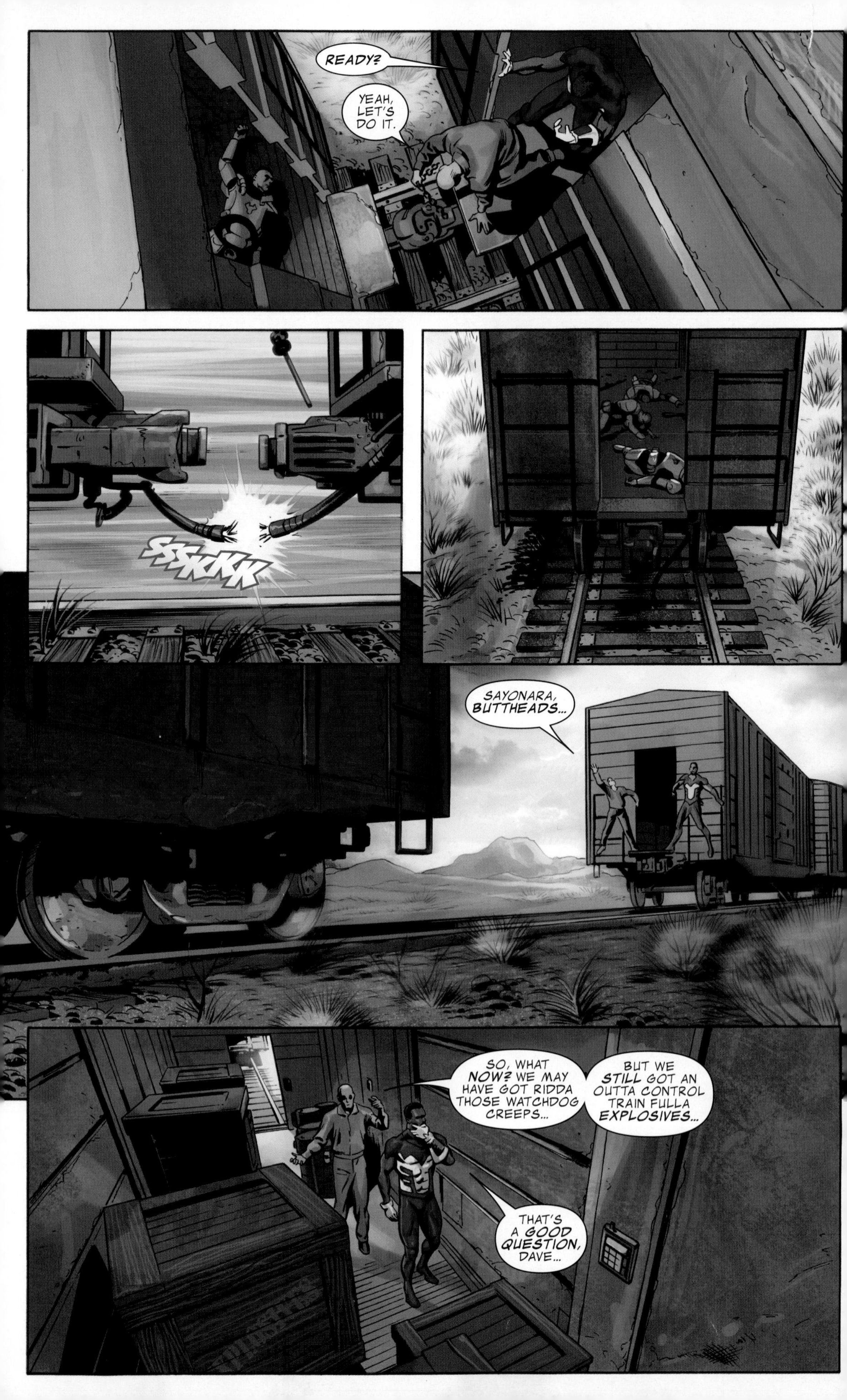
READY?
YEAH, LET'S DO IT.
SSSKKK
SAYONARA, BUTTHEADS...
SO, WHAT NOW? WE MAY HAVE GOT RIDDA THOSE WATCHDOG CREEPS...
BUT WE STILL GOT AN OUTTA CONTROL TRAIN FULLA EXPLOSIVES...
THAT'S A GOOD QUESTION, DAVE...

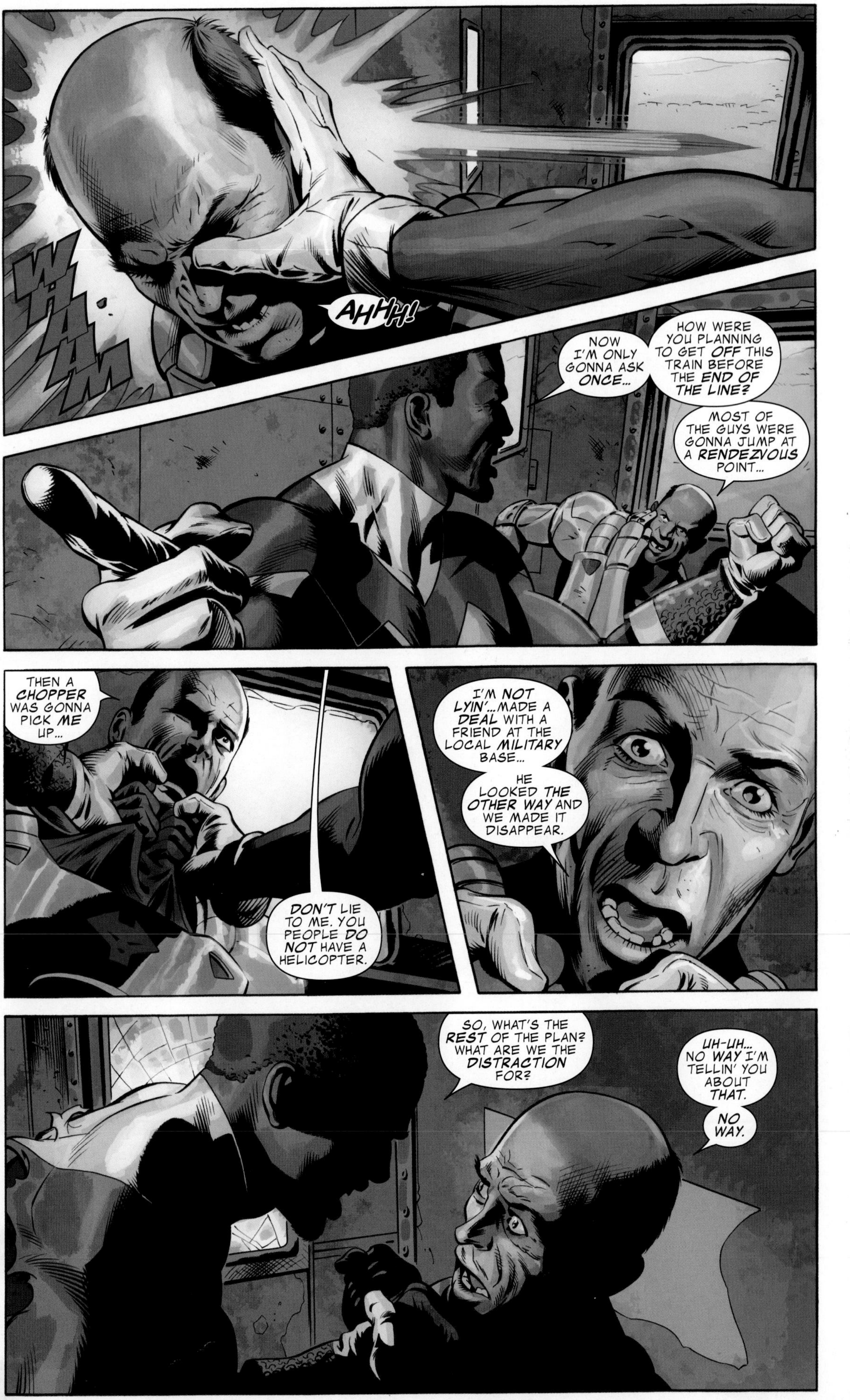
WHAAM
AHHH!
NOW I'M ONLY GONNA ASK ONCE...
HOW WERE YOU PLANNING TO GET OFF THIS TRAIN BEFORE THE END OF THE LINE?
MOST OF THE GUYS WERE GONNA JUMP AT A RENDEZVOUS POINT...
THEN A CHOPPER WAS GONNA PICK ME UP...
DON'T LIE TO ME. YOU PEOPLE DO NOT HAVE A HELICOPTER.
I'M NOT LYIN'...MADE A DEAL WITH A FRIEND AT THE LOCAL MILITARY BASE...
HE LOOKED THE OTHER WAY AND WE MADE IT DISAPPEAR.
SO, WHAT'S THE REST OF THE PLAN? WHAT ARE WE THE DISTRACTION FOR?
UH-UH... NO WAY I'M TELLIN' YOU ABOUT THAT.
NO WAY.

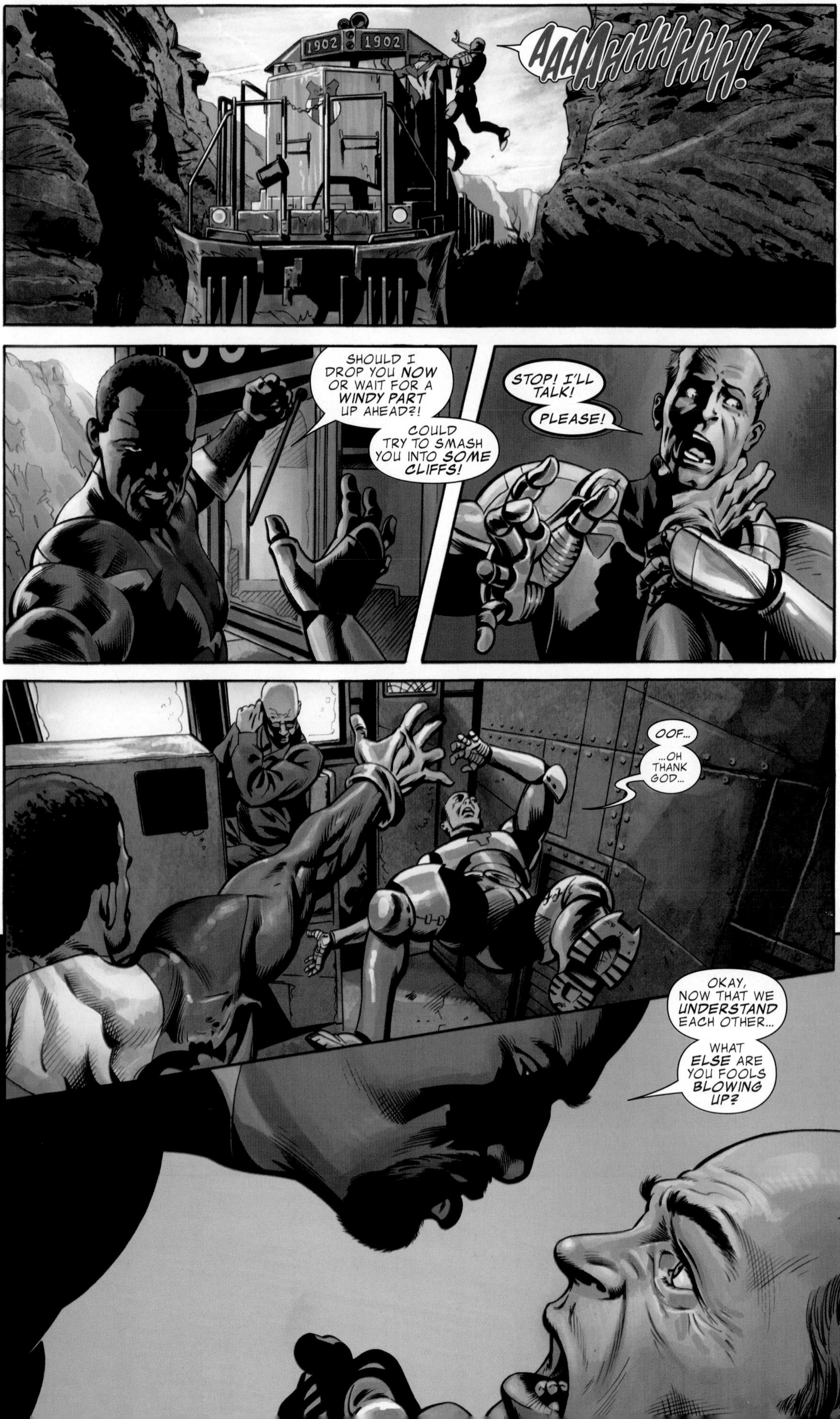
1902 1902
AAAAHHHHHHH!
SHOULD I DROP YOU NOW OR WAIT FOR A WINDY PART UP AHEAD?!
COULD TRY TO SMASH YOU INTO SOME CLIFFS!
STOP! I'LL TALK!
PLEASE!
OOF...
...OH THANK GOD...
OKAY, NOW THAT WE UNDERSTAND EACH OTHER...
WHAT ELSE ARE YOU FOOLS BLOWING UP?

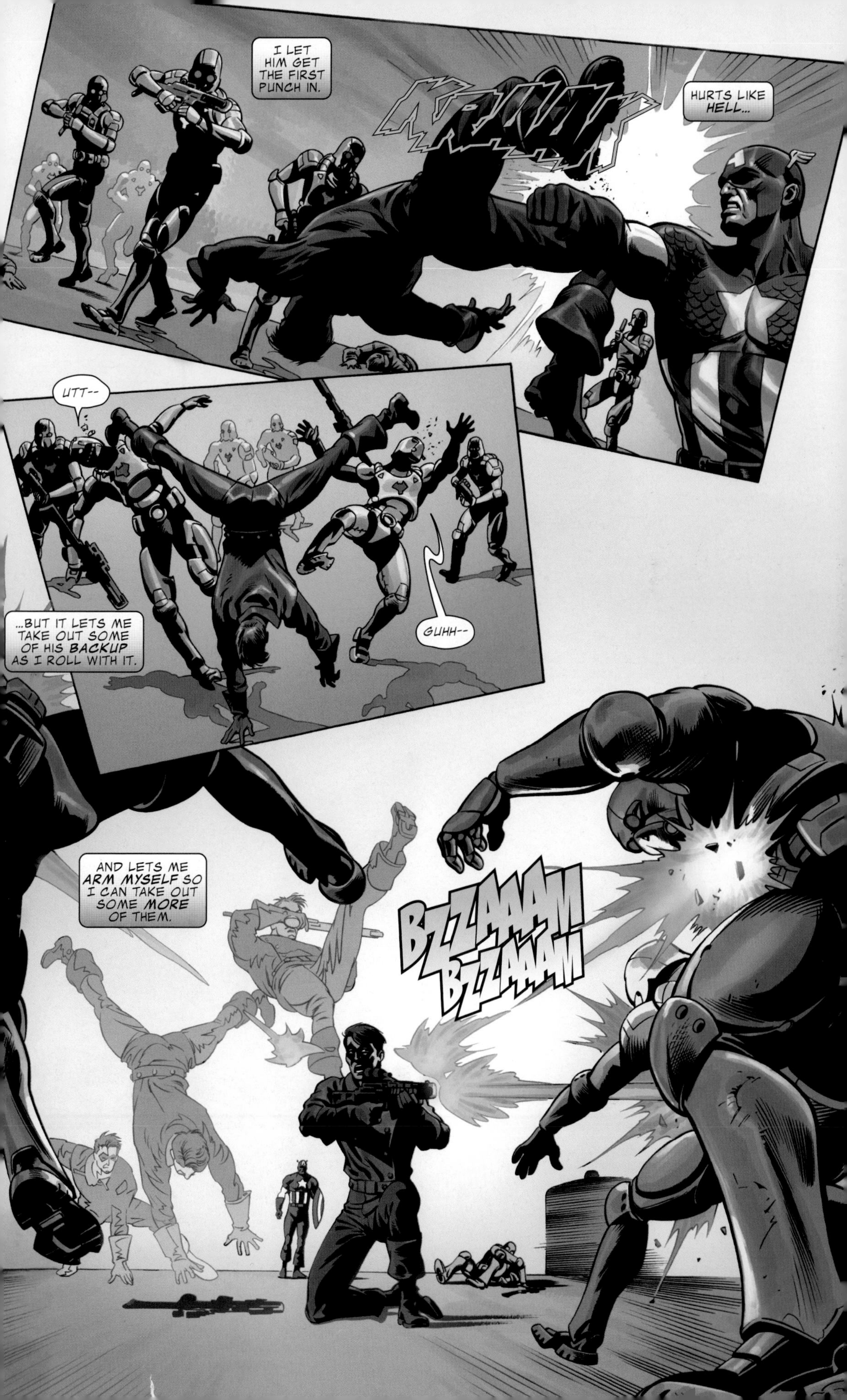
I LET HIM GET THE FIRST PUNCH IN.
HURTS LIKE HELL...
UTT--
...BUT IT LETS ME TAKE OUT SOME OF HIS BACKUP AS I ROLL WITH IT.
GUHH--
AND LETS ME ARM MYSELF SO I CAN TAKE OUT SOME MORE OF THEM.
BZZAAAM!
BZZAAAM

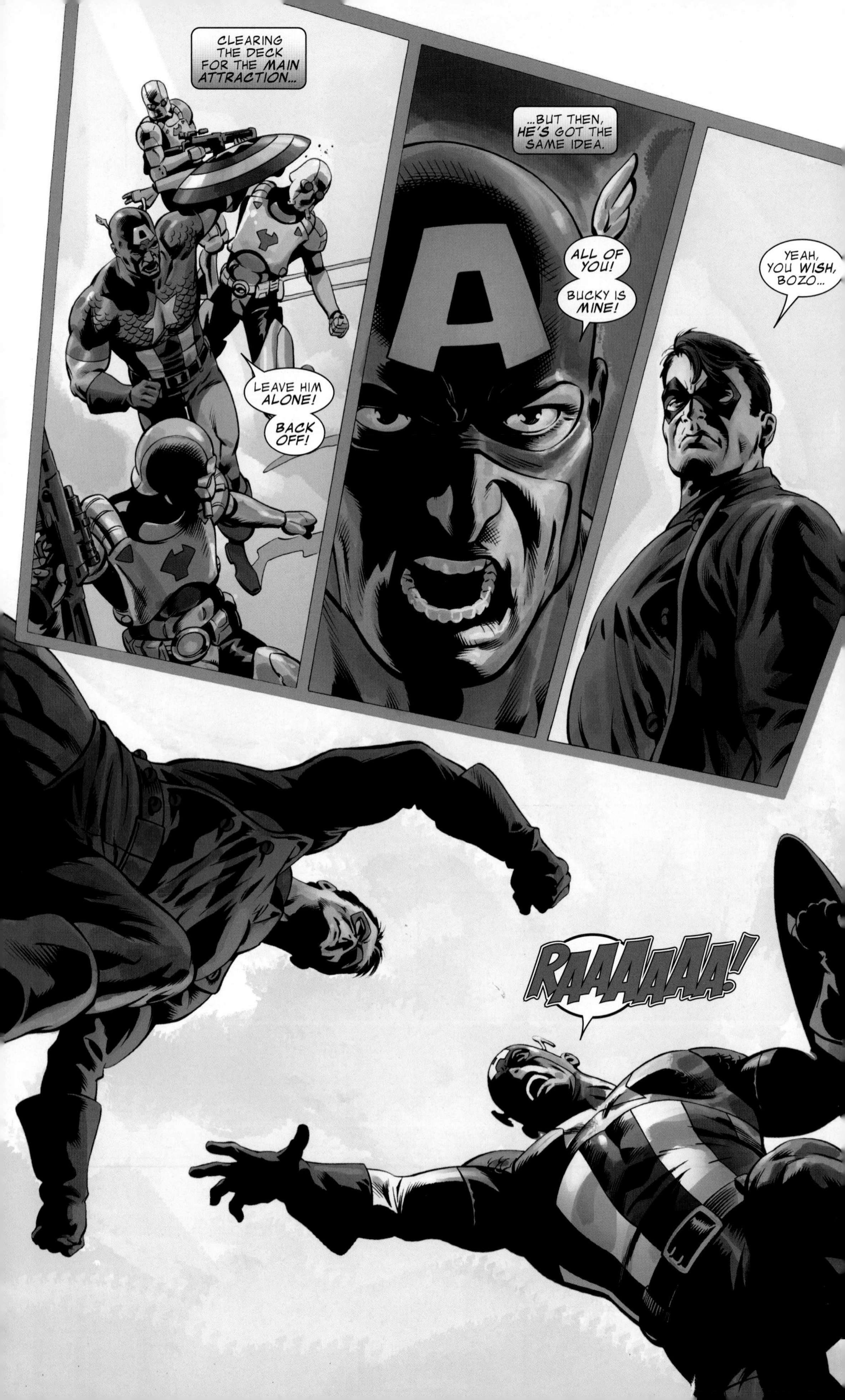
CLEARING THE DECK FOR THE MAIN ATTRACTION...
LEAVE HIM ALONE!
BACK OFF!
...BUT THEN, HE'S GOT THE SAME IDEA.
ALL OF YOU!
BUCKY IS MINE!
YEAH, YOU WISH, BOZO...
RAAAAAA!

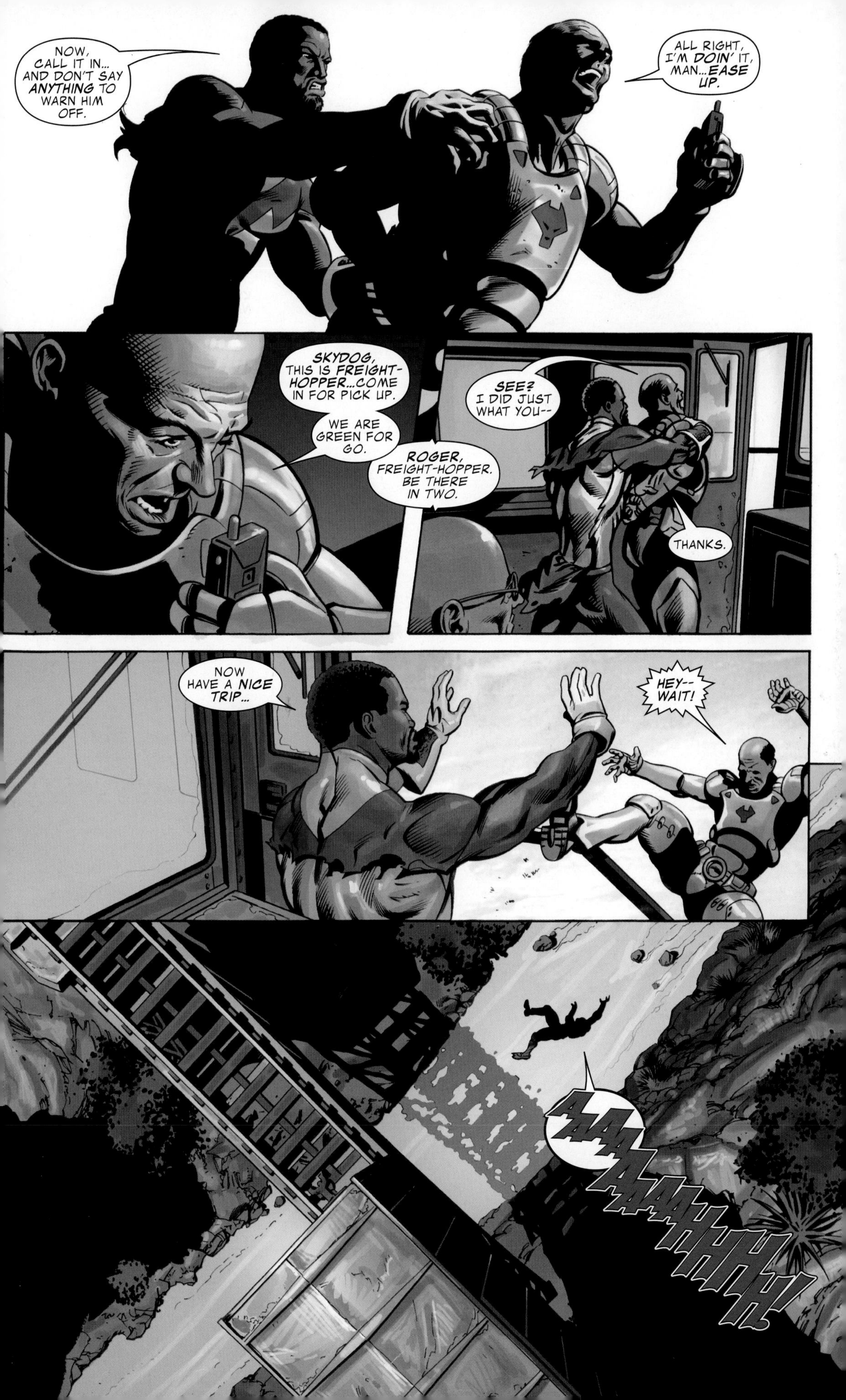
NOW, CALL IT IN... AND DON'T SAY ANYTHING TO WARN HIM OFF.
ALL RIGHT, I'M DOIN' IT, MAN...EASE UP.
SKYDOG, THIS IS FREIGHT-HOPPER...COME IN FOR PICK UP.
WE ARE GREEN FOR GO.
ROGER, FREIGHT-HOPPER. BE THERE IN TWO.
SEE? I DID JUST WHAT YOU--
THANKS.
NOW HAVE A NICE TRIP...
HEY-- WAIT!
AAAAAAAAHHHH!

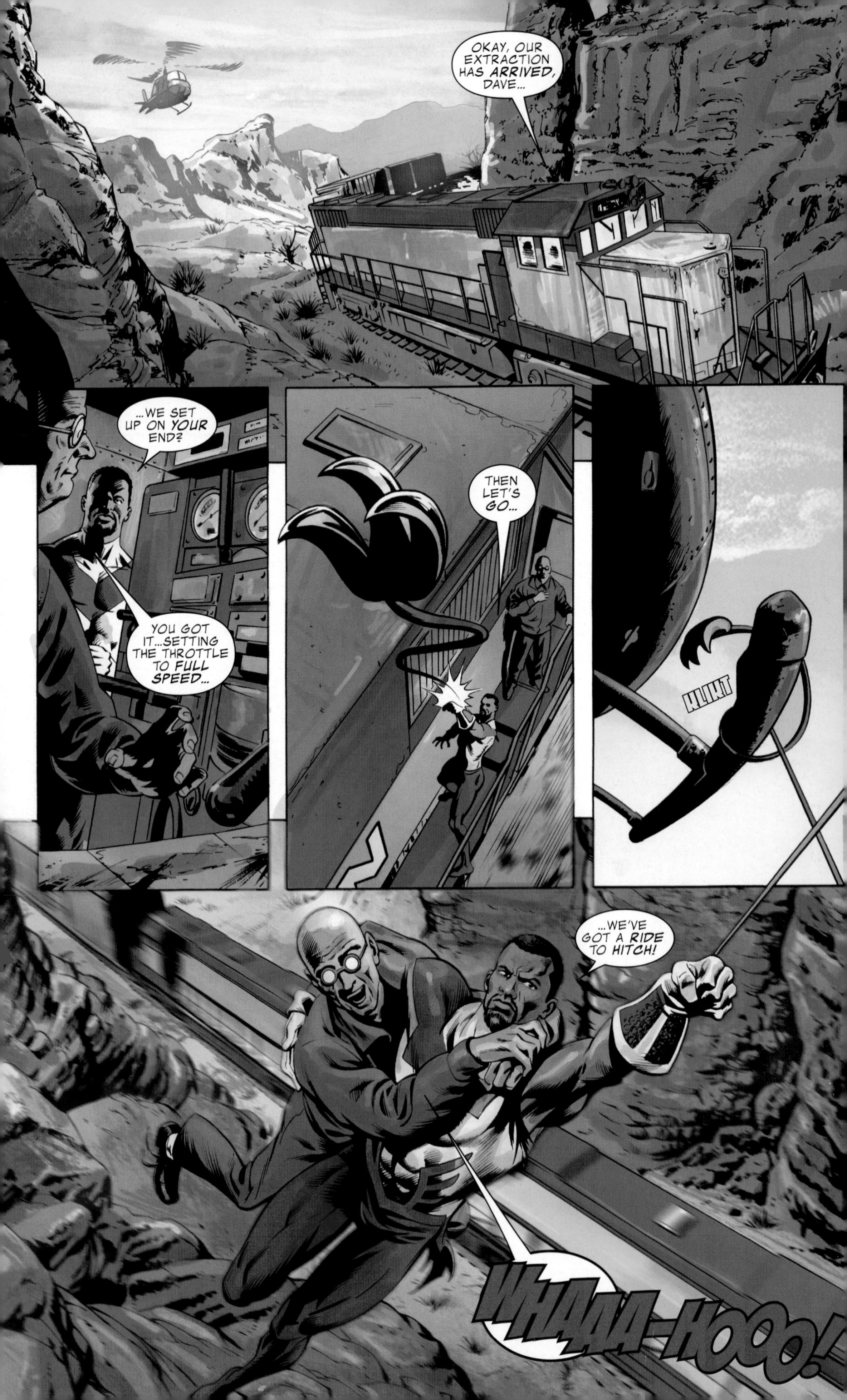
OKAY, OUR EXTRACTION HAS ARRIVED, DAVE...
...WE SET UP ON YOUR END?
YOU GOT IT...SETTING THE THROTTLE TO FULL SPEED...
THEN LET'S GO...
KLIKT
...WE'VE GOT A RIDE TO HITCH!
WHAAA-HOOO!

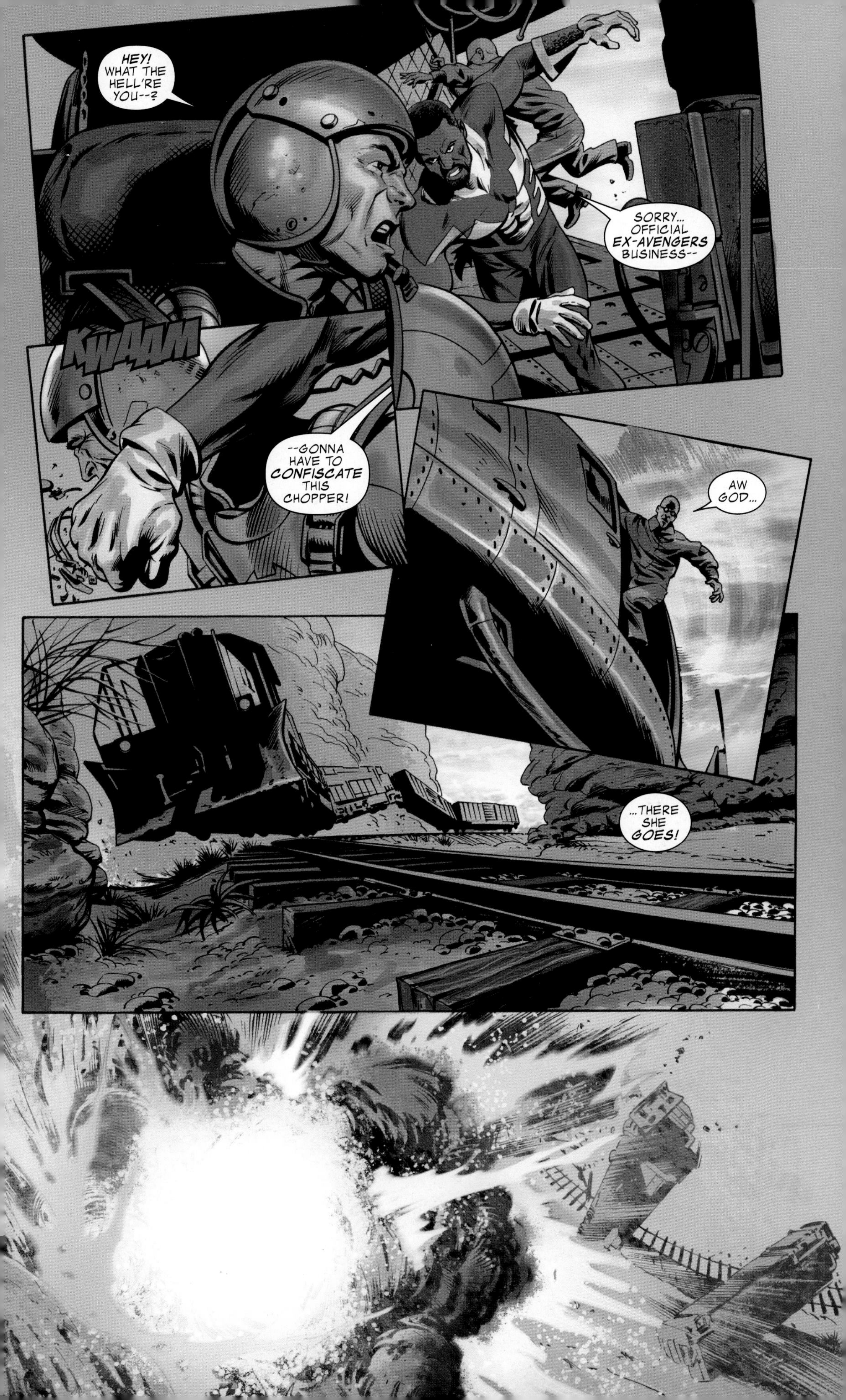
HEY! WHAT THE HELL'RE YOU--?
SORRY... OFFICIAL EX-AVENGERS BUSINESS--
KWAAM
--GONNA HAVE TO CONFISCATE THIS CHOPPER!
AW GOD...
...THERE SHE GOES!

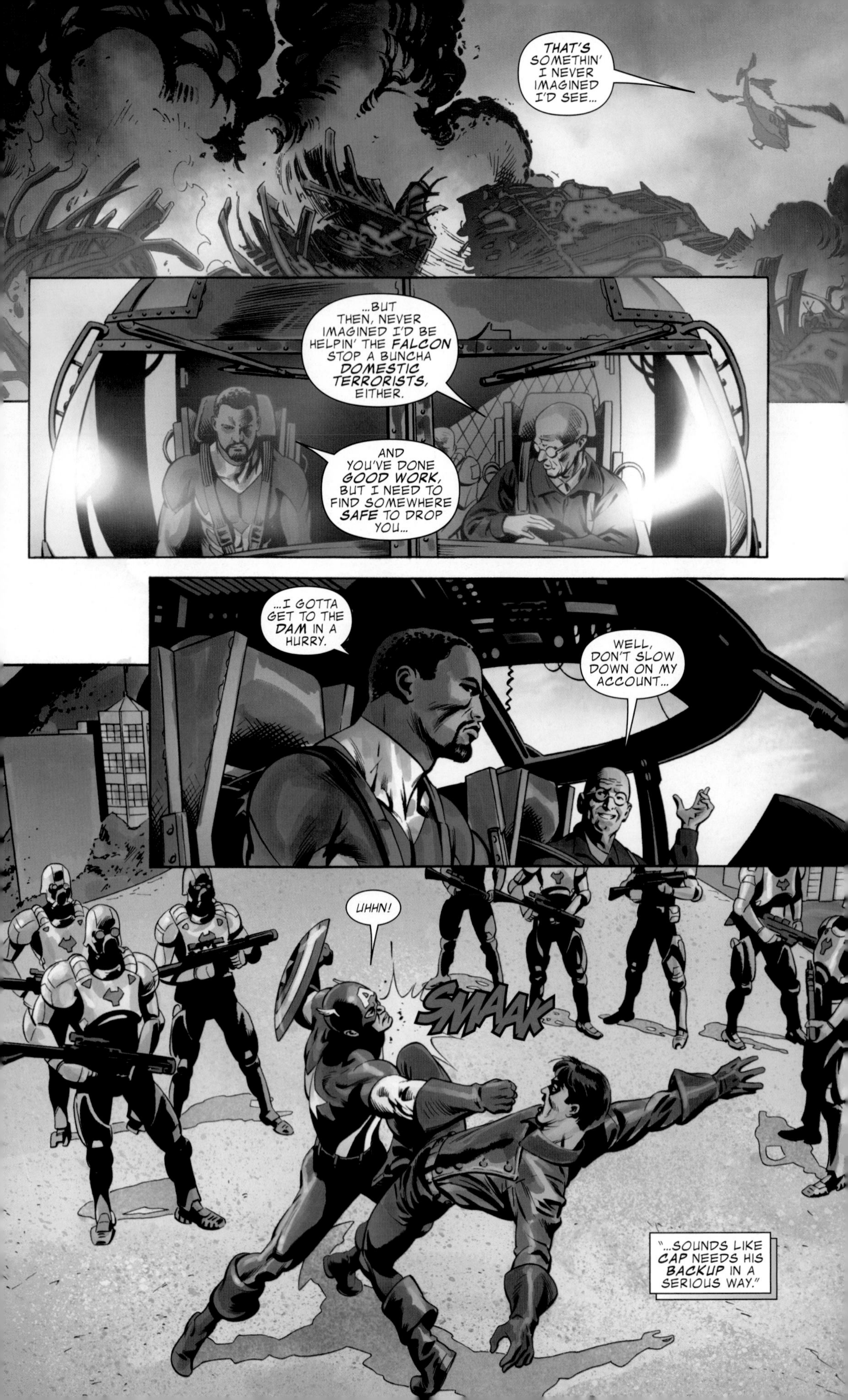
THAT'S SOMETHIN' I NEVER IMAGINED I'D SEE...
...BUT THEN, NEVER IMAGINED I'D BE HELPIN' THE FALCON STOP A BUNCHA DOMESTIC TERRORISTS, EITHER.
AND YOU'VE DONE GOOD WORK, BUT I NEED TO FIND SOMEWHERE SAFE TO DROP YOU...
...I GOTTA GET TO THE DAM IN A HURRY.
WELL, DON'T SLOW DOWN ON MY ACCOUNT...
UHHN!
SMAAK
"...SOUNDS LIKE CAP NEEDS HIS BACKUP IN A SERIOUS WAY."

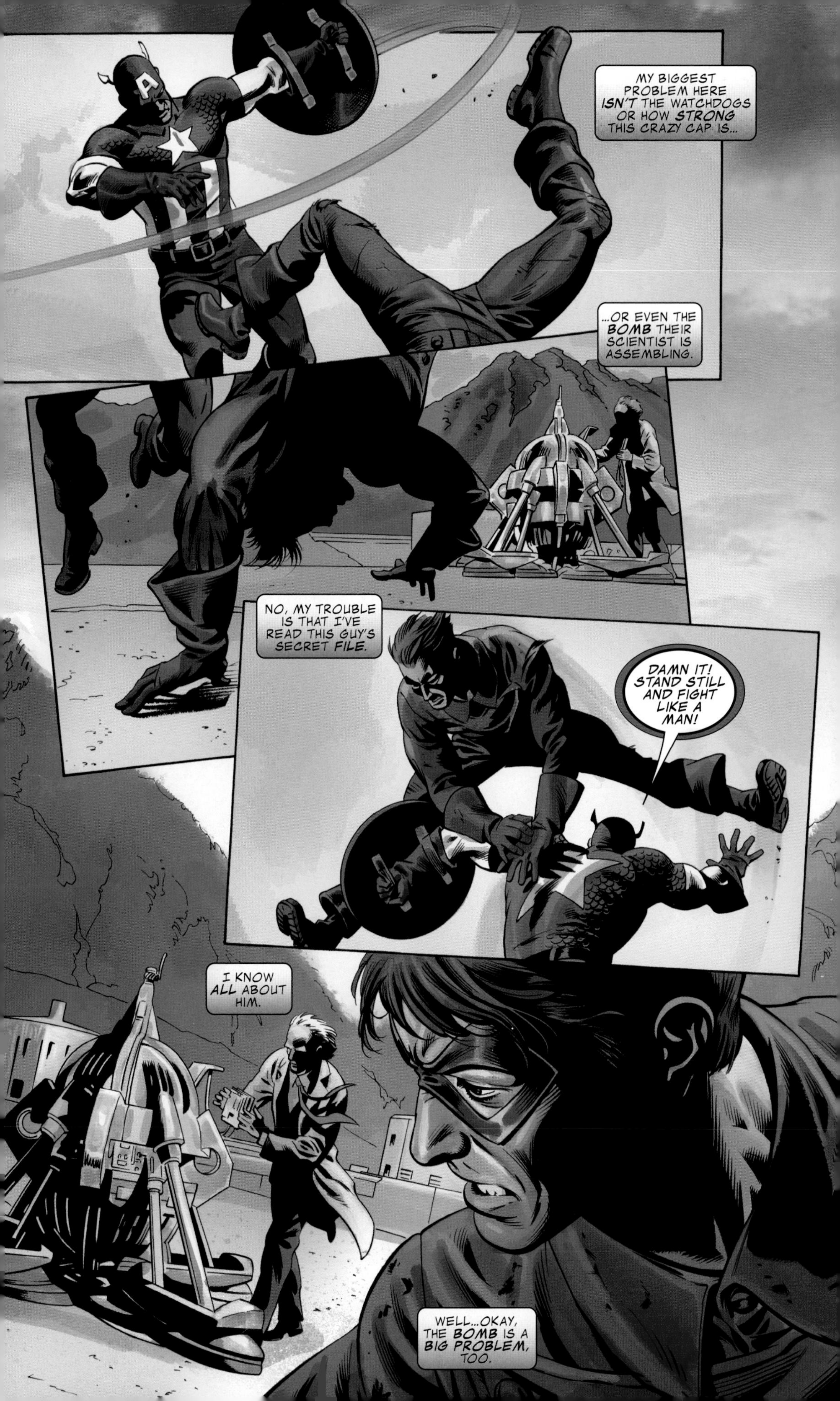
MY BIGGEST PROBLEM HERE ISN'T THE WATCHDOGS OR HOW STRONG THIS CRAZY CAP IS...
...OR EVEN THE BOMB THEIR SCIENTIST IS ASSEMBLING.
NO, MY TROUBLE IS THAT I'VE READ THIS GUY'S SECRET FILE.
DAMN IT! STAND STILL AND FIGHT LIKE A MAN!
I KNOW ALL ABOUT HIM.
WELL...OKAY, THE BOMB IS A BIG PROBLEM, TOO.

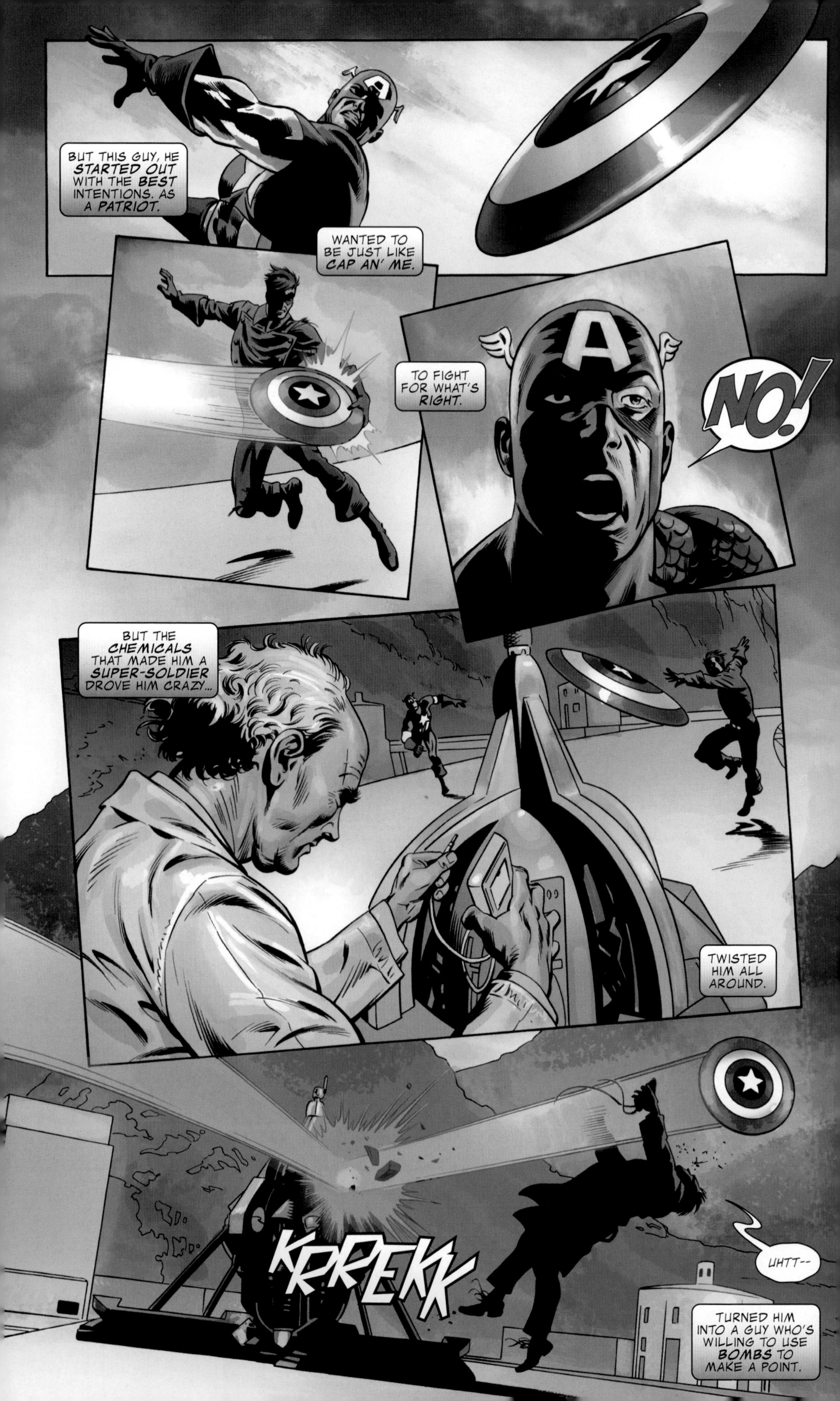

BUT THIS GUY, HE STARTED OUT WITH THE BEST INTENTIONS. AS A PATRIOT.
WANTED TO BE JUST LIKE CAP AN' ME.
TO FIGHT FOR WHAT'S RIGHT.
NO!
BUT THE CHEMICALS THAT MADE HIM A SUPER-SOLDIER DROVE HIM CRAZY...
TWISTED HIM ALL AROUND.
KRREKK
UHTT--
TURNED HIM INTO A GUY WHO'S WILLING TO USE BOMBS TO MAKE A POINT.

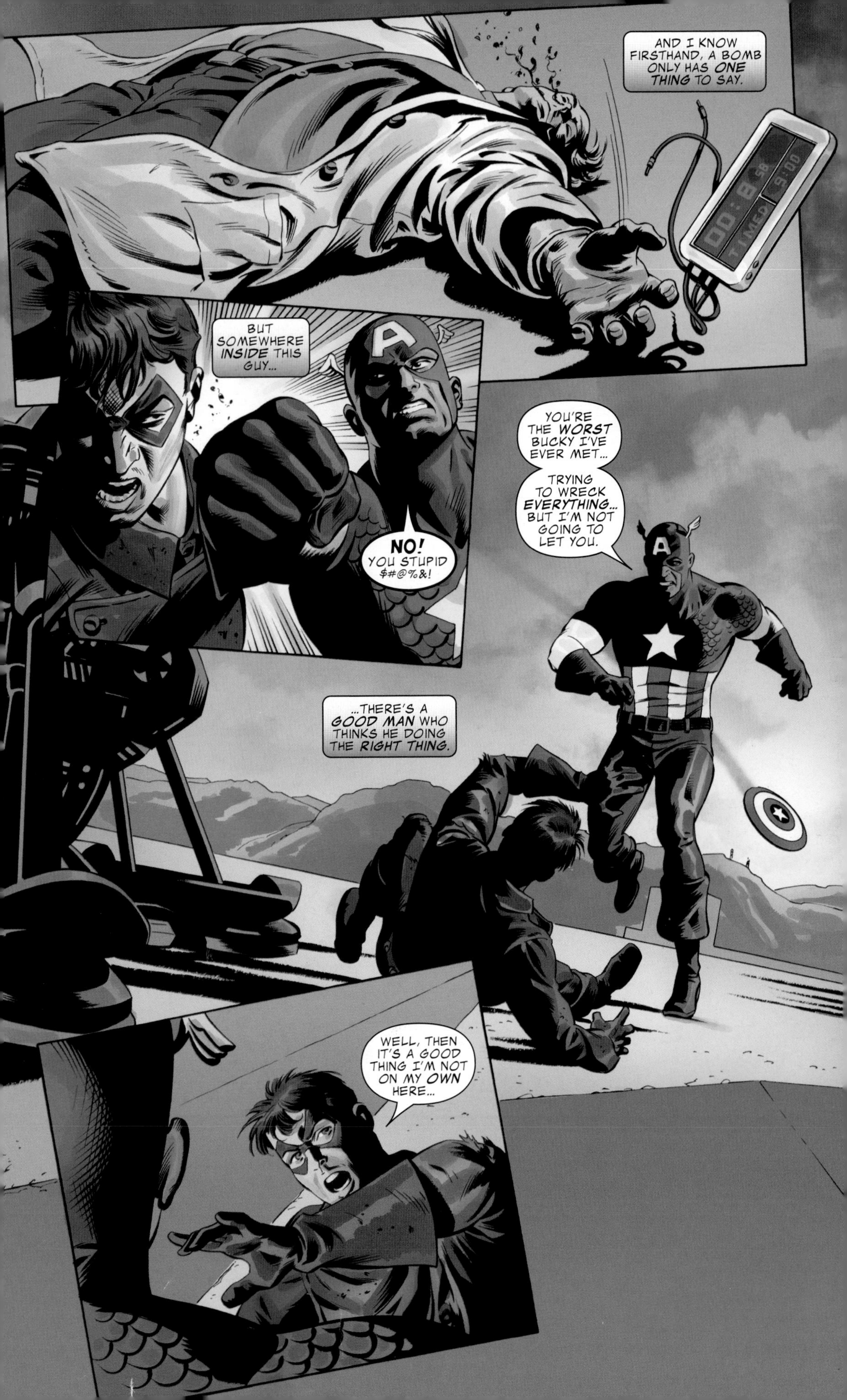
AND I KNOW FIRSTHAND, A BOMB ONLY HAS ONE THING TO SAY.
BUT SOMEWHERE INSIDE THIS GUY...
NO! YOU STUPID $#@%&!
YOU'RE THE WORST BUCKY I'VE EVER MET...
TRYING TO WRECK EVERYTHING... BUT I'M NOT GOING TO LET YOU.
...THERE'S A GOOD MAN WHO THINKS HE DOING THE RIGHT THING.
WELL, THEN IT'S A GOOD THING I'M NOT ON MY OWN HERE...

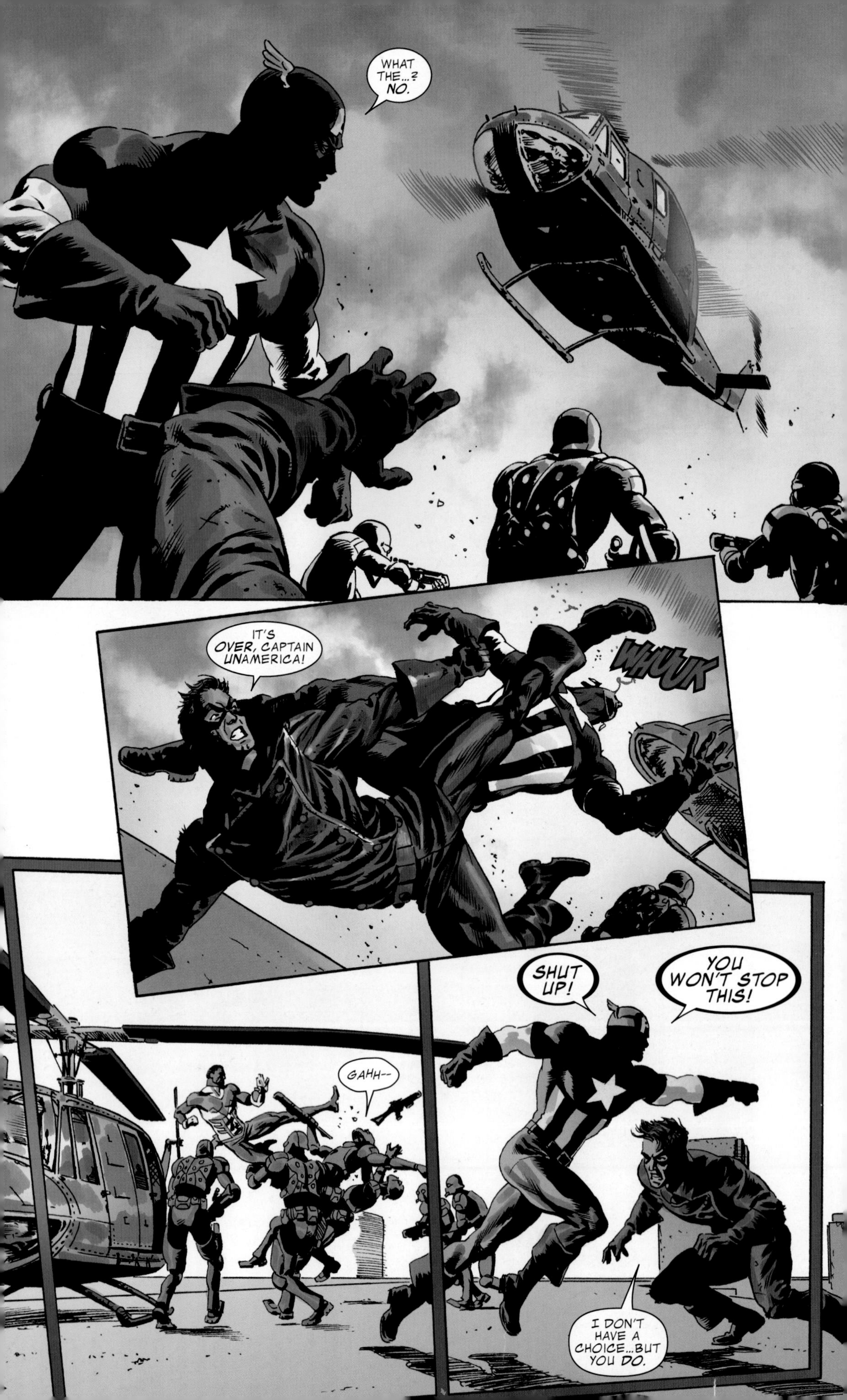
WHAT THE...? NO.
IT'S OVER, CAPTAIN UNAMERICA!
WHUUK
SHUT UP!
YOU WON'T STOP THIS!
GAHH--
I DON'T HAVE A CHOICE...BUT YOU DO.

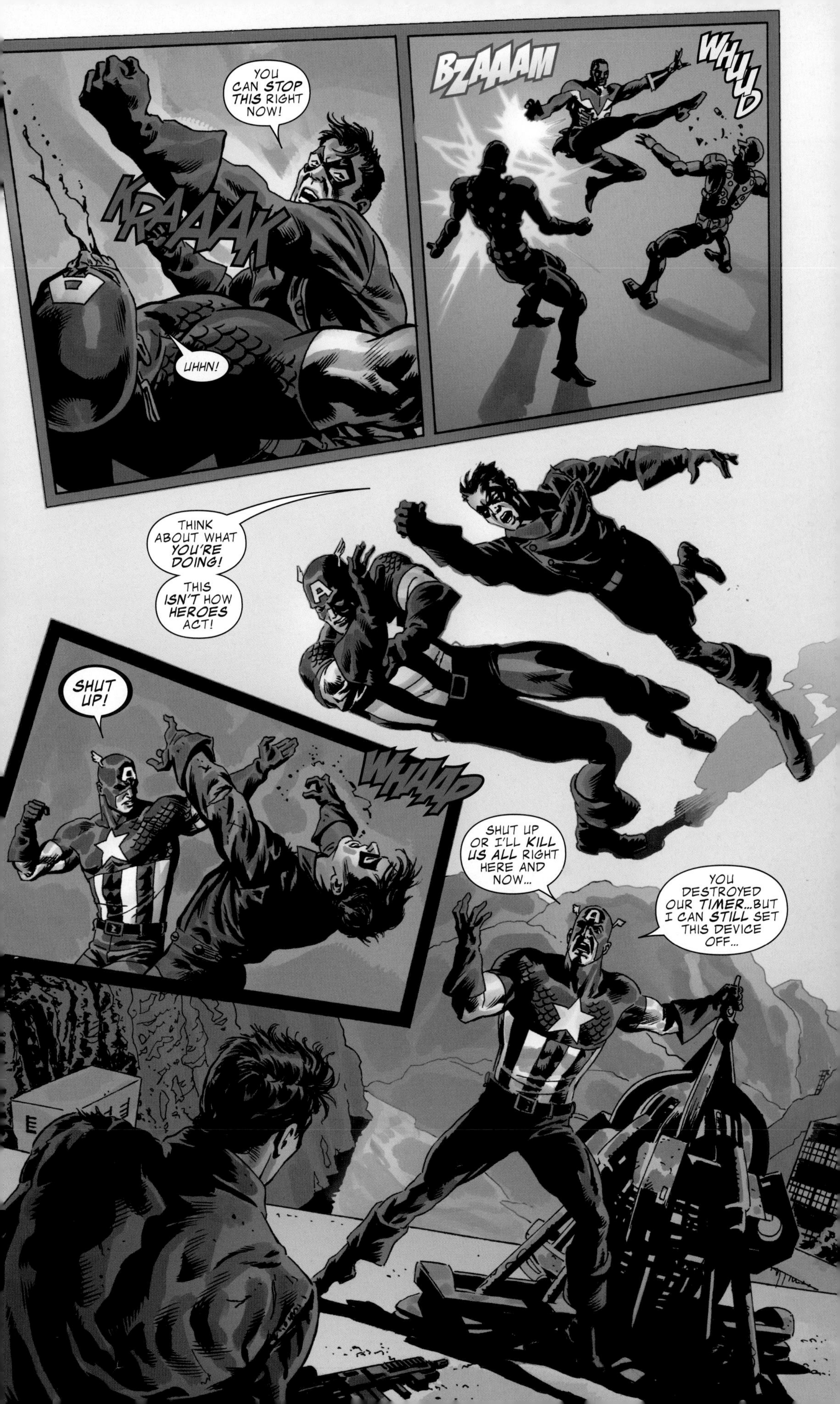
YOU CAN STOP THIS RIGHT NOW!
KRAAAK
UHHN!
BZAAAM
WHUUD
THINK ABOUT WHAT YOU'RE DOING!
THIS ISN'T HOW HEROES ACT!
SHUT UP!
WHAAP
SHUT UP OR I'LL KILL US ALL RIGHT HERE AND NOW...
YOU DESTROYED OUR TIMER...BUT I CAN STILL SET THIS DEVICE OFF...

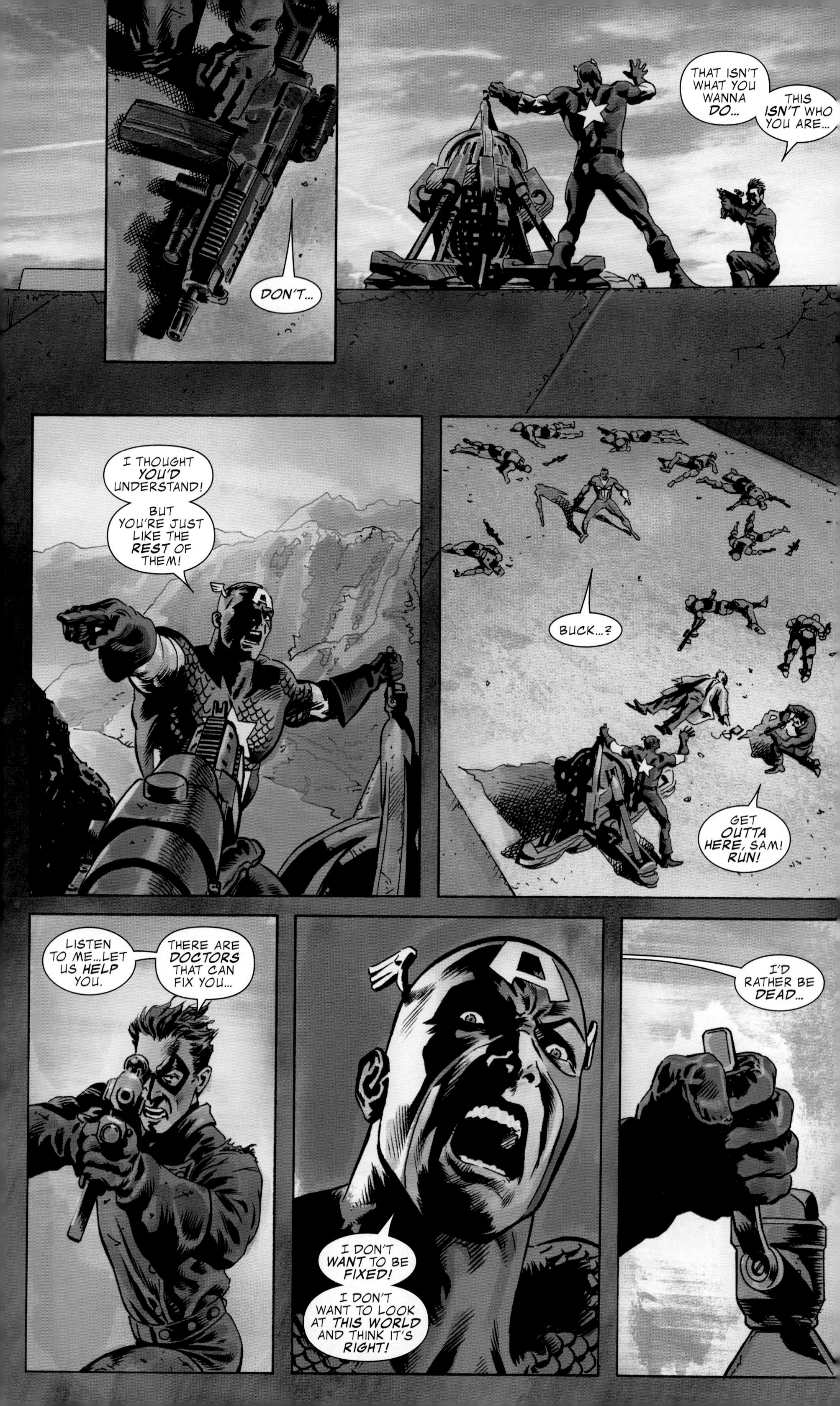
THAT ISN'T WHAT YOU WANNA DO...
THIS ISN'T WHO YOU ARE...
DON'T...
I THOUGHT YOU'D UNDERSTAND!
BUT YOU'RE JUST LIKE THE REST OF THEM!
BUCK...?
GET OUTTA HERE, SAM! RUN!
LISTEN TO ME...LET US HELP YOU.
THERE ARE DOCTORS THAT CAN FIX YOU...
I DON'T WANT TO BE FIXED!
I DON'T WANT TO LOOK AT THIS WORLD AND THINK IT'S RIGHT!
I'D RATHER BE DEAD...

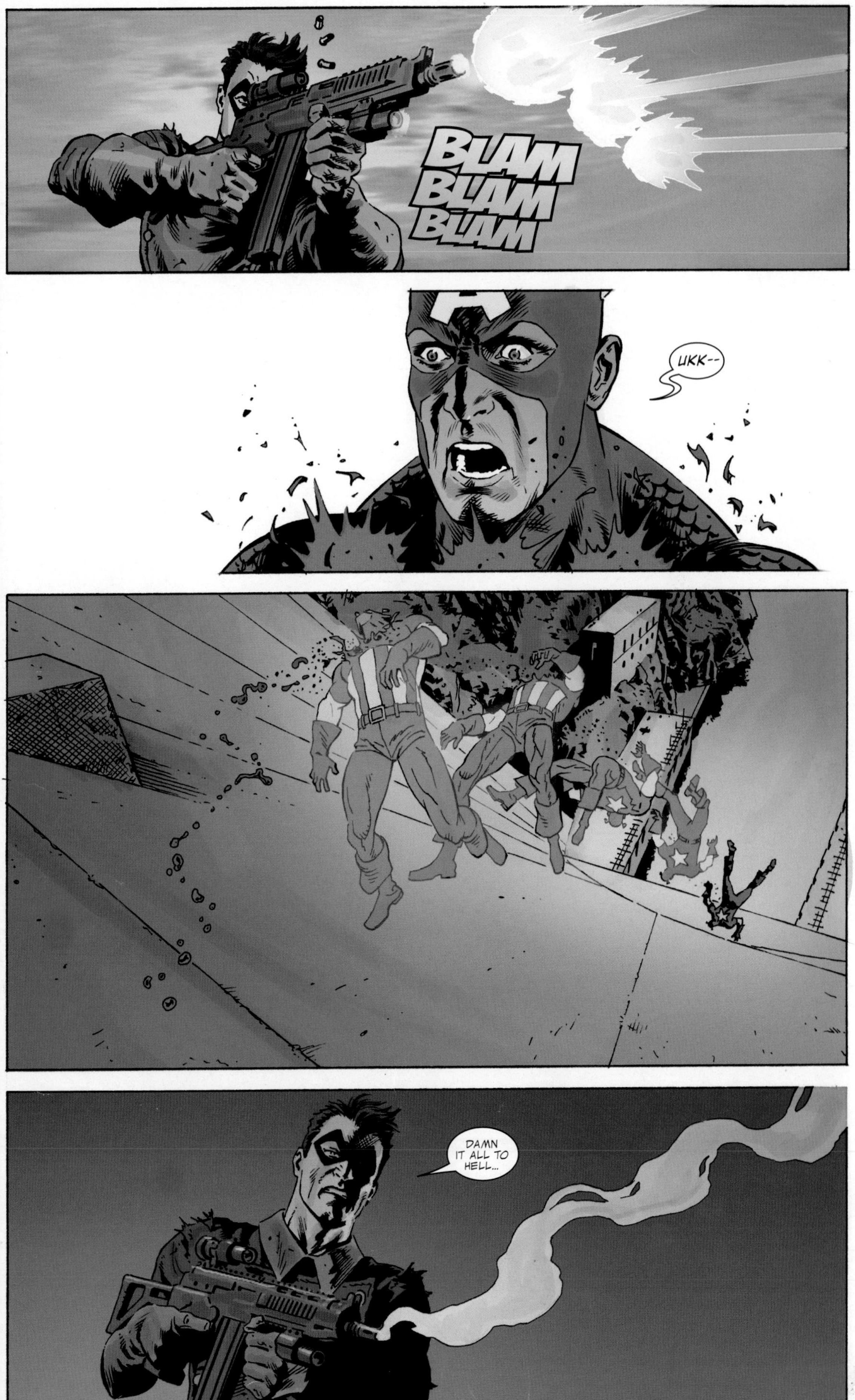

BLAM
BLAM
BLAM
UKK--
DAMN IT ALL TO HELL...

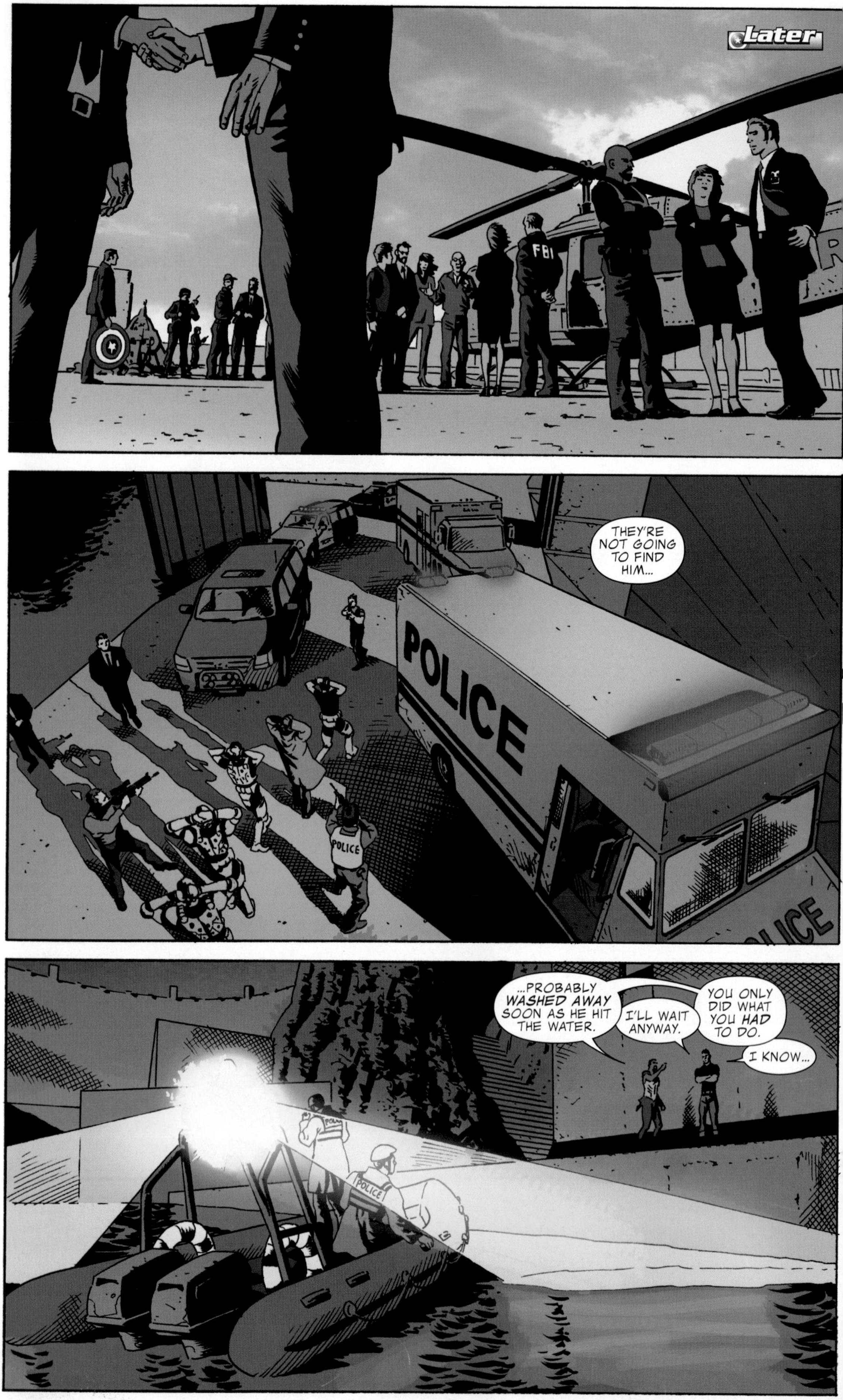
Later
THEY'RE NOT GOING TO FIND HIM...
POLICE
...PROBABLY WASHED AWAY SOON AS HE HIT THE WATER.
I'LL WAIT ANYWAY.
YOU ONLY DID WHAT YOU HAD TO DO.
I KNOW...

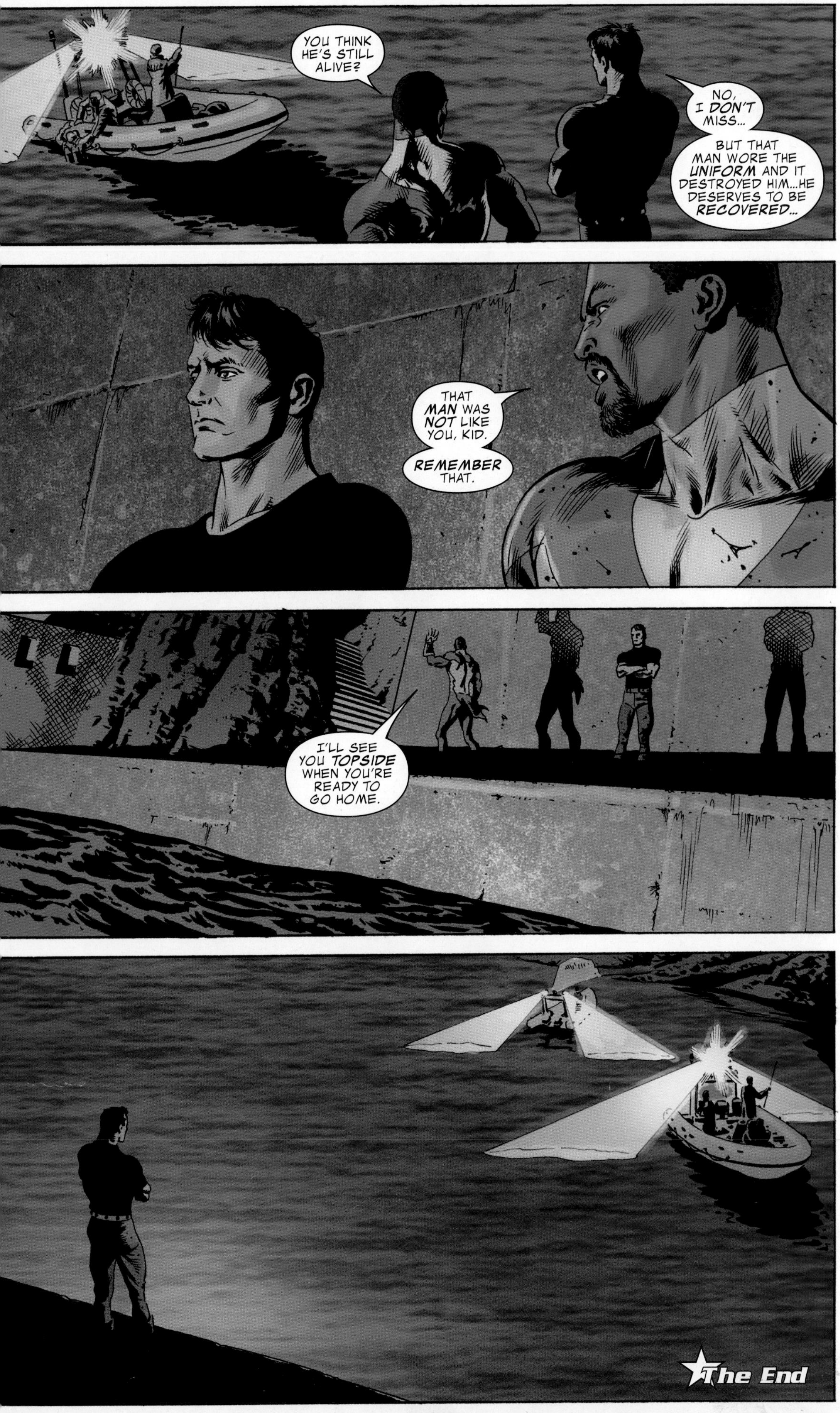

YOU THINK HE'S STILL ALIVE?
NO, I DON'T MISS...
BUT THAT MAN WORE THE UNIFORM AND IT DESTROYED HIM...HE DESERVES TO BE RECOVERED...
THAT MAN WAS NOT LIKE YOU, KID.
REMEMBER THAT.
I'LL SEE YOU TOPSIDE WHEN YOU'RE READY TO GO HOME.
The End

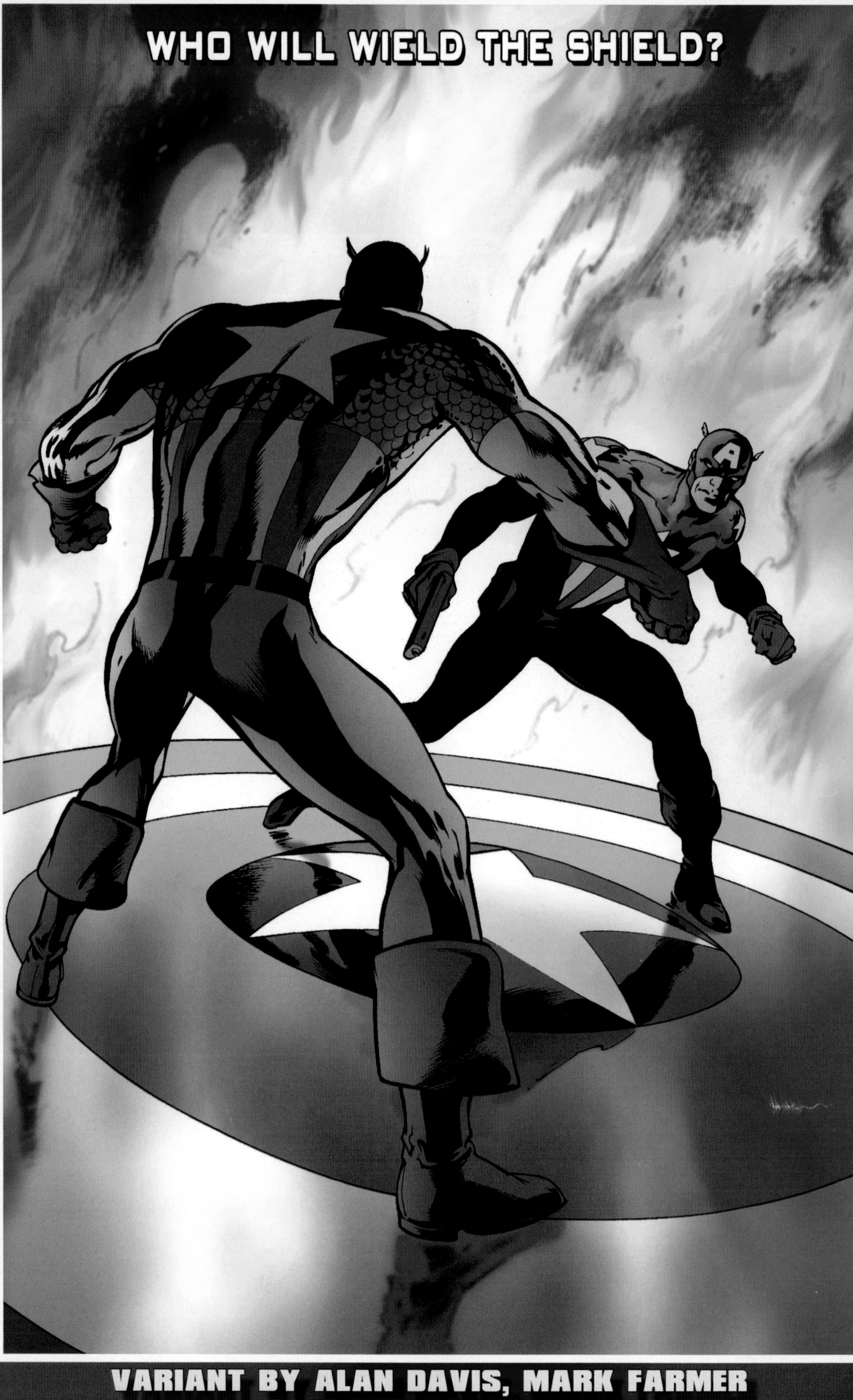
WHO WILL WIELD THE SHIELD?

VARIANT BY ALAN DAVIS, MARK FARMER
& JAVIER RODRIGUEZ

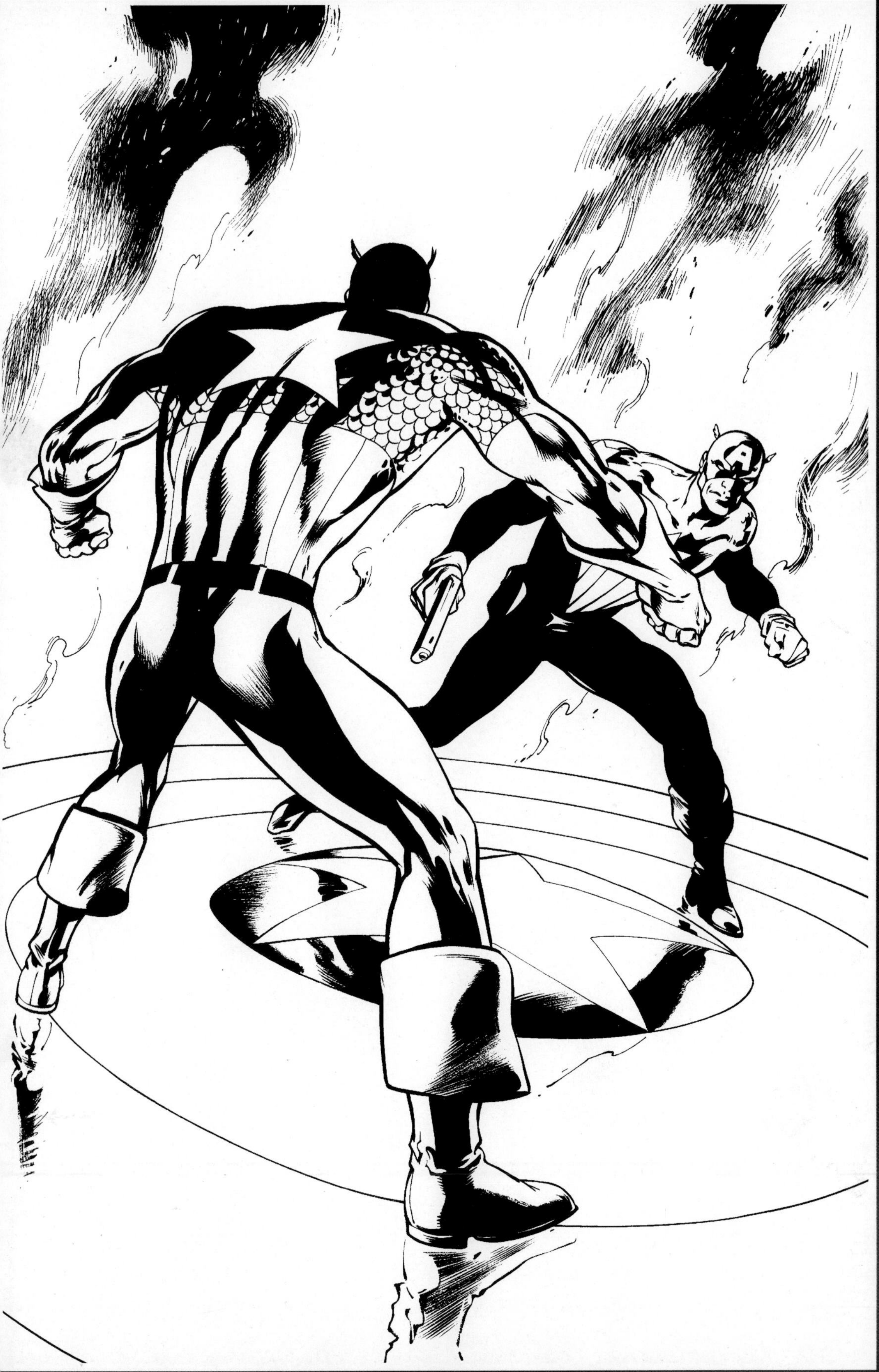

VARIANT INKS BY ALAN DAVIS & MARK FARMER

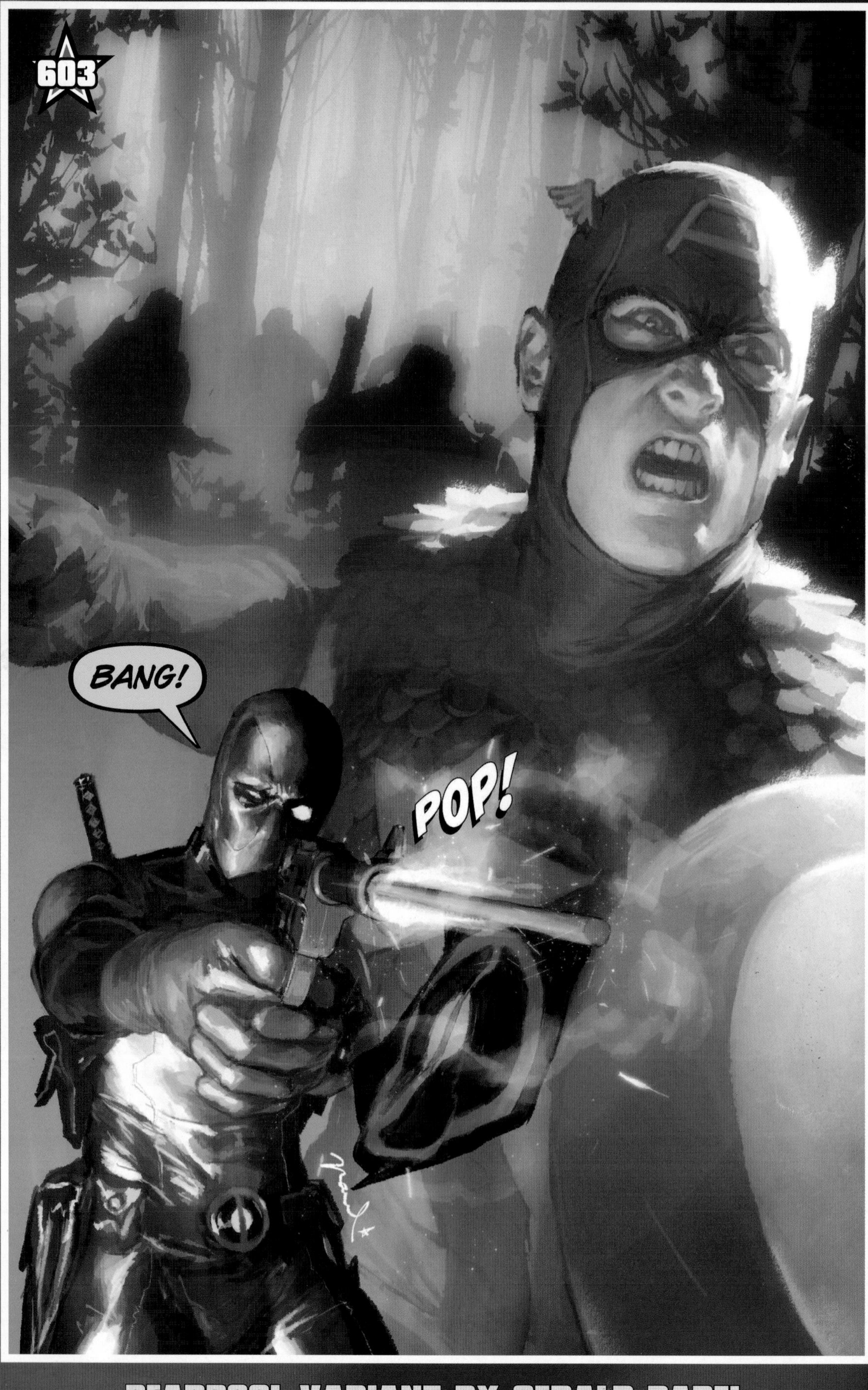
603
BANG!
POP!
DEADPOOL VARIANT BY GERALD PAREL

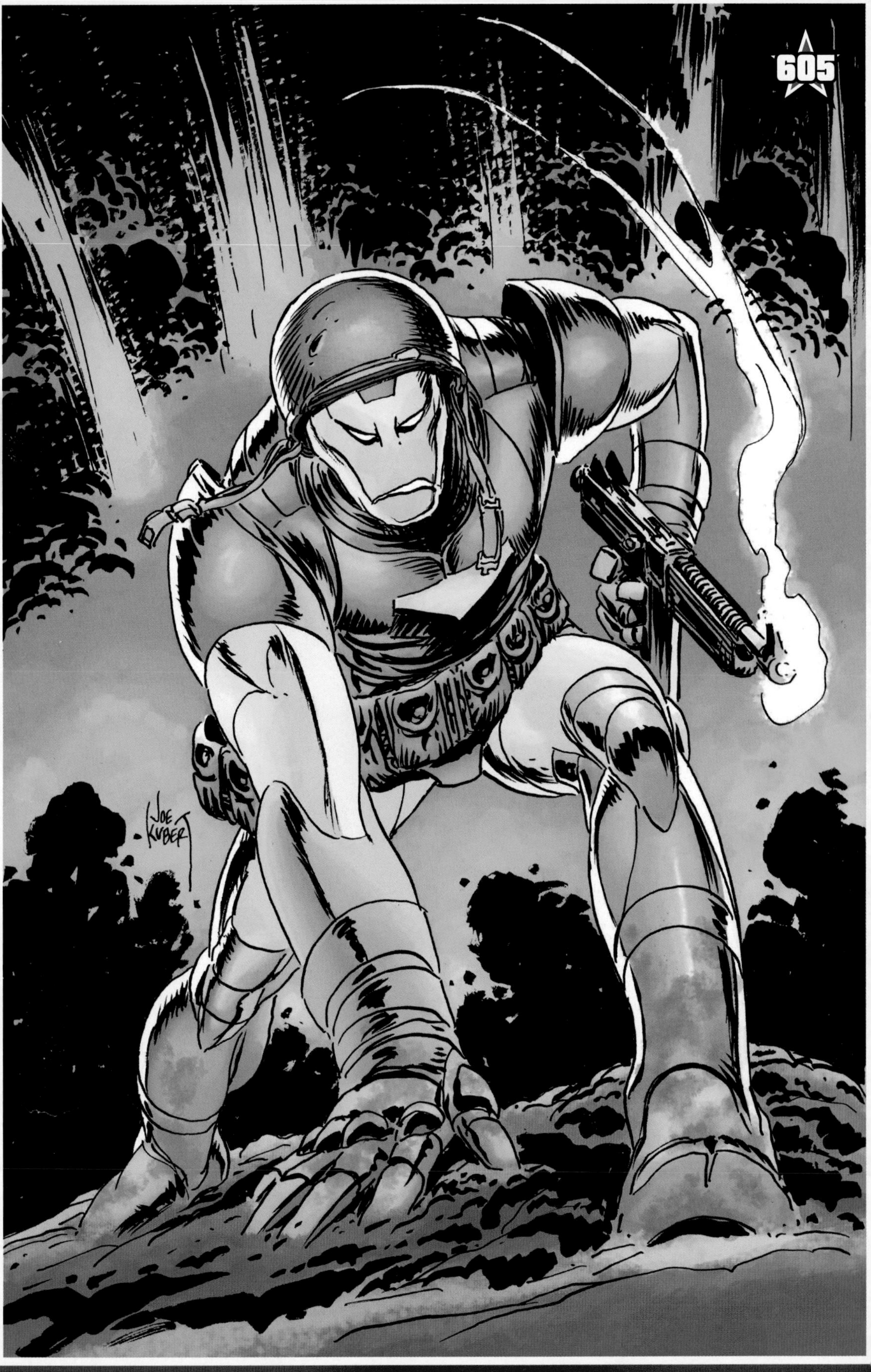
605
JOE KUBERT

IRON MAN BY DESIGN VARIANT BY JOE KUBERT